THE RED DRAGON CAST DOWN

Blessing Sora!

Jim Webb

THE RED DRAGON CAST DOWN

A REDEMPTIVE APPROACH TO THE OCCULT AND SATANISM

E. JAMES WILDER

Foreword by Dr. Neil T. Anderson

Chosen Books

A Division of Baker Book House Co
Grand Rapids, Michigan 49516

Published by Chosen Books
a division of Baker Book House Company
P.O. Box 6287, Grand Rapids, MI 49516–6287

Printed in the United States of America

Library of Congress Cataloging-in-Publication Data

Wilder, E. James, 1952–
    The red dragon cast down : a redemptive response to the occult and Satanism /
E. James Wilder ; foreword by Neil Anderson.
        p.   cm.
    Includes bibliographical references and index.
    ISBN 0-8007-9270-X (pbk.)
        1. Occultism—Religious aspects—Christianity. 2. Satanism. 3. Family—
Religious life. 4. Community—Religious aspects—Christianity. I. Title.
BR115.03W53   1999
261.5'13—dc21   99-21769

For current information about all releases from Baker Book House, visit our web site:
http://www.bakerbooks.com

To David, Peter and Jennifer
Snatched up to God's throne—away from the red dragon,

and to Nathan Sanders
who never drew a breath but taught me how to love them.

Each held by God's messengers until we meet.

Contents

Contents

Child: learns to take care of self.

Adult: learns to care for two or more at once.

Parent: grows children by giving sacrificially.

Elder: grows a community.

Maturity requires individual and community effort.

As dependent creatures we must receive before we can give.

To live and mature we must both receive and give.

Humans have been given dominion over their individual and community maturity by the creation order. Inherent in this dominion is their capacity as people to understand and accomplish maturation. That is, we can know how people "grow up" and how to bring about this growth. This is our business and not beyond our capacity. We are capable of knowing how our families and communities mature and of directing this growth in a coherent manner. This is our dominion and within our grasp. Maturity for ourselves and our world is the normal object of human activity.

4. Some Aspects of God's Redemptive Work
   Regeneration: We receive a new heart.

Sanctification: We are restored to our true identities.

Healing: We are healed of the traumas of sin.

Spiritual adoption: We receive a spiritual family.

Deliverance: The assaults of evil on us are stopped.

Spiritual gifts: We receive the means to participate in God's redemptive work.

God's redemptive work is one of restoration. Because of our fallen state, we are plagued by corruption, which blocks and perverts our attempts to produce maturity. Decontamination from this evil is beyond our capacity to achieve, direct or coordinate. Redemption is not our dominion; consequently we lack the capacity to effect or grasp the entirety of the project. Redemption is the normal object of divine activity. Specifically we are told by the apostle John about a search made throughout heaven, earth and the underworld, after which only the Lion of the tribe of Judah was found worthy to make sense of all calamities, evil, war, terrorism and suffering (see Revelation 5:1–14). This is "Lion" territory and dominion.

We are incapable of understanding the big picture of redemption. Our inability is due not to randomness or incoherence of the redemptive work, but rather to the magnitude of redemption and our own finitude. Surprisingly the redeemed still play a significant part in redemption. This participation is a bonus or gift from God. Consequently the means by which we accomplish these tasks are referred to as spiritual gifts. Because we are not able to direct the work of redemption, these gifts often take us in unexpected directions, serving both to teach us about redemption and simultaneously to accomplish its purpose. As a partial result we are returned to our normal dominion: producing maturity.

Our dominion is restored by at least three means: deliverance, healing and adoption. Our participation in these three aspects of restoration is guided by our hearts, souls, minds and communities, through prayer and by the indwelling of the Holy Spirit, from whom we receive all we need.

Deliverance is the act of war by which the assault on us is terminated. While the police may suffice to deliver us from a burglar or abusive spouse, and an army may deliver a nation, full deliverance includes stopping the spiritual assault as well as the lesser onslaughts. The Lion directs our intelligent and prayerful participation in this battle.

Healing is the restoration of our capacity to receive and give life. The privations and assaults of evil create real losses. Damaged through acts of war against us, our capacity to live is greatly diminished until we are healed as individuals and communities.

Adoption reconnects us with others with whom we receive and give life. Once able to receive and give life, we need sources and receivers of life around us and connected to us. By this adoption we become part of the family of God. Adoption is also described as being grafted into the one true Vine. It connects us to life so that we might bear fruit—our spiritual offspring, obtained through the work of the Holy Spirit in adoption.

Adoption is the aspect of redemption tied most closely to the normal human task of maturity. Often referred to in ministries of evangelism, healing and deliverance as "aftercare" or "discipleship" or "follow-up," adoption attaches us to the spiritual family in which we mature.

I am choosing the term *spiritual adoption* rather than *community-building* because in the spiritual family, I refer to more than neighborly relationships. Spiritual family is God's provision to heal type-A traumas caused by the absence of loving bonds in our lives. Spiritually bonded relationships challenge and change the natural family bonds by exposing their failings. This accounts for much of the resistance spiritual adoption receives in the Church, as well as many of its abuses in cults.

In this book I am making three assumptions. First, I am assuming familiarity with most aspects of the *LIFE* Model, beginning with the essentials of maturity for both individuals and communities. I mention sources in the text directing those who want further reading. Second, I am assuming familiarity with the Holy Spirit's guidance of individual and community life through the heart that Jesus Christ gives. Like Jesus we do only what we see the Father doing. Third, I am assuming that the many books on healing and deliverance will provide the necessary teaching on those components of God's restoration. This book focuses on spiritual adoption in a way that should add to, rather than substitute for, these other aspects of redemption.

Why Does This Book Focus on Spiritual Adoption?

Spiritual adoption may be the most ignored aspect of redemption in contemporary American Christian thought—but it is central to cult thinking. If true Christianity is composed of truth, power and relationship, then post-modern American Christians are strong on truth, just beginning to discover power, and lost when it comes to relationship, according to Dr. Charles H. Kraft.[2] Truth and power without loving relationships are denounced by the apostle Paul in 1 Corinthians 13. Beyond that, we will see that the truth contained in our symbols is interpreted through our relational bonds (see chapter 6). Relationship, power and truth belong together.

If we require a spiritual family to tell us our true identity, and the redemptive work of God's spiritual adoption to recover from traumas, then spiritual bonds are central to proper development as well as to recovery from evil. Counseling (or pastoral care) and raising children will aim for maturity while seeking God's redemption through healing, deliverance and spiritual adoption.

To this end we will examine the often ignored and deeply threatening implications of spiritual adoption. Perhaps the most threatening is its denial of a caste system of spiritual superiority or belonging. All believers are adopted. There are no natural children except for the Son. No one is exempt from these claims and requirements.

For this reason adoption cannot be attached to any existing system of maturity-building (counseling, psychotherapy, pastoral care) without radically changing the bonds in that system. Spiritual adoption severely challenges most current counseling and pastoral care models. Here is the simplest and most profound way to say this: After our adoption, all bonds are permanent, all relationships are real, all business is conducted between family members. Rather than stay detached, we must carry our responsibilities toward all in a mature manner. Doctors must treat patients as family and family as patients.

Adoption is neither optional nor unnecessary. We cannot omit adoption without giving evil the upper hand. Doctors ran the Nazi death camps and psychiatrists designed the gas chambers because they had learned how to have "as-if" relationships instead of real bonds.[3] Failure to accept adoption opens us and others to the ravages of evil. Spiritual adoption, healing and deliverance transform our individual and community identities redemptively so that once again we can build maturity as our natural function.

Although we take maturity with the greatest seriousness, we are also aware that without redemptive help we shall not succeed. Nothing will, in the end, turn out as we have planned—thank God.

and sense of self of a caring person will be threatened and altered by the mere exposure to evil in its more concentrated forms. Imagine, then, what actually living through evil can do! Since I like to help people get better from their traumas, writing a book that would hurt the reader does not appeal to me.

There are risks, however, in diluting evil.

First, one may create the mistaken impression of performing a public relations campaign for evil by making it look better. Let me say clearly that in sparing you, I do not wish evil well in any way. The second risk in reducing your exposure to evil is that I may lose credibility with those who have been there and know how much worse the matter really is. Third, those who venture into battle with evil may feel set up and betrayed when they find out that it is not nearly so nice as this book might imply. Fourth, titrating evil does not allow good to demonstrate its full force. When life overcomes death, we know the strength of the resurrection, the foundation of our salvation.

Christians are called to be a life-giving community in a killer world. In order to give life, we must know what is killing us. If we choose to oppose evil, we need to know what we are fighting. This is part of the necessary cost of our struggle. The price to each who joins the fight is both real and imaginary.

Imaginary, in that it costs us our false sense of security built on the groundless hope that we are not like other people. It costs us our imagined isolation from evil. Evil, we find, is close around us— in our churches, communities and even our families. Knowledge of our enemy also costs us the luxury of contentment with minimizing, questioning and believing we have done enough.

It costs us these imagined advantages, and in return delivers some real pain. When we discover that as families, churches and communities we are in some sense our brothers' and sisters' keepers, we will be pained when they are not well kept. But we will be pleased each time we learn it is not too late to confront evil.

A Few Remarks to the Devil

Since my Master has defeated you and given His servants authority over you and your kingdom, you are no longer the ruler of this world. Since you were created to reflect God's glory, you cannot help but be a glorious creature. Still, because of your rebellion, you distort everything about God, and it is for the purpose of correcting that distortion that this book is written.

Jesus the Christ, my Master, has come to destroy all your works. His Kingdom is now among us and I love it and am devoted to it. You and your kingdom are forbidden in Jesus' name, therefore, from interfering in any way with those who are reading or distributing this book.

Readers with wisdom, who know that you are rebellious by nature, will insist that you obey these instructions.

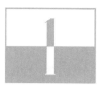

THE STRUGGLE

A CHRISTMAS GIFT FOR SATAN

IT WAS Christmas Eve, one of the best times of the year in our house, and probably in yours. This evening the fireplace was all mine. By creating a masterpiece of warmth I would soon draw every family member into my circle of love. As I cleaned the grate I recalled my last year of seminary.

When mid-December arrived that year, Kitty and I had only fourteen dollars left after paying the rent. Fourteen dollars for food, gifts and whatever a family of four might need. Our two sons Rami (pronounced Rayme) and Jamie keenly appreciated toys in the way that only four- and six-year-old boys can. Kitty got tears in her eyes as we talked about buying gifts, but there was nothing to be done. Adult and child realities were about to crash.

That year Kitty replaced gifts with a holiday tradition. It grew into a custom as rich as we were poor. An old tree branch became a yule log. On Christmas Eve we brought our mattresses out to the living room and lined them up next to a scrawny Christmas tree.

27

The lights on the tree's eight uneven branches stayed on all night while our radio played continuous Christmas music.

We lit the yule log before lying down, hoping the warmth would last as long into the night as possible. Miraculously the log burned all night. Tiny flames still flickered from the mound of embers as the boys awoke. Neither boy remembers what he got that year (with good reason!), but it became the best Christmas we ever had.

When we bought our first house we made sure it had a fireplace. Each year after that we tried to find a yule log that would burn through the night—without success.

This particular Christmas Eve the boys had just helped select a yule log when the phone rang. On the other end of the line Ted Cooper's voice sounded distressed. Ted was a successful businessman who had sought counseling for his marriage. But nothing in graduate school or seminary had prepared me for his next words.

"We have been contacted!" he exclaimed. "My father-in-law, who is in a satanic cult, is coming over tonight to hold a human sacrifice in our house. They have the child for the death ritual already. They say we have to join them or they will kill our children. What shall we do?"

Ted's words contrasted sharply with the peaceful scene around me. Suddenly, brutally, what I was seeing and what I was hearing seemed from two different worlds. Outside my children examined the yule log happily and speculated about how long it would burn. But tonight, on my favorite night of the year, Ted was telling me that, while his family participated, a child was scheduled to die.

Ted and I contacted the police but they were not interested in helping unless a crime had already been committed or was in progress.

The evening dragged on with a long series of frustrating phone calls. I was consumed with feelings of agitation and powerlessness. Finally the Coopers found a family from church who took them in for the evening so they could be safe from the threats against their children. Ted's father-in-law would not show up, we figured, where there were witnesses. This church family was willing to share the Coopers' anguish and change their private family Christmas into a Christian family Christmas.

The phone calls on Christmas Eve had not attracted much attention from my family. Now, with the Coopers safely tucked away, I tried to return to Christmas celebrations. Something was going on in my mind, however, that would not disappear and about which I did not want to tell my family. All night, lying in front of our yule log, my mind was haunted by thoughts of a child dying as a Christmas present for that old red dragon, the devil. Great sorrow wrapped itself around my soul as I tended the fire, although somehow I was able to smile for gifts and children on Christmas morning.

Christmas is the day we remember for God traveling for us from one reality into another. But that day found my mind caught between two realities—one I liked, one I hated. It was time to share with my family the reality of a joyous day. But to be faithful to God's trip to earth, I also needed to visit Ted Cooper's reality of a dreadful night.

My wife and children understood in a general way what was going on around them. Our evenings were often interrupted with calls from agitated individuals. Upset people would sometimes show up at church and act odd and frightened. Slowly Kitty and Rami and Jamie began to learn more about living in the war zone between good and evil. It was time for them to share my reality of the ugliness of evil and the importance of righteous action. We were in a battle for lives, and my children needed to know how we planned to win the struggle. They needed to know the meaning of Christmas.

Fighting for Our Children

Several years before, I had selected a documentary to begin the educational process for my family. No one had nightmares after we watched *America's Best Kept Secret*—a good videotaped documentary on the subject of Satanism.[1] There was not even much discussion at the time. Sitting between Kitty and me, Jamie and Rami learned about bad things. Through the video both boys saw we were struggling against evil and seemed pleased to be part of the solution.

My sons had known about Satanism before they were out of grade school because the basic ingredients that would pull them into evil were already present in their lives. They needed a broader view of reality. The boys had to learn about life-stealing dangers from sexually perverted people, drugs, divorce, greed, AIDS and Satanism, because those realities surrounded them and they needed to know there is a life-giving alternative. Kitty and I stayed close to our children as we led them out into a sometimes-dangerous world.

The benefit of being close to our children and being open about the world came from addressing their concerns together. We joined in our children's reality and invited them to join in ours. In so doing, we believe, we gave them life.

Our sons wanted to understand the battle between good and evil. They needed to know about realities that differed from their home. It made them harder to fool.

There were subtle influences toward danger in our community. Take music. The house across the street had been used for rehearsals by a heavy metal rock band before the prostitutes moved in. After that some missionaries took the house. Then the missionaries' oldest son became a heavy metal fan with a vengeance. Our boys played with his brothers and sisters. They needed to understand our reservations about playing at his house, that we were not afraid but concerned.

Other influences emerged as well. The church elder who kept us under his care wore a cap that his son had found touting Ozzy Osbourne, the heavy metal rocker whose satanic themes and stage appearances have created much controversy. When we took a vacation together, this elder's kids wanted to watch movies depicting satanic ceremonies. The bright, sociable son of the director of evangelism and Christian education at our church came over to teach the boys how to play his new game of "Dungeons and Dragons." By junior high our older son, Jamie, found that the other students in Spanish II were playing with a Ouija board in class when they ran out of work to do, which was every day.

Once, while my sons were getting haircuts, a woman came into the shop, held up a pentagram and cast a spell on the owner. The owner laughed and told the boys the woman was a witch who did not want to pay her bill, and threatened to curse her. This left an impression on them, however, along with many questions: Would the spell have any effect on them? Should they be concerned about the effect of the curse on the owner?

Soon our children started asking us tough questions. Should you buy a Natas (Satan spelled backwards) skateboard? Most children seemed to know what it meant, even if parents did not. Should we sing Christmas carols at the house with only one upside-down star on the door?

Still, these discussions did not prepare us for what was to come.

Fighting for Our Community

One warm November afternoon a tan truck slammed up over the curb and roared after Rami, our younger son. Rami was on his way home from elementary school with his friend Mark. Neither boy had seen these two men or the truck before. As the boys raced out of range, the driver turned around for a second pass. Together the boys fled into a house with an open door, finding shelter from strangers as the truck screeched past, leaving the cul-de-sac as quickly as it had come.

While comforting our frightened boy that night, Kitty and I wondered if this strange incident might be related to the all-night vigil we had held recently to support nine of the people we were helping to leave or recover from Satanism. We had been warned of reprisals after we had gotten involved in the healing of these souls. Was this one of them or were we getting paranoid?

Other counselors were talking about hiring private investigators to discover what lay behind strange encounters they were experiencing. We heard reports of poisonings. Several ex-Satanists feared being attacked in their homes. One pastor friend found dead animals regularly on the same spot in his yard. This was not what I had expected when I settled my family in a quiet residential neighborhood just blocks from the Rose Parade!

One wintry night not long after, we gathered our sons by the fireplace for a book-burning. The volumes due for combustion consisted of the occult library of a woman named Rose who was coming to terms with her multigenerational background in Satanism. Rose wanted her books destroyed. We had a fireplace. Rami now had the motivation. So our family gathered around Rose as a spiritual family to help her through this moment. We jointly incinerated some of the volumes we suspected of inspiring men to drive their way into our lives almost a month before.

The pastors at our church got wind that I was helping people from Satanist backgrounds, and began to talk about what they knew. Differing realities were crashing behind the scenes in church. There proved to be a remarkable number of folks in our congregation going in or out of Satanism, even though, naturally, there was not much open talk about it. It was interesting to see what happened when word got around that I knew about other realities, especially secret ones.

A shy, lonely teenage boy approached me one Sunday morning after the service. He talked to me occasionally because I knew he was always fighting with his parents and still did not hate him for it. Now Greg pulled a folded piece of paper from his pocket.

"One of the Satanists[2] at school gave me this to help me find a girlfriend," he said. "It's a love spell. Do you think I should try it? Do you think it's real?"

The page contained a carefully worded invocation to Isis that included a pledge to serve her in return for her favors. Instructions were included on how to perform a ritual to make the spell work. It was complex enough that I had to look up some of the names later. Whoever wrote it had some resource books.

Greg took the paper back and squirmed. He needed a girlfriend because his churchgoing parents had driven his last one away with their screaming, shouting and swearing. Here at last was help when he needed it. Or was it? He was glad the Satanist in his class had understood his loneliness and seen past the outside reality of his Christian family to the inside reality of a lonely, rejected, angry boy, and joined him there. Greg was also glad he could talk to me.

When we were finished he threw the paper with the spell into the trash. But the next day he stole his parents' car and went to visit his old girlfriend.

I wish I could say the story had a happy ending. Neither his pastor nor I could induce Greg's parents to change their way of life. They continued to alternately scream, hit and quote Scripture at each other. Nothing short of having a strong, life-giving Christian stay with the family would have stopped the war; and no volunteer could be found. Perhaps no one else could see the problem. Many people's view of reality has no room for parents who act like Greg's yet still go to church.

Before he turned fifteen Greg was living in Canada with a cultist who thought himself the messiah. It was much quieter there. Greg still did not have a girlfriend. But with no Christian community to support him, he had turned to a cult to be his family.

Greg was not the only child being drawn away from church. The Christian mother of a thirteen-year-old boy getting into Satanism came to church desperate for help. Her alcoholic husband was driving the boy away from home, God and church with his drunken anger, and she needed men to be father substitutes for her son. Then, when she discovered the boy had bad intentions toward his little sister, she turned desperately to the elders of the congregation. She needed a life-giving family, one without little girls at home, that could provide immediate care for her son while she protected her daughter. She longed for someone who could see in her son the boy she loved and the menace he had become. These two realities had a way of obscuring each other.

What could we learn from the people getting out of Satanism, I wondered, to help those just going in? That search to understand the Satanist's mind and to provide a better choice for those getting involved has helped me see how we set up ourselves, our friends and our children to receive evil. In many ways we, like Greg's screaming parents, unwittingly pave the way for people to join cults or follow the devil.

Is There a Real Problem with Satanism and Destructive Cults?

The only agreement among experts on Satanism is that none of them has the whole picture. I doubt any expert can completely separate fact from fantasy from fear. Experts disagree about how bad the situation has gotten. Some folks fear an international conspiracy of Satanists, poised, organized and ready to take over the world. Others report highly secretive family cults going back for generations.

Cult expert Dr. J. Gordon Melton suggests that Satanists are created by the Church. "There is no group of Satanists that survives from generation to generation to carry on the tradition," he says.[3] Instead, he argues, Satanists appear as a reaction to negative personal experiences with Christianity.

While that does not seem to fit all the evidence I have seen, Melton raises a serious question: Are we part of the cause or the cure? The door between good and evil does seem to swing both ways.

I have less of an answer to that question than others do because, as a minister and counselor in "weird" California, I see only the problems that come to me. What walks through my door creates most of my world.

Imagine my surprise over the years as mothers, teachers, musicians, nurses, salesmen, missionaries and office managers have all told me they were trying to come out of Satanism. That did not fit my view of reality! None of them appeared psychotic. Most were long-time church members with families. All told horror stories of multigenerational satanic cults—some going back more than half a century, others very recent. According to these church members, people from the community and counselees, there are respected members of society living sinister lives without being detected.

All such stories suffer from a credibility problem. Even a cursory discussion of these reports begins with bone-chilling, disgusting accounts of murders and rapes that defy most people's ability to stay objective. Bizarre cults can be an incredibly ugly subject. It is difficult to believe that civilized people would do the things some cultists are accused of doing. In addition, if they are killing, torturing and eating people, why are more of them not being apprehended and convicted in court?

The discussion of facts disintegrates in a variety of different areas: law enforcement, courts, witnesses, evidence, media, memories, evil and mind control. One question is asked frequently: If cults are murdering, raping, torturing and eating people in America, why aren't there more arrests and convictions? Here is a brief discussion of each of these areas so you can make better sense of the material you hear on cults and crime.

The Law

Why are there not more arrests for ritual abuse? Only five states have laws making ritual abuse a crime. For all the other states that means ritual aspects of a criminal case are not elements of the crime. If there is no ritual abuse law, no arrests or prosecutions will be recorded. Instead of being charged with ritual abuse, those arrested are charged with rape, murder or child abuse. Even if a cult uses rape for religious rituals, punishment of members or coercive persuasion, they can be arrested only for rape. No law, no crime, no arrests, no records.

Also, law enforcement is generally unconcerned about the religious beliefs of suspects. Since the U.S. Constitution protects freedom of religion and freedom of speech, all cults in this country are legal. Police departments do not keep official files of Satanists—

or Lutherans, either. Nor does the government track crime committed by what it considers a particular religious association, such as Satanism.

The Courts

Trial court verdicts of "not guilty" in ritual abuse cases have sometimes been misconstrued to say that the crime did not take place. When the McMartin Preschool trial defendants were found not guilty, for example, most Americans concluded that no crime had been committed.[4] That conclusion is wrong. The McMartin jurors were not asked to decide whether the children had been abused. Some jurors even said after the trial that they were certain the children *had* been abused—a view shared by the examining doctors, prosecutors and parents, as well as by the children. All we can conclude from the verdict is that we are not sure who did it.

It is wrong to use the McMartin case, therefore, to argue that ritual abuse does not exist. When O. J. Simpson was found not guilty, no one concluded that Nicole was still alive, only that there was insufficient proof to show that Mr. Simpson committed the crime.

Most criminal cases involving Satanism come to court as murder trials or as alleged child sexual abuse. Murder cases like that of "Son of Sam," Charles Manson or the "Night Stalker" can be tried without bringing up the religious aspects of the case. When the crime is sexual abuse of children, prosecution becomes far more difficult because of problems with children's testimony. Prosecutors try to find children who will testify only about sexual crimes without mentioning rituals. This has led law enforcement experts to say that the existence or prevalence of ritual crime should not be judged by conviction rates.[5] In spite of these problems, there have still been convictions in court of crimes with ritualistic motives.[6]

There are other reasons we cannot rely on criminal justice records as proof that no ritual crimes have been committed. Many cases of what seems to be ritual crime, like that of "Baby X" of Rupert, Idaho,[7] remain "unsolved" and never go to trial. Law enforcement officers do not investigate crimes they do not believe exist; prosecutors do not prosecute crimes they do not think the jury will believe were committed; and the jury is unlikely to believe in crimes they have not heard of. We are no safer than our own community's level of awareness.

The Witnesses

The witnesses in cases involving destructive cults are either victims or experts. Both groups have credibility problems.

If the experts talk to the victims, there are allegations of brainwashing. The experts for the defense in cases of alleged child sexual abuse claim it is therapists who make up satanic ritual stories and insert them into the minds of children.[8] But cult and child abuse seem to be the only crimes in which brainwashing witnesses into believing they are victims is an issue. If someone talks to a victim of a bank robbery, no one claims brainwashing. Perhaps since most victims are children or people with a psychiatric problem (such as post-traumatic stress), these victims cannot perceive reality.

But that would be news to me.

Certain "expert" witnesses suffer from credibility problems of their own.[9] The involvement of one expert witness in particular has set the stage for legal, media and public opinion.

Dr. Ralph Underwager has been an expert witness for the defense in court cases alleging satanic ritual abuse of children. He was present for the founding of VOCAL (Victims of Child Abuse Laws)[10] and has been vocal for some time in the area of child memories and brainwashing. Dr. Underwager is also a co-founder of the False Memory Syndrome Foundation (FMSF) and a one-time member of their Scientific Advisory Board. He is sometimes credited with creating the phrase *false memory syndrome*. The FMSF, like VOCAL, exists to defend people accused of sexually abusing children. The foundation's position is that satanic ritual abuse "simply does not exist."[11] Therapists, they believe, create memories in the minds of unsuspecting adults, which accounts for every known report of abusive satanic rituals.[12]

Dr. Underwager testified as an expert witness in a Jordan, Minnesota, court case that children reporting satanic abuse were programmed by their therapists with techniques that "conformed precisely and in exact detail" with the techniques used by the Red Chinese, North Koreans and "oppressive tyrants everywhere." When questioned about these statements during a deposition in Florida, he was unable to answer questions about how the Red Chinese would program someone, and was unable to list one technique from the Chinese, North Koreans, North Vietnamese or tyrants in general that had been used in the child interviews he had studied.[13]

It raises a credibility problem, to say the least, when Dr. Underwager claims scientific evidence for a "syndrome," yet cannot produce any. In fact, Dr. James Friesen demonstrates in his book *The Truth about False Memory Syndrome* that no such syndrome can be established on scientific or medical grounds.[14]

Dr. Underwager has also become an apparent advocate for pedophiles—those who have sex with children. In an interview with *Paidika: The Journal of Paedophilia*, Underwager affirmed pedophilia as a "responsible choice," then went on to say:

> Paedophiles can boldly and courageously affirm what they choose. They can say what they want is to find the best way to love. I am also a theologian and as a theologian I believe it is God's will that there be closeness and unity of the flesh, between people . . . What I think is that paedophiles can make the assertion that the pursuit of intimacy and love is what they choose. With boldness they can say, "I believe this is in fact part of God's will."[15]

The claim by FMSF (the organization Underwager helped found) that Satanists cannot be considered responsible for any reported cases of ritual abuse is even more interesting in light of the tendency on the part of prosecutors to try for convictions based on pedophilia. The defense need only highlight the "religious" aspects of the crime to remove a child's credibility, since most jury members disbelieve sexual abuse with religious motives. But Underwager, an ordained Lutheran minister, has helped establish this very point. Sexual contact with children, he purports, is religiously justified behavior for God's followers.

If this expert witness and Christian theologian with a doctorate supports sex with children to please his God, can we be absolutely certain that no Satanists would molest a child for theirs?

Underwager's claim that children are being programmed by therapy interviews or police questioning into claiming falsely that they have been sexually abused, so that these children should not be believed in court, needs to be reexamined. It does not make sense to deny that children's reports of pedophilia are real and then call pedophilia a "responsible choice" for adults. Sadly, however, none of the court cases influenced by this kind of testimony will be reexamined. Their verdicts will remain as proof in popular culture that nothing happened to those children.

The Evidence

One of the most bizarre twists in the investigation of stories related to Satanism is the rejection of information from emotionally damaged individuals who claim to be victims of ritualized abuse. Their testimony is ostensibly invalid because they show signs of mental instability.

The effects of extreme evil on the mind should predict just such a result. Nazi concentration camps produced mental instability in their prisoners. Rejecting reports because of mental distress is like rejecting the testimony of a woman who claims she was hit by a bus because she is mangled, in shock and has a fractured skull. It is more logical that we believe someone who shows signs of being in an accident than to dismiss the story outright.

Before understanding the damage, let's understand and accept the source. If a young man were to tell us he had been shot by a gun-wielding gang member in Los Angeles, we might progress with the investigation differently than if he claimed to have been shot by a ray-gun-wielding Martian. If we do not believe a certain evil exists, then we will not recognize the wound it creates. Our protection, as I said earlier, is only as good as our community's understanding of evil. When someone's damage is not understandable, then his story is not believable; but we must ask, before rejecting his story, whether our reality is too small. The investigation starts with the realization that we do not know everything.

Some Satanists claim (not surprisingly) that Christians make up these awful tales. With the fact-finding methods of Tomás de Torquemada in our heritage, it is hard to claim total innocence. Tomás was a Spanish Dominican monk appointed grand inquisitor by the Pope during the Spanish Inquisition. An agent of the Church, he and the rest of the Inquisitors were masters of torture, dismemberment and murder. They made the answers come out the way they wanted. Their behavior indicates that evil is not limited by a person's religious label. It is historically proven that people do torture each other for religious purposes and that intentional, methodical, complex and even elaborate methods can be developed by people of faith.

The only question remaining is, Are Christians the only ones capable of such cruelty?

The Media Debate

Some believe the Satanism problem has been created by sensationalized journalism. There is lurid journalism, to be sure, and some reporters lie. We have Leo Taxil to thank for his help along these lines.[16] A century ago this unscrupulous reporter created stories about an imaginary satanic high priestess. His deception created a decade of commotion. Obviously he had a nasty imagination. But today there remains scattered support for the idea that if we could simply rid ourselves of Christians, journalists and therapists, the world would be a better place.

Current media interest has been stirred by television. Oprah Winfrey's two shows on Satanism, two by Sally Jesse Raphael and two by Geraldo aired between 1986 and 1991.[17] These hosts have a flair for the sensational. Does that account for all the evidence? It does prove that reporters are capable of thinking terrible thoughts and promulgating them to others—but are they making it all up?

There is a trend in America to establish truth through the media, public opinion polls and call-in shows on talk radio. This often assumes that if you present both sides, you have been impartial. But it takes more than that to uncover a lie.

Journalism currently favors the view that reporters are impartial while therapists, law enforcement officers and doctors concoct stories and blame cults. True, satanic rituals, sexual perversions, murders and child abuse do go together, according to some therapists, reporters, law enforcement personnel and doctors. Most therapists report, however, that they heard an account first from a client before they ever imagined that such cruelty existed.[18]

Is it safe to conclude that these ideas spring up only in the minds of helpful people but never captivate the imaginations of Satanists?

The Memories

We will consider the recovered memory debate here because it always accompanies discussions about abuse. It is not really related to this book because I have not used recovered memories to make my case. Ted Cooper, for instance, the businessman whose father-in-law was coming over on Christmas Eve to hold a human sacrifice, was in the present when he called.

We will discuss memory and trauma later in this chapter, but first let's ask some questions. Are one hundred percent of these memories implanted? Is implanting memories that easy to do? Have you ever done it to someone by mistake? How easy would it be for someone to make *you* believe you had killed or had sex with someone? Could you implant the memory of something you had never thought possible into someone without knowing you were doing it? There are no courses for doctors and police on how to do this, you know.

Marie came to see me with flashes of memories of people in robes and masks, being tied down, lights, a baby being killed. She thought maybe she had been abducted by a UFO or by Satanists. No, she had aborted her first child. Do you doubt the abortion happened?

Marna had been to primal therapy, where she had seen images of dead babies and people on crosses and had horrible terrors. Her therapist told her these proved that Marna had been ritually abused. As a result she stayed away from her family. I asked her if I could test her with the recognition signals used by Satanist groups, and she could not recognize a single one. She also did not know their symbols and had no emotional reaction to them at all. Yes, Marna had also had an abortion, but when she no longer thought she might be a Satanist, the images disappeared. With the removal of a medication she had been taking, the terrors left.

Five-year-old Molly woke up with graphic dreams of sex and human sacrifice. She described them in anatomically correct detail that few people but a surgeon would know. She and her parents had moved just before these dreams started terrifying Molly, so her family suspected she had been ritually abused in the town they just left. Soon after, a neighbor mentioned that the people next door were witches and had cursed Molly's new house. Without the girl's knowledge, her parents invited a prayer team to the house to cleanse it. From that point on Molly had no more bad dreams.

No argument about memories, or even scientific research, will answer a fraction of the questions about what people experience. We do know a lot about memory, but it requires definite study to understand it more completely. We should not simply believe because people remember or disbelieve because they do not.

Mind Control

Thus far we have been examining a kind of human behavior claimed to occur at satanic rituals. While denied by most Satanists, we know it has been done by some Christians. It involves the sex-

The results of terror on the human mind have been studied carefully in the wake of the Jewish Holocaust at the hands of the Nazis.[21] The result of these studies suggests that victims of torture do *not* recall clearly and describe accurately every detail in a logical and coherent way. There are reasons why.

Right and Left Hemisphere Memory Systems

Do you remember being born? It was a big event!

It does not bother you, of course, that you cannot remember, because most people do not—but why is this? It is because the brain's librarian, called the hippocampus, does not develop sufficiently until a person is two or three years old. Until then everyone has "infantile amnesia."

We still learn a great deal before age three, however, much of which is stored in right hemispheric memory (not controlled by the hippocampus). This memory system in the brain is called implicit memory.[22] Right hemisphere memory, which is *not* mediated by the hippocampus, is:

- Implicit
- Nonfocal
- Not suggestible at all (no one can implant ideas)
- Lacking a subjective sense of being recalled

What we usually call *memory,* on the other hand, has a subjective sense of being recalled. We can tell we are remembering. We recognize that something is a story or event from the past. Left hemispheric memory, which is controlled by the hippocampus,[23] is:

- Explicit
- Focal
- Conscious
- Very suggestible (one can implant ideas)
- Has a subjective sense of being recalled
- Autobiographical, with sense of space and time
- Cortically consolidated (after age eight) during rapid eye movement sleep

Just as you cannot explicitly remember your birth because your librarian was not developed enough to create a left hemispheric story of the event, you also lack left hemispheric memory of anything that happens when the hippocampus is asleep, unconscious, drugged or overloaded.

Certain situations can overload the librarian.[24] When any of these happen, we call our lack of explicit memory *amnesia*. The hippocampus is blocked by three conditions:

- Massive discharges by the amygdala (alarm centers of the brain)
- Split attention
- High levels of cortisol (stress hormone) in the blood

Cortisol secretion is caused by prolonged stress. Repeated or prolonged trauma stimulates cortisol secretion. Cortisol destroys new nerve connections, thus causing to be "unlearned" or "unremembered" whatever led to the stress. High cortisol levels can also cause us to forget, over a period of days, many details of newly learned explicit memory.

When the brain is young and still developing (particularly before three years of age), cortisol secretion also destroys whatever part of the brain is new growth. Thus, high levels of cortisol during development of any brain system leave a permanent lesion in that brain structure. Trauma between two to three years of age, for example, leaves a "scar" in the hippocampus, which is developing at that time.[25] It will not work right after that.

Because right hemispheric memory does not use the librarian, it is possible to have right hemisphere memory for events that have no left hemisphere counterpart. The right hemisphere carefully records all events that overwhelm the hippocampus librarian. But in right hemispheric memory, events are not associated with thoughts and words, so they cannot be retrieved by thoughts, words and questions. The information is in the mind but not retrievable by thinking about it. The story cannot be spoken with words.

If the left hemisphere learns how to retrieve right hemisphere memories, and then sends them to the librarian for processing, it produces voluntary, conscious recall of events (as one reconstructs them.) Because right hemisphere memory cannot be focused, it is impervious to suggestion and interpretation. The same is *not* true for the left, so reconstructions can be very faulty and have many details that have arisen from suggestion.

Repression or Dissociation?

I was in third grade and my brother was in second. We attended a one-room schoolhouse with a handful of other children. Linda was one of the kids I remember well because she was the first girl I ever kissed. She was also humiliated before the whole school.

It happened one afternoon when Linda was a first-grader. Fifteen minutes before school let out, she raised her hand to go to the bathroom. Miss Clarabelle refused to let her go. Then, just as we were standing to be dismissed, Linda could not hold it anymore and made a puddle. The class was furious with Miss Clarabelle and Linda was completely distraught.

A few years ago I ran into Linda again and we began to talk about grade school. I told her how bad I felt about her embarrassing moment.

Linda said, "That never happened to me!" Then, after a moment's pause, she added, "Now that you mention it, I vaguely remember that happening to another girl in school, but it wasn't me!"

She laughed happily at my confused memory.

Realities were colliding in my head.

"Are you sure?" I asked. "I could have sworn it was you."

"No, no," she said, "it wasn't me." She puzzled for a moment and thought. "I just can't remember who that other girl was."

That evening I called my brother.

"Tim, do you remember when we were in Miss Clarabelle's class and a little girl wet her pants? Who was it?"

"Oh, sure," he said immediately. "That was Linda X."

"I thought so," I said.

Tim added, "Yes, she asked to go but Miss Clarabelle wouldn't let her. We were standing to be dismissed when she went on the floor. I remember how mad we all were at the teacher."

Linda had been so convincing in her denial of the incident that she had almost persuaded me to disbelieve my own memory. On the other hand, she could clearly remember breaking her arm in third grade just fifteen feet from the spot where the first grade incident took place.

The media might say that Linda "repressed" her memory, but most people have no idea what the word actually means.

Repression is the slow removal of a memory. This is very hard to do. Dissociation is another way to "not remember." It occurs while an overwhelming event is happening and the librarian/hippocampus files this event under a different reality. Dissociated events are impossible to assimilate right from the beginning. Dissociation occurs instantly during overwhelming events, whereas repression takes place afterward. Dissociation helps us function in normal life by blocking thoughts of overwhelming, confusing and disabling circumstances, particularly if our survival depends on our quick wits.

If an event is so overwhelming that it shuts down the librarian completely, it will be stored in right hemisphere memory, where it can come back as "flashbacks." These memories are experienced as though the event were happening again with no subjective experience of remembering.

Linda's recall today, for example, could be triggered by similar events. While standing for prayer, she might suddenly feel as if she were wetting her pants. If her humiliation afterward had been intense and long-lasting, Linda could have created cortisol and dissolved details of the memory until the story was forgotten and her emotional stress disappeared. This would remove much of her left hemisphere memory but probably not all of it.

If Linda tried mentally to suggest to herself a different and false version of the memory (like "That never happened"), we would say she *repressed* her memory. Most likely, however, Linda did not put the story into permanent memory at all, since she was only six years old and since the ability to permanently store left hemisphere memory does not develop until age eight. Long-term memory holds information for only a few months, so it was gone by the time she was old enough. By then we schoolmates had stopped telling the story, so Linda's left hemisphere memory probably faded and only the right hemisphere version remained.

What people can remember, you see, is a function of many things: their age, their condition, the event, what followed the event and the response of the community around them.

Memory Retrieval

Trauma memories, whether dissociated or right hemispheric, may come back to mind only under certain environmental cues,

As for me and my family, we have decided it is well worth the pain to find out we are winning the war with evil. Join us. By examining the road in and out of Satanism, you and I together will participate more fully in the preventive and restorative work of the King, in whose presence is fullness of joy. Perhaps we will find more of what it means to be His family.

THE DRAGON'S LURES

CATCHING YOUNG ADULTS
WITH UNMET NEEDS

WHERE have you been?" Julie cried over the phone. "I'll never trust you again! I needed to talk to you and you were away, so I called Sixty-three. He said you don't care about me at all, or you wouldn't go away for the weekend. He says I'm special to him and that he'll be there for me day and night—that I just need to come back."

Clearly I could not truthfully make the same promise as Sixty-three, a Satanist. Although Julie had the name of someone to call both days I was gone, she knew that person was not me. The same was not true for the competition. Because they used numbers, not names, the handler on duty was able do the rest. He could promise that everything would be perfect if only Julie returned to the next ritual, whereas I could not promise that everything would be perfect if she stayed with God.

Julie did not want to hear that.

Sixty-three (not his real number) had one enormous advantage going for him that

50

We are at the mercy of our communities to help us know who we are and what we need. When our communities are wrong we die.

People entertain other mistaken views that have the same impact on them. A friend in advertising said that the secret to getting people to buy something they do not want is to make them think they need it. Drugs and sex are two such lures used by criminal cults to catch young adults.

Those Who Have Lost Hope
That Their Needs Will Be Met

It should not surprise us that many people in destructive cults are angry, cynical, hopeless and contemptuous of loving relationships. They get what they want in other ways. Some have lost hope and turned to hate. These are the leaders. But many, like Julie, are simply clinging desperately to their last hope. She bit hard.

People who cannot meet their own needs feel powerless and wish they had more personal power. Cults offer power. A cultist can become somebody through esoteric knowledge, secret laws and controlling spirits, and more obviously by money and influence. More about this later.

Those Who Deny Their Needs

Because our needs can leave us vulnerable, many attempt to deny or cover them up. They teach their children to protect themselves by denying and covering their needs as well. Because we cannot simultaneously deny needs and learn to satisfy them, this protection leaves a terrible susceptibility. Those who do not know how to satisfy their needs are open to deception. Those who deny their needs and teach their children to lie to themselves about theirs have created not a defense but a weakness.

Hungry Fish Keep Biting

We all have real needs. It is unavoidable. We were created with needs and we stay that way throughout our lives. What we believe about ourselves determines the ways we will go about trying to meet those needs. If we have an accurate sense of who we are, we will respond appropriately to our needs. Our identities guide our search—identities formed by our families and communities, identities that structure our reality. Our identities should reflect that we are dependent creatures with needs.

The Dragon Goes Fishing

When the dragon goes fishing, he is looking not for people who think they need drugs or spells, but for those who do not know who they are as individuals or groups. When he finds unmet individual and group identity needs, he pats his creel and licks his fangs. These fish will bite on almost anything.

Most cults—and Satanism is no exception—identify people in need and offer answers. Young adults need both an individual and a group identity, so they are twice as easy to catch. Isolated, lonely, needy people will often try almost anything to meet their needs. Without a supportive community, people do irrational things. Julie illustrates how unmet needs are used for cult recruiting.

Group Identity Needs

Julie wanted relationship. She greatly feared the secrets she carried that kept her isolated and alone. Satanism provided an appealing answer. They would receive her no matter how bad her secrets might be. In fact, worse secrets were better. They would get close to her, even have sex with her (that, by some standards, is really close). They would give her drugs to help her feel better and get very involved in her life. It was just what she needed—companionship and acceptance at last.

Social misfits lack a group identity. They do not know how to meet their own social and personal needs. By keeping to themselves, they help others avoid them. Such people are easy to spot because of their hesitancy with others and their tendency to withdraw. They are easy recruiting targets for cults of all sorts. Unhappy, lonely and isolated people have a hard time turning down any offer of companionship. In addition they have a harder time uncovering false claims by cult groups because they lack the relationship resources of a life-giving community to verify or disprove the cult's claims about what they need.

Singles bars and singles ministries around the country attract people with these needs. Many people, particularly those raised in institutions or by distant, uninvolved or divorced parents, feel the need for more relationships. Missionary children raised in boarding schools in which they were never held feel isolated and alone. Some were touched only when adults hit them for punishment. Others experienced companionship only when approached sexually. All of these have strong needs for companionship with no viable solutions. They were reared in Christian communities that did not recognize many of their needs and provided inadequate ways to meet them.

These unmet needs, then, are a kind of trauma caused by the absence of necessary good things.

If Julie missed church no one called. But Sixty-three let her know she would always be someone important to him, and that gave her a much-needed group identity.

Personal Identity Needs

There is one need that cults address effectively, while many Christian communities seem oblivious to its very existence: A person needs an individual identity. It is important to be someone. A person who feels that his or her self or identity is inadequate is constantly searching for ways to get a better one. Nothing attracts us more than the chance to become the selves we always wanted to be. Then we could meet all our needs!

At points it is more important for adults to have an identity than to preserve their lives. A "tough guy" gunman will not back down from a fight that could kill him because his identity is worth more to him than his life.

When cults recruit needy people, these people are not destined for greatness. They have something the group wants, like children or a body. They are promised greatness. They are told that in the cult they can be somebody important. They join in the hope that people who can recognize needs will know how to meet those needs. They want to be needed; they want to be somebody. Instead, religiously abusive groups force people into roles, making them become no more than what they can do.

All life-giving communities share a trait in common: They help their members develop strong identities. Our ability to be satisfied depends on knowing who we are. If we do not understand ourselves, we will try wrong solutions in the hope that they will work. Many people eat when they feel lonely or afraid. Does food cure loneliness or remove danger? Hardly! But that does not stop many of us each day from trying to make the formula work.

Finding a Good Spot to Fish

To find followers, look for people with unmet needs. It is not hard to find them. They have regular gathering places like counseling centers. In fact, recruiting in mental health clinics is a method used by organized satanic cults.[2] There have been four reported instances of unsuccessful Satanist recruiting in a center where I work. Although all four recruiters claimed to be Satanists, only one stated that she was under orders from her cult to recruit in our center. We did not phone the cults to verify any of the claims.

Our counseling clinic was a community center founded by a church that recognized people's unmet needs but had other ways of recruiting members. No one would contest that the clients contacted by Satanists in our waiting room and parking lot had unmet needs. The center provided a community where the clients had a chance to compare the satisfaction offered by differing solutions. It was a place where the two ways of meeting needs competed.

What Are They Biting on Today?

My Uncle Bode, a game warden, taught me how to fish at his cabin on Fishhook Lake. We caught bluegill and sunfish mostly. Tricking fish with bait on hooks was easy for me as a boy to understand, but lures really intrigued me. Why would fish bite a metal spoon with an obvious hook? They would fight and flop and gasp and bleed and die. Then, when we had caught a mess of keepers, my uncle fried them up for supper.

Catching people is also an art. It is hard to catch the old wily ones, but young adults will often bite on pleasure, sex, drugs, music, control, special knowledge, spiritual power and belonging.

Lured by Pleasure

It is frequently said that you can have drugs without Satanism but you cannot have Satanism without drugs. Drugs give pleasure or help a person feel no pain. They are an effective way to avoid experiencing needs or pain, at least for a while. This provides relief for people who cannot meet their own needs or who cannot find their way back to joy. Drugs also obscure the damage being done.

New recruits to Satanism often start by attending a sex party. Here they can get all the pleasure they want. This must be heaven— but they are told God disapproves, so this is actually what hell will be like without a God to bother them.

Sexual pleasure lures people into activities for which they can be shamed, blackmailed and manipulated. Careers, political aspirations, marriages and police records can all be at stake. Like drugs, sexual pleasure also obscures the damage being done.

Sexual pleasure is a powerful lure because it is tied so closely to good things about us. It touches our need for relationship, to enjoy and be enjoyed. It also touches our need to be the source of something good to others. Linked inseparably to sexual pleasure is our ability to be life-giving.

Pursuing pleasure does not help meet these needs, however, and damages our capacity to do so. In later chapters we will see that the reason sexual activity plays such a large role in Satanism has less to do with pleasure than it does with controlling this life-giving ability, and other hidden objectives. Unfortunately, many people believe that whoever gets the most pleasure is the smartest, luckiest, most successful person. Under these conditions it is dumb to miss any pleasure.

A life-giving community teaches that pleasure fails to meet needs because pleasure alone is not life-giving. Nor is life-giving always a pleasure. Yet life-giving is what satisfies, and when all is well, then life-giving is a pleasure.

Lured by Power

While pleasure is a theme for Satanist writers like Crowley and LaVey, generally it is only bait on the hook or a "benefit" for the true follower. Power forms a far more central theme than pleasure for the serious occultist. The two, in their carnal expression, are remarkably interrelated, as we shall see.

Have you ever been seduced by power? Bill's parents were. His father and grandfather were both policemen. His mother liked nice things and dreamed of being popular but had married an alcoholic. The family members claimed to be close but hated each other. Emotional power was abused because everyone who could got into powerful rages. A contact at a country club brought Bill's father into Satanism. It was, he was told, a way to get more money than any cop would ever see. Money and influence were hard to turn down but proved even harder to find.

Bill was born cute. His mother soon recognized the potential for him in commercials and television. By the time he was ten, Bill had paid for much of his parents' home and was included among his mother's lovers. Bill's every move was regulated to keep him cute and marketable. His mother kept tyrannical power over her small domain. By thirteen Bill was lost to drugs, and by eighteen to wild sex. By 35 he could not keep a friend and was afraid he had AIDS. He felt very insecure, just as his mother and father had before him.

SECURITY THROUGH POWER

Security is a strong need. Power is a counterfeit way to find it. Power is deceptive because it seems that just a bit more will cause us to prevail and be secure. But with a whole universe threatening our security with its awesome power, we never have enough; more power is always needed. Formulas or powerful allies are required if one is to be the strongest.

Control of elements, universe and spirits provides just such a goal for those learning occult crafts. They hope to gain power that most people do not even know exists. The ability to control becomes the measure of power.

Perhaps the three most appealing occult powers for young adults are clairvoyance, divination and telekinesis. Knowledge of the future or of other's thoughts can be quite an advantage. They certainly provide options for great fantasies. Moving objects with thought power also would impress almost anyone.

While the fight rages fast and furious over whether these abilities are real or illusory, the appeal of their power is obvious. One feels more secure with a secret weapon. There is confidence that comes from an advantage. A boy on a bicycle feels free to challenge a flock of boys on foot to a race. Similarly, if one can get a Ouija board to tell the future, one feels a certain advantage betting on a horse. Knowledge, then, can be power.

Knowing what others are thinking would also give us an advantage in meeting our needs for companionship. Julie might have liked that to give her some security. Matters of the heart provide much of the incentive for special powers. If we could make others love us, our sense of security might improve. Love spells and potions are popular among those who lack prestige, possessions and pulchritude. Having had two teenage boys, I can vouch for how much time and energy teens spend trying to figure out what others think about them. Finding and using love spells, then, is a major attraction to Satanism for the high school crowd.

POWER TO CONTROL THINGS

Most occult, magick (sorcery, distinct from stage magic or illusion), alchemy and parapsychology studies are directed at control of the elements and at forces of the universe. Of the two, controlling forces is more appealing to occultists because those are far less understood. Consequently occultists can make up whatever theory suits them with little threat of being disproved. They are enabled to step beyond the frontier of science into deeper knowledge, or perhaps nonsense—but who can tell the difference?

James Webb notes that occultists have long wished to be seen as scientific.[3] They go to great lengths to develop formulas that are reductionist and allow the practitioner to control forces in predictable ways.

Dan Korem, a professional magician, believes there is little real power or control available from spirit beings. Instead there are many illusions by people who stand to gain by convincing others that they have powers.[4] Korem devotes much time and thought to understanding how the mind can be fooled. He finds many deceptions and little evidence of real power.

Telekinesis or "mind over matter" is an entry-level attraction to the occult world. Mind over mind, mind over body and mind over spirit are far less visually captivating than mind over matter. Consequently deceptions are so commonplace with telekinesis that it hardly bears looking for a real event. Even if someone were to demonstrate such mind power, he or she would need to do more than move pencils to interest a serious Satanist. They want power to control people.

POWER TO CONTROL PEOPLE

Power to control others appeals to all of us occasionally. There were times when Kitty and I wanted a switch on the back of Rami's head that we could flip and start him cleaning his room. These "harmless" desires seem helpful to us. By controlling others, we hope to ensure that our needs will be met. And if we fear others or ourselves, such control looks tempting.

One common personality style that wants to control others is the authoritarian. We have three reasons to examine this kind of controller: First, many cult leaders are authoritarian. Second, authoritarian parents, teachers and church leaders contribute to the rebellion that sends young adults toward cults. Third, the personality style itself develops as a result of problems in the young adult years. The person with an authoritarian personality tries to solve problems by an application of power. The propensity to see relationships as power equations is motivated largely by fear.

According to Dr. Bob Altemeyer, "It turns out such persons tend to be highly fearful. They tend to see the world as a dangerous place where we live at risk. Many [authoritarians] believe they are God's designated hitters on earth. This explosive combination of fear and self-righteousness can produce many kinds of hostility."[5] Fearful people who feel the need to keep the world right for themselves are drawn to power. Whatever they need to do, if they end up on top, is approved. To them all they do seems right.

The hall monitor on a dorm floor was a junior who, so he believed, was there to help the freshmen get up to school standards. Larry was vigorous in his application of the rules; he even inspected rooms more frequently than the schedule required. He insisted on silence in the halls and, of course, no running. Sinks, tubs, floors, mirrors and even the trim around the base of the walls were never clean enough to avoid being rewashed. In short, the freshmen grew to love and appreciate his "help" the way most of us appreciate the oversight of the IRS. Larry liked to have power over others.

Authoritarian people seem to develop their personalities from encounters with unfair or frightening people in their community during adolescence.[6] Parents have less influence on this trait—evidence that we share responsibility for the healthy development of all those in our communities. Authoritarian personalities develop when young adults see their communities as dangerous instead of life-giving.

Mrs. Brahma, Rami's sixth-grade teacher, told him to bring his papers to her desk. As Rami stacked his papers carefully, an office worker entered the classroom and began to talk to the teacher. When Rami reached her desk a few seconds later, Mrs. Brahma yelled at him, "Go back to your seat or I'll tear those papers up!" Mrs. Brahma was an authoritarian who liked power over others.

People who like to have power over others tend to create people who also want power. Rami wanted to fight back so he stopped doing homework because this made her mad. Being at the abusive end of power in action often makes us wish for more power than our nemesis.

The Downward Spiral of Control

The desire for power is not limited to adults. Even grade school, like any society, has its power-hungry members.

Martin dominated the skyline at my school. Martin was known for flushing children's heads in the toilet if they did not do what he commanded. He carried a slingshot and aimed it at children's tender places to assure the action he demanded.

I am ashamed to say that I adapted to Martin by joining him. Often I would talk him into leaving kids alone, but sometimes I joined him in tormenting youngsters like Steven. Steven got the worst of what Martin and I had to offer. He was sensitive and intelligent—qualities bullies hate. Adults liked Steven; they disliked Martin. In fact, the whole grade school disliked Martin. Eventually a group of us got slingshots and together—although individually none of us was as ruthless as he—we deposed him. Soon after that Martin left the school.

What surprised me, however, was that with Martin gone, I became even meaner to Steven than Martin had been. Fearful that Steven would report what Martin had done, with my complicity, I was determined to control him. But Steven was not going to be pushed around again, and I got really ugly.

Every attempt that failed to control Steven left me more exposed to being reported and required something even worse to follow. By the time I succeeded in intimidating Steven, I had tied him to a thorn tree, lit a smoldering fire around his feet, poured red ants on his arms and rubbed stinging plants on his neck. The results left me with neither satisfaction nor a sense of power. I was afraid of myself and feared by others. It was a most regrettable success.

Mind Control

The person who chooses to control has started into an intensifying spiral of intimidation. He or she needs to escalate the level of control to more dramatic levels each time in order to feel powerful. As the spiral continues, obtaining control over others by the direct use of threats quickly becomes dissatisfying. Sex given at gunpoint pleases only until it becomes obvious that anyone with a gun could get the same results. Since it is hard to feel attractive while forcing others to give pleasure against their will, one is compelled to force them to more extreme actions. Eventually these actions must become unnatural and repulsive to make clear that the person is being controlled. It is easiest to demonstrate control by forcing others to perform acts they would wholeheartedly avoid on their own.

It is impersonal to use a gun or knife because anyone with a weapon could obtain the same results. It begins to feel as if the gun itself has power rather than the individual. This limitation can be overcome, however, by switching from weapons to mind control. Mind control allows the criminal to feel special personal power in forcing people to obey without a direct application of force. The more unnatural, painful or repulsive the activity, the better it proves the power of the one in control.

Since control is unable to make the controller feel special as a person, at best only powerful, the activity coerced is often designed to be pleasurable in some way. This results in the combining of physical pleasure with the most loathsome and painful activities imaginable. This is sadistic abuse.

The result of such perversion on the perpetrator and victim alike is to convince them of their unattractive, degenerate state. In the absence of visible threats, both parties begin to believe they must want and like this somehow. They start to believe it is what they need and, even worse, who they are. Their identities are now being destroyed.

Because of our inner search for satisfaction, mind control is often the next step after sexual and physical control. To describe these facets of control in this fashion is misleading, however, because they do not always come in this sequence. These three arenas of control—sexual control, physical control, mind control—seem to spiral downward in the criminally perverse mind to progressively worse activities. Organized mind control cults, by contrast, recognize the end result and tend to pull their recruits, as either children or adults, directly into the mind control as quickly as possible. Like most activities, once you have mastered it, what counts is how quickly and effortlessly or intricately you can bring it about.

For mind control to succeed, the controllers must disrupt the human identity of their victim sufficiently that the target of their control stops knowing who he or she really is. To do this means separating the heart, soul and mind. That these elements can be separated is seen in Jesus' command that we love the Lord our God with all our heart, soul and mind (see Matthew 22:37). If these could not function independently, there would be no need to list all three.

In biblical terms, our heart is the organ of discernment or spiritual knowing. It is through the heart that we know truth, who we really are and who God is. Mind control is obtained by destroying what the heart cares about so that the pain is too intense for the soul to bear. When the soul retreats, the mind will also disconnect, because thinking about the truth brings the heart and soul together again. Once this is accomplished, the mind can be deceived, or even divided, fairly easily. Since the will is a function of the mind, it, too, can be divided and used against itself. James 1:8 reminds us that a divided mind is unstable in all its ways. Thus the fear of pain becomes the basis for deception and mind control.

Mind control can be avoided or overcome only by strong love. Strong love bonds are the basis of a working identity for individuals or groups. For Christian faith to work, it, too, must be based on bonds of love, and not just any kind of love; it must be "all-our-strength" love. We are to love the Lord our God with all our heart, soul and strength (see Deuteronomy 6:5).

The same is true for our individual and group identities, for we must love our neighbors as ourselves. In case we think neighbor love is a lesser love, John reminds us that if we do not love our brother whom we have seen, how can we claim to love God whom we have not seen (see 1 John 4:20)? Those who are not held by "all-our-strength" bonds look like easy catches to the dragon.

There is still greater control for those willing to take the next step. From a mind control perspective, causing people to witness or participate in murders has profound effects. This is particularly true if individuals are attached to the persons they are murdering and feel responsible for their suffering or deaths. For these psychological reasons alone, murder is a valued part of terrorist activities.

What we do not want to believe is that some people are studiously and creatively getting better at mind control.

POWER OVER LIFE AND DEATH

One Satanist woman told me over breakfast that her first human sacrifice was the most intense rush and most religious experience of her life. Nothing compared with this power in the two Christian services she had attended.

Even thinking about death in this manner upsets most of us. We are deeply aware that the power to end life belongs to God.

Life and death control is the greatest power available to humans. This is particularly true when we are speaking about human life. We have been given the gift of creating life, but for odd reasons many people feel more power in taking it away. The very act of ending the life of a human being conveys a sense of power.

Nowhere is the interest in death more evident than in human sacrifice. The most common and consistent charge leveled against destructive cults is that of ritual sacrifices. Animals, people and particularly children are murdered in exchange for great power. The act is final and irreversible. Some of the appeal of suicide also comes from exchanging one's life for power.

No doubt the reactionary nature of sin and occult thought makes the taking of life more central than the creating and sustaining of life. After all, God commanded us to multiply and fill the earth and not to murder. If power is to be found by breaking the rules, then killing is more powerful than saving.

There are benefits to stealing God's power. For many it is the satisfaction of eliminating an enemy, the need for justice or the desire for security through obliterating a threat. For others, people stand in the way of what they want, and people are easy to kill.

All this power is destructive. It is faster and far easier to destroy than to build. Wrecking a car is easier than building a car. Shooting someone takes far less skill and time than helping that person heal. Raising a healthy child takes far more work than traumatizing one. Ah! But which one makes us feel more powerful? Wrecking things is powerful—but empty.

Destruction and even potential destruction have a useful side effect: They produce fear. Fear gets quick results. Since power and speed are so closely related, fast things seem powerful. This makes type-B trauma—recall from the Professional Preface that this is the bad that happens, as opposed to type-A trauma, the absence of necessary good things—useful to those who want control. Picture every movie you ever saw with some man waving a gun and demanding instant results. Now picture every movie you ever saw with some man offering love to get quick results. Fear is the faster motivator. Christians have been known to lean on fear to motivate others.

Which do you rely on when you need results?

Ultimately control is futile. It cannot be achieved without destroying the value in others, and for that reason will fail to meet our needs. Our needs are met through receiving and giving life, not by taking power. Power used to control deceives the one in control.

Lured by Knowledge

Knowledge looks harmless enough. We expect that more knowledge will always be helpful. Almost every book I have seen on Satanism recommends obtaining more knowledge on the subject as a major step in solving the problems. But remember, humans got into trouble because we chose knowing good and evil over the tree of life. Knowledge is not life.

COMMON KNOWLEDGE

There is a difference between common knowledge and occult (or hidden) knowledge. Common knowledge is the basis for our educational system and has a few problems of its own. Many wealthy people and missionaries have selected knowledge over family life and sent their children to boarding schools. Science, the cult of common knowledge, is often wrong, bringing a constant need for new knowledge.

UNCOMMON OR HIDDEN KNOWLEDGE

Watching the dragon work this lure would make one think occult knowledge is really special stuff—not for common folk. For thousands of years mysteries have provided enticement to occult religion. In recent centuries science has performed most poorly on the mysteries we would most like to understand: Who am I and what will happen to me? From the far fringes of knowledge comes the repository of rejected knowledge with promises to provide the missing details about our future.

Such knowledge is available through channels of enlightenment. This is the world of the serious occultist.

There are three major kinds of occult knowledge: esoteric knowledge, practical (or power) knowledge and personal knowledge. Each has its own appeal.

1. Esoteric knowledge for the disillusioned. Mystery/occult knowledge provides an alternative view of the world. It is unlikely that anyone but a first-generation occultist would ever publish such knowledge openly. First-generation adult participants are rebelling against the world in which they were raised. As such they have reason to let that world know how wrong it is. They and their ideas experience rejection together. These are the writers, poets and artists with a message to us.[7]

Esoteric Satanism and witchcraft are both the realm of the multigenerational cults, who have no reason to write to us, and an intellectually disenfranchised elite, who have every reason to publish.

The occult crafts are generally suited to the intelligent mind. Their traditions in alchemy and esoteric lore are complex. The ideas and data needed to understand and control the universe within or without the human mind must, by necessity, be complicated. For those who postulate a spirit realm beyond the physical, the topic becomes even more intricate and varied. Once we become convinced that not everything has been explained by our current paradigms, there is room for knowledge that will not fit the mold. Knowledge that exceeds our current limits can prove either brilliance or trash. Occult knowledge proposes to explore such mysteries.

James Webb notes that "the obsessive quality of occult beliefs results almost invariably in their domination of the possessor's mind."[8] That is to say, once you start to think about these subjects, they tend to consume you. The more peculiar the outlook, the more time and energy it takes to understand or explain it. I suspect this is part of what the apostle Paul had in mind when he referred to "doctrines of demons" (1 Timothy 4:1, RSV).

It appears that esoteric knowledge forms much of the attraction for the professional community. Many doctors and nurses who deal with children's deaths and acts of cruelty have great difficulty with their feelings. Science seems insufficient for understanding their depth of grief and despair. Similar reactions are found among law enforcement and criminal justice personnel. They have difficulty believing in a loving, all-powerful God who would allow these atrocities.

2. Practical knowledge for the action crowd. Most occult information is of little interest to the teenage Satanist, who is more concerned with knowledge that produces results. He or she wants knowledge with power. The same can be said for criminally sociopathic Satanists who use these practices to protect their crime or further their own perversions.

Teenagers collect occult knowledge for certain games. These games require a practical working knowledge of spells and rituals for action or for the destruction of enemies. Players must master vast amounts of knowledge of spells and spirits, and those who become proficient need to learn the knowledge of the occult worldview. This practical knowledge varies considerably from the esoteric knowledge that attracts older audiences.

There is a large controversy over the connection between fantasy role-play games like "Dungeons and Dragons" and teenage Satanism. Investigators claim that Satanists use such game networks for recruiting.[9] Players who tend toward social isolation and difficulty in relationships are better than average targets for Satanism. Again, every young adult needs a group identity.

Freemasons and Shriners attract followers to their secret traditions with more of a view to action than knowledge. In secret societies it is who you know that matters. Occult knowledge becomes a way to exclude outsiders and identify resource people. Occult knowledge brings rank and power within occult groups. Some dream of belonging to a new world order.

3. Personal knowledge for the lonely. This use of occult knowledge is personal, seeking answers about my life, my future, my lovers, my money. Love spells decrease a teenager's chance of rejection if he or she possesses the secret knowledge of how to work the spell.

In general, then, it can be said that there are three sorts of occult knowledge that appeal to different groups: esoteric knowledge for the intellectuals and experts; practical knowledge for the action crowd; and personal knowledge for those who still hope to relate to others. This latter group can be caught with New Age lures. Those who hate the opposite sex but like their own are often attracted to witchcraft. Those who despair of any powerful love cannot resist one of the dragon's daredevils—Satanism. The hope for a loving relationship with a real person is without a doubt the single-largest deterrent to Satanism.

Lured by Spirits

The need to be comforted or connected to others brings many to their first séance or medium. Often people want to connect with those they love or admire but who have died. Others come seeking knowledge and power from powerful spirits. Mediums or channelers would protest, strongly and correctly, that they are not Satanists but spiritists. Communing with "superior" beings gives spiritism its appeal. These beings ostensibly supply knowledge about history, the future, people's identities and destinies and "how things work." Consider, then, the position of those who believe they have access to the answers to such questions. Only cost could induce someone to pass up the offer.

If these spirits are so helpful, however, it makes me wonder why their consultants work in such seedy places. I would think their spirit guides, using their superior knowledge, might help them obtain better accommodations.

Spirit guides appear to prefer the past to the future, while humans seem to want the opposite. Possibly the future holds the threat of making spirit guides look stupid when they miss their guess, whereas the past holds no such risk.

Spirit guides provide an entrance to the occult realm. In some cases they offer a form of relationship to rejected or abandoned people. When a high-status spirit being seeks them out, it makes them feel special. Being known is itself a deep need that we never outgrow.[10]

Several people tell stories similar to that of Irene Park[11] about spirits who taught them from childhood and led them toward Satanism. While I tend to disbelieve most of what I hear along this line, the stories are believed by many of those involved in the occult.

This subject is so fraught with deception, con artists and charlatans that it will never get untangled. Many want to hear from spirits so badly that there is a ready market to help them to do so. If a person believes that his or her needs will be met by spirits, finding guides is an easy job. Satanists are among those who market this service.

A certain elitism may be observed among those in occult leadership who claim they were taught by spirit masters rather than by people. Since Satanism is a pseudo-science, the idea of being taught is far less prevalent than in other occult circles. These occultists want to control spirits. The idea of discovering how to control spirits by one's own experiments and investigations allows far greater emphasis to be placed on the human as master. Who wants an ascended master when the person himself may ascend to be master? Not that this motivation is lacking in New Age thinking, but when we are all gods, there is a distinct loss of individual control that the Satanist would rather retain.

It seems to fit the nature of malevolent spirits to seek those who do not want them and to allow charlatans to exploit those who do seek them. The end of either one is deception. Spirits are not our community and they are sterile. Humans are meant to give life.

The Catch

- People take the bait only when they believe their needs will be met by a counterfeit.
- Lies are most compelling when the liars themselves believe the deception.
- The extent to which a belief system or group becomes dangerous is tied largely to how distorted its solutions to our real needs have become.

One salient feature of cults is that they act as if they have more solutions than problems. This concept is challenged by outsiders but believed by the group. It might be fair to say that the measure of a group's belief in its solution can be found in its response to needs. This belief is separate from its actual accuracy in matching needs to solutions. One must look no farther than the failure of Communism to see that.

Genuine need plus a false self-concept leads to deception. It is because we believe (incorrectly) that we need to know the future, to become wealthy, to control others, to be normal or perhaps to be better than others that we can be deceived. If we are convinced there is something missing from our identities, then almost any bait starts looking good. We will always be drawn to those who have what we think we need.

Obviously there is much disagreement about what people really need. At the center of this controversy is the basic view of how human beings work and who they are. I contend that our needs change across our lifetimes but are always present.

What we need at any moment is determined by our maturity and injuries. Babies and children spend all their time meeting their own needs. Adults meet each other's needs in a fair way. This is when their group identity develops. Parents meet children's needs without seeking to receive in return. Elders are parents to their community, meeting the needs of those who lack families of their own. Throughout the process each person continues to face the challenge of meeting his or her needs, in addition to meeting the new demands of his or her development. To do so requires an increasing ability to avoid isolation and draw on supernatural, social and internal resources. None of us is ever free from these demands while we are alive.

Immature people, however, are frequently ignorant or mistaken about what they need. They are easy to lure. People without resources will settle for what they can get. What each solution costs us to achieve becomes the issue of the day. One author believes there are few blacks in Satanism because they have discovered there is no such thing as a free lunch.[12] Perhaps the common experience of matriarchal power among American blacks or the prevalence of Nazi and Aryan supremacy thought in Satanism are other influences. Hell, it appears, is to be ruled by whites—or, at least, fewer blacks believe hell will meet their needs. That makes them, on that lure, harder to catch.

The Real Needs of Young Adults

A life-giving family and church community teach us what will satisfy our needs through each step of our lives. Since young adults are particularly vulnerable to cults, let's examine what they need to become life-givers rather than destroyers.

The needs of young adults can be divided into three categories: relationship, power and truth.

Relationship

From the beginning of the teenage years, friends, dates, groups, teams, sex and all sorts of relationships take center stage. During this time teens grow from individuals to members of groups and society. Those who are received into groups develop the sense that there are causes and purposes bigger than they are.

It is particularly important for young adults to express this group identity and even defend it. Gangs use graffiti. Others use clothes and uniforms. Some use drugs or activities to announce who they are. Cults are quick to allow young adults a group identity and the chance to proclaim it. Many groups use young adults as missionaries, which meets their need to proclaim who "we" are.

Many churches and communities do not recognize the need for their young adults to form, declare or defend their group identity. This leaves an unmet need.

Power

Young adults are learning to use power and are attracted to it. These are the years of strength and action. Most of the action and service recorded in Scripture is attributed to young adults. Cults, as we have seen, particularly the destructive ones, are interested in power.

Many churches and Christians, on the other hand, practice a religion without power. Furthermore they are often engaged in power struggles with teens and are reluctant to give them any real power. Because young adults are treated as trivial, they disappear in droves from churches. This leaves them with unmet needs for power within their communities.

Truth

Young adults have a third need, which is truth. The truth they seek most desperately is that of their own identities. They want to know who they are as individuals, couples, friends and groups. They want to know who they are as male and female.

This is a relational kind of truth, so it should be no surprise that the power they seek most is also relational. Young adults want to have a real effect on others. This can be accomplished with a gun in a schoolyard or by prayer in the cafeteria; by wearing sexy clothes or by looking buff. Each one is seeking the true power of

71

their group, as seen in its effects on others. Those who do not know their true identities are easy lunch.

The Failure of Christianity

The three primary needs of young adults are also crucial components of genuine Christianity.[13] Loving the Good Shepherd is a relationship. He is Truth and provides true identity through the hearts He gives us. The King of kings also has all power and authority. Dr. Charles Kraft, the noted missionary anthropologist, once commented to me, as I mentioned earlier, that American Christianity has revered truth, rarely experienced power and practically ignored relational aspects of the Gospel. As a consequence many young adults go elsewhere to find their truth, power and relationships.

In this chapter we have seen how unmet needs and a poorly developed group identity leave young adults vulnerable to cults. In the next chapter we will see how these young adults got this way. The problem often begins much earlier.

Preparing Children for the Dragon

Fear-Based Identities

GOOD PEOPLE while trying to do the right thing, can actually prepare children for the dragon. If their efforts were intentional they could repent, but most are accidental or, worse yet, a result of misguided helpfulness. Many of these hurts are minor, but through them the dragon seeks to shape our identities around fear.

Our identities are open only to those with whom we bond and whom we need. Only those we need can really touch our core. They alone have permission to shape our identities. To succeed, the dragon must sneak fear into children.

Kitty sat on her little chair listening to her dad. Across the room Mommy was combing her hair. Carefully repeating each word her father said, Kitty prayed the sinner's prayer, accepting Jesus into her five-year-old heart. She knew this was very important. Her dad had never been so attuned to her. Her parents had never seemed so pleased.

This wonderful moment eclipsed the past week's excitement about starting school.

Kitty was the oldest child on their African missionary outpost and this would be her first year. She did not really understand the concept of going to school, but tonight all that slipped from her mind. Her parents' joy was immediate and real. She could feel their approval.

The next morning Kitty and her little suitcase were loaded onto a plane. Her father was no longer attentive. He talked to the pilot and very little to her. Then, before she knew it, she was waving goodbye to her family. She had a stomach-dumping flight—alone. The pilot got angry when she threw up on his plane. It was scary.

Although she would not be able to recall it later, she was told what happened next. For two weeks little Kitty wandered the halls of the missionary boarding school, crying. The girl with pixie-length blonde hair carried her dolly and called, "Mommy!" as she walked. She searched every hall, room and corner she could reach.

Then the crying stopped. No mommies heard or came in this scary new world. Aunties came. They would spank bad girls. Aunties seemed angry. They talked about Jesus—the same One she had let into her heart. It had made her parents glad before they sent her away. In time she would learn that Jesus had sent her parents away from *their* mommies and daddies. Jesus did that to all the children she met in this school. She feared this place where He had sent her, and she feared He would continue sending her away. She began to see Jesus as Someone who sent little children away instead of calling them toward Him. Distrust began.

After four months in first grade Kitty returned home. She was glad going to school was finally over. She was so happy for Christmas. Christmas was the time when family was more important than Jesus' work. Even the Africans could be sent away that day. School was behind her and she was home to stay. Her punishment was finished. Now Mommy came when she called. Kitty was entitled to a family again.

The day after Christmas, however, she found out she was going back to school. Her heart almost stopped. Preparations for her send-off began. She felt confused and lost. Why was she the only one sent away from home after Christmas? Why could her brother and sister, the dog, the Africans and even the crazy *mahaukachi* stay? What was so bad about her?

To the adults around her, this school was a great improvement for missionary children. Thanks to the vision of an adult missionary child, children could now see their parents twice a year. Until then school-aged children were left Stateside and saw their parents every four or five years. Parents hid their sadness from the children and tried to celebrate this real improvement, but it was not a complete solution. Fear and pain still found their way into the best plans and into Kitty's identity.

No one noticed that controlling hundreds of children produced, for many of them, a fear-based world. Trying to keep from being punished became inordinately important for some. Others feared disgracing their families, missions or God. Fear governed much of their actions and stunted their growth, curiosity and identities.

By the time I met Kitty in college, she had little idea of what she liked. She could not decorate a room or cook a meal. She had no idea she was a person with individual tastes, opinions or feelings. Since there was no music in the dorms, she did not have a taste in music. She did not know there was more than one kind of cheese. It took me three or four years to help her overcome her fear of milkshakes enough to try a sip.

Kitty was afraid of the unknown. She knew what she feared but not what she wanted. She avoided anything she did not understand and everything that might make someone angry with her. She was terrified that people would think there was something wrong with her. She hid all her flaws and worked hard to be good. She had a fear-based identity.

Fear-Based Identities

Every distortion of our true selves leaves a weakness to be exploited through fear. Injuries to our identities are the most painful and debilitating damage we can sustain. Every incorrect accusation or attribution by those we trust leaves pain, confusion and weakness. These false labels cause fear that makes children see themselves, in spite of others' intentions, as the dragon wants them to. The power of life and death is in the tongue.

Knowing our true identities in Christ is an impenetrable defense against evil. This identity is based on love—a love so solid it can endure all pain. God is certain that if we know Him, we will love Him.

The dragon, on the other hand, prefers that our identities be based on fear; he does not expect to be loved. He knows we fear pain.

I once had opportunity to ask a man who had been a high-ranked leader in a cult which was the more powerful force, love or fear. Without hesitation he responded, "Fear." What do you believe? Those who believe fear is stronger will organize their identities around fear itself. They admire the scariest person, force or being. Because fear is the main motivator for Satanism, they bond their identities to the very things that scare other people to death.

Pain is the simplest way to produce fear. This is so simple that you may miss the impact. Those who want the power that comes from fear must produce pain. More pain means more fear, which means more power over others—except over those who do not fear pain. Who does not fear unbearable pain? The dragon likes pain and fear, and his followers find them useful.

What about good people? Surely they do not want to help the dragon. They are not attracted to fear or pain, but they may fear pain. Fear of pain is natural and expected, but there is danger in using this fear to get results from children, and good people actually prepare children and friends to serve the dragon when they begin to use the fear of pain for motivation.

Good Christian people are as likely as anyone, I believe, to be motivated by fear and to use fear as the main way to motivate others. This prepares people clearly and directly to respond to the pull of cults. The practice is so widespread that we are practically unaware of it. In many places it is preached mistakenly as sound biblical childrearing and discipline. It is the power of fear. It is enforced by pain. It is diabolical.

What motivates you, when push comes to shove, and what motivation do you use with others?

It is absolutely inevitable for us to experience both fear and pain. Do not ask me to explain why. This problem is felt so intensely that many people get upset and confused merely from the introduction of this topic for discussion. Fear and pain are both unavoidable and necessary. We are even required at times to be the source of pain in the lives around us. A good parent teaches children how to understand pain and to endure or remove it without fear.

Yet here is a double trick: Those who try to save their children from all pain are teaching them to fear pain as much as those who use pain to produce fear in their children. Both overprotective and controlling parents produce the same fear in their children. Whether you say, "Don't do that, it might hurt," or, "If you do that, I'll hurt you," the same fear grows.

In a general way we can say that the instruction and experiences we have with fear and pain will either prepare us for cults or immunize us against them. The path into destructive cults is a spiral into the power of fear and pain. This principle becomes important the first time a baby experiences fear or pain, and it continues throughout his or her life.

Many a child has been born crying. Pain and fear occur in the womb, but we know little about their effects. In nonabusive homes every effort is made to relieve children's fear and pain. Children in these homes learn that pain means comfort is on the way. Almost everyone treats newborns this way. It is not until the child begins to appear to have a will (somewhere between six and eighteen months, depending on the parent) that good parents begin to consider the judicious use of pain and fear to motivate their children.

The threat, the upraised hand and the phrase *Mommy spank* mark the beginnings of change. This may interest you because you were a small child at one time. Most of us do not remember clearly what happened to us as toddlers. Some of us have our own toddlers or anticipate having small children. We want to help them grow without letting fear and pain provide even a small place in their identities for the dragon's teeth.

Normal Identity Formation

Before we can discuss the parents' and community's roles in forming or correcting identities, we must take time to study the process of individual identity formation. In chapter 2 we studied how young adults form group identities. Now we will examine how infants and children form individual identities.

We need a mental diagram of the way their identities are formed. Until we know how it works, we cannot compare methods, although we all notice the results.

I remember deciding to fix the emissions control equipment on my car. Smog systems are far simpler than children, more standardized, easier to understand and they come with manuals.

77

Equipped with my trusty manual, I traced several parts but soon arrived at a canister that did not show up in my book at all. It got worse after that. The car had hoses and square things where none was shown. Parts were absent from places the diagram assured me they could be found. The tubes were arranged a little like the California diagram, a little like the mountain version and a little like the variation found only in England. Fortunately, twenty dollars bought me a different version of the diagram with certain "later variations."

Children have almost infinite variations to their identities and no diagrams. There are, however, consistent objectives. We want a car to pass the smog check and to run. We want children to have their true identities. There are constants, patterns, principles, critical periods and essential tasks that will lead to corrupted or accurate identities. Children can be built many ways; some prepare them to know God and some cause them to think like the dragon.

Children are born not knowing who they are. Actually most of the identity regions of the brain have not yet been formed at birth. Most of these areas grow in the first two years in response to joy. This brain growth is tied directly to how much joy the parents share with their children between six and eighteen months. Research has shown that this growth depends on parental stimulation.[1] The amount of joy shared by parent and child sets the strength and size limits of the baby's identity and respective brain structures.

At a neurological level, joy means, *Someone is glad to be with me. That person's face lights up to see me.* Joy is the only emotion that infants seek on their own during the first year of life. Joy is the basis of normal identity growth. With proper stimulation our joyful identity structures in the prefrontal cortex of the brain can eventually grow to become 35 percent of the adult brain. These structures are responsible for love bonds and how we see ourselves. But this growth is over before we can speak fifteen words.

At the neurological level we see ourselves reflected in the facial expressions of others because that is what these prefrontal cortex nerve cells store. Our identities are created from the relationships among the face that represents us as babies and the faces we bonded with that are looking back at us. We see ourselves in the mirror of the faces looking at us. We know ourselves not as *I* but as *us* or *we*. Research has established that there are at least two faces, mother and child, in this brain image,[2] but theory predicts that there must

who have begun to see themselves as God sees them can see their children with heaven's perspective.

As children grow older the process of correctly matching who they are, how they work and what they are worth, to the way they think about themselves, is often called building self-esteem. We also refer to it as developing a positive self-image or a good self-concept.

These terms, however, are a bit misleading. *Primary ontological security* is more accurate but leaves most people in the dark. Confusion about these terms arises from the positive tone of their message. For an identity to be solid, it is more important that it be accurate than either pleasant, nice or positive. We all sense things about ourselves that are painful, shameful or bad. But many parents try to build self-esteem and save their children from pain by telling them nothing but good things about themselves.

The encouragement that "you can do anything you put your mind to" is bogus and every child suspects it. "You're the smartest girl in the world" is cute but will not hold past recess. "That's a beautiful picture! You are such an artist!" breaks down almost as quickly when teacher says, "Try to stay in the lines next time."

Equally deadly is the trap of acknowledging the bad but forgetting the child's value. Many parents, in the mistaken impression that they are being encouraging, point out only the mistakes or errors in their children's efforts. They would not neglect their children's discipline for a day but do forget on many days to bless them in God's name and announce their little ones' value.

Humanists say, as a rule, that all bad is imposed from the outside, since the self is good. Christians believe the self has evil in it, but beyond that, opinions vary greatly. Whatever else may be meant by *sin*, it refers to not acting out of our true selves—the selves we were created to be. Sin means it is now possible for us to both act like ourselves and not act like ourselves. We can receive and give life or we can destroy. Original sin means it is inevitable that we will fail to act like our true selves because we will be like our parents.

The result of neglecting either the evil or the value within a child is that he or she will develop an identity that cannot accommodate both. Either way his identity will not fit what the child knows to be true. The truth is, he is both good and bad, and he will become vulnerable to the first person to recognize this truth in his soul and do something about it.

Children who have an accurate sense of self, including both good and bad, are, in my view, far less susceptible to occult influences or experiences. Further, their desire for cult involvement decreases because they can relate to others realistically with far less need for irrational solutions. People with an accurate sense of self are less motivated to have their worth reappraised. After all, if we know and accept that, despite all our faults, we are God's children, having a higher seat in hell will not mesmerize us.

Type-B Trauma and Identity Formation: When Bad Things Happen

After examining normal identity development, we can now begin to study how fear and pain can alter the basic structure of a person so completely that he or she can be built around fear rather than the joyful flow of life into and out of him or her. Fear comes naturally with trauma and pain. Trauma has huge effects on identity, especially on incomplete child identities.

Before we look at the more subtle forms of this problem, let us tell the truth about the blatant forms. Some Americans abuse their families. For their own benefit, they put their families through emotional and physical pain so they can control them through fear. The biggest difference between this and the way Satanists in multi-generational cults raise their families lies in the nature of the self-deception justifying the torture. The joint creativity of cult groups makes them more effective, but there are cases in which solid citizens have come close to matching cult cruelty.

The now-elderly son of a university professor and political leader tells of more than ten years of physical and sexual abuse from his father. The boy was enrolled in a private Christian school where his father was held up as a model to the community. The father, a devout churchman, punished imagined crimes, such as the possession of a stolen quarter, by combining tortures. (The quarter was not stolen but was a gift from a friend.) First the dad beat his son with a wire until the boy's back was lacerated and permanently scarred; then he drowned him to the point of unconsciousness; and he finished with an anal rape.

This level of punishment did not, in the family's view, merit medical treatment, but more serious infractions like interrupting the father's work could land the boy in the hospital. The assaults continued and increased steadily in severity over the years. They were so devastatingly effective in producing fear that the abuse continued even after the boy was an adult. Many of his organs and body parts were damaged so extensively that they required surgical removal. The young man was frequently sodomized from age six to eighteen in a manner that included the abusive use of laxatives. This "discipline" was necessary, so the boy was led to believe, lest he become a thief or liar.

I applaud the father's stated goals. Don't you?

There were no reports made, no arrests and no convictions in this case. I am shocked and horrified because the family, church and community allowed this father to "train" his son in this way. At one point or another responsible members of each group were made clearly aware of what this Christian man was doing. Grandparents, mother, police, doctors and clergy all failed to take action. Each and all were *afraid* to get involved. The man had influence, power, money and prestige. He was the American dream—and obviously dangerous. He knew and used the power of fear.

His son, now 72, makes almost all his daily and long-term decisions based on fear. He achieves what he wants from others through his temper and through others' fear of getting him mad. He is still consumed with avoiding pain.

People from all walks of life know how to use pain and fear to control others. A librarian actually prostitutes her children for gambling money she owes to the wrong people, afraid of what they will do to her otherwise. She makes fear-based choices based on her fear-based identity. Her children now fear what their mother and all men will do to them. A judge pushes his pregnant wife out of a moving car so she will learn to spend less money. Her mind floods with fear for herself and her child, but she is more afraid of leaving than of staying. She does not think she can take care of herself. Her husband's crime, therefore, goes unreported.

These traumas all produce the same results: pain and fear. While the abuse is extreme, it is unfortunately not rare.

Threats to maintain silence are also based on fear of pain. "If you tell anyone, it will kill your dad," for instance, exploits a child's fear of loss and abandonment. Victims are trained to avoid seeking help from others through fear. Their identities allow very few choices.

Herein lies the secret to much of spouse abuse. Violence and threats are often directed toward keeping the spouse isolated. If he or she sought help, it would become too easy to escape the control of the perpetrator. By combining fear of pain, therefore, with such indirect fears as shame and guilt, it is possible to obtain a high degree of isolation, even when help is readily available.

Fear-Bonded Obedience

With children, pain and fear can be used to create trance states that abusive parents call "obedience." This obedience arises from an altered state of consciousness in which the frightened child focuses on pain to such an extent that he or she will not consider alternate solutions or behavior. Such obedience is mind control—fairly easy to create in most children by combining spanking with yelling. This training causes the mind to run in tight patterns that preclude creative thinking. It produces a fear-based identity.

The main problem is that such obedience occurs only in the trance state. Parents must threaten the children repeatedly, therefore, to the level of fear needed to induce the trance before they get compliance. Then they say, "I don't know why I have to threaten him within an inch of his life before he'll do what he's told." This is fear-based motivation.

The ability to enter such a trance state decreases rapidly with age unless the child is abused. Adults abused as children are far more susceptible to altered states and hypnosis. The ability to enter a trance is excellent preparation for enduring abusive cults successfully. A child abused "for Christ" (to make him or her good) is even more susceptible. The anger alone pushes him or her to seek a different god. Satan represents freedom to those who think of God as controlling.

Trauma during childhood influences worldview formation and identity development, and it frequently leads to demonization that affects both identity and worldview. Trauma leads to fear of the world and of other people. Trust becomes difficult, and without trust it is hard to feel loved. In addition, since traumas attract evil spirits, which do not tell the truth about who we are, it is possible for children to develop bizarre ideas about themselves. Not uncommonly they come to believe they need a spirit force for a companion since no one else will "help." It is reasonable to expect any spirit influence to lead a young person toward occult activities rather than toward God.

A central psychological influence of childhood trauma is perceiving oneself as a victim. Victims, who have a fear-based identity, make decisions based on fear. Victims always try for the least scary choice. It is easy to trap and manipulate victims because most good choices include some risk. Victims make good cult recruits.

Preparing Children to Accept Mind Control

Type-B trauma can go beyond creating victimization to altering the structure of children's brains and personalities. Children become unable to manage their own emotions. When the pain becomes too intense, prolonged or methodical, children's minds begin to focus on fragments of reality. Life becomes irrational. This is the beginning of mind control, which as we know is practiced by tyrannical governments as well as by abusive parents. Pain and fear are used to shape identities based on fear that gives no choice but compliance.

Slap! went the big hand across the little face, sending the little head against the floor.

"Who do you think you are?" bellowed the big voice.

As the salty taste of blood grew in the little mouth, the answer came. It was the only answer that would stop the big hands and voice. "Nobody, Daddy. I'm nobody."

He did more than say it. The little boy became "Nobody" in the part of his mind reserved for beatings. Since he was only four, he took his identity to mean that he had no body. That meant that the parts of him that bled and hurt were not his own but some other little boy's. It was confusing if he thought about it, so he did not.

When he was six, he heard about ghosts and started to wonder if he was one of those.

As a teenager Little Nobody had real identity problems. He became a flasher. His body, which did not seem quite real, produced strong reactions in people when he exposed it. He was obese but did not seem to notice. Some part of him was fighting being a nobody by getting as big a body as possible.

As Nobody grew older, he began to think of himself as a nobody in the more usual sense, so he dropped out of school, even though he was bright. Nobody kept menial jobs, even though he was capable of much more. He never used his considerable artistic talent. Whenever he felt threatened he ran away. That resulted in several outstanding warrants against him. To everyone but the sheriff, his drug dealer and his victims, he had become a nobody. His fear-based identity was full of dragon bites, and Nobody was dragged places he did not want to go.

Building a Fear-Based Identity

By combining pain and specific messages, parents can use fear to shape their children's identities. When parents cause a child to associate certain messages with fear, these messages will replay themselves loudly whenever the child feels fear. This sense of identity will guide the individual's future choices and thoughts whenever he or she feels afraid.

Mom sexually abused her daughter with a broom handle.

"You like it, don't you!" she screamed and called her a filthy name related to a sexual act.

The five-year-old girl learned well. The screaming, the pain and her mother's intense emotions captured all of her attention. Her mother was teaching her who she was and what she liked.

Christie could not sleep all night and could scarcely move without crying out. Through the dark hours she heard the echo of her mother's words and actions again and again, telling her who she was and what she liked. It crashed against something in Christie that knew she disliked pain. She had thought when she sat on Billy's lap—Billy was her mom's off-and-on boyfriend—that she only wanted a story read. But her mother knew better, and in a fit of rage sent Billy out of the house and taught Christie a lesson. Christie discovered painfully how little she really knew about herself.

Christie was receiving a new, fear-based identity. Mommy was teaching her, in a lesson that could not be ignored, who she was, what she liked and how she wanted to be treated.

In the years ahead, this and similar lessons would make it hard for Christie to find people like her in church. When Juli Blackman sat on the Sunday school teacher's lap for storytime, Christie called her the same filthy name her mother had used and was sent out of the class by a horrified Mrs. Butler, who then told Christie's mother.

That led to more lessons for Christie. The little girls at church, it seemed, were not like her at all.

In time the youngster came to learn there were other places to go. In high school and even junior high, Christie became one of those girls your mother warned you about. Loneliness drove her toward people who knew who she really was down inside. One day an older, scruffy-looking man with a van spotted her; another day a jerk on a bike recognized her.

Christie fought to finish school. Some of her teachers, like Mrs. Butler, believed in her; and, as is often true with children whose identities have been distorted by their parents, she was saved by people in her community who saw value in her. Christie fought hard and eventually became a teacher herself, but it did not bring peace to her identity, because the dragon's teeth had been driven in with a broom handle.

The war for Christie's identity extended into the community. Some saw a good Christian teacher; others saw her as her mother had and slept with her in degrading ways or treated her badly. When people seemed to love her and respect her work, Christie almost panicked. She could not take the pressure between her identity and her image. *If they only knew!* her mind would scream. She was not the nice teacher in a wonderful Christian school that most people had been fooled into seeing. Then Christie's sense of who she was started to fall apart, causing severe anxiety. She had a fear-based identity. The dragon's teeth would pull and tear, dragging her toward anyone who could see the real Christie, as her mother had.

Anxiety would trigger each quest to find someone to repair her identity the way her mother had taught her. Before long one of the dragon's men would find her. As they began she would say, "Talk mean to me. Make it hurt. I love it when it hurts!" Then she would go away deep inside her mind. Afterward she would crawl away alone. It always ended that way. She knew she really belonged alone in the dark with dark forces.

Other people have become repulsive, stupid, hot-tempered and homosexual—not because they needed to be but because that was what came to define their identity. If something becomes your identity, you see, you do not even have to act on it for it to stay true. Our identities are always with us.

Type-A Trauma and Identity Formation: The Absence of Good Things

Now that we have examined how the more blatant forms of fear and pain push people toward the dragon's solutions, we can examine the covert influences.

Just as severe pain and fear can cause people to focus so narrowly that their identities change dramatically, so lesser amounts of fear and pain can permanently distort a child's understanding of who he or she really is. Subtle influences can often have the most lasting results because they go unnoticed and uncorrected. Neglect (also known as type-A trauma) is harder to spot than abuse. The absence of necessary good things produces its own profound terror—the fear of nothing.

Left to raise themselves in a vacuum, children use the vacuum to define themselves. Children who lack help at crucial times in identity formation come to believe they deserve to be alone or that they possess unusual characteristics that make them different from children who are loved.

It is upsetting to be unsure who one is, for we have to be someone. We fear having no identity more than having an ugly one. We would rather have a bad description to define us than none at all. Neglect leaves a huge hole in a child's identity. How children try to fill the hole is determined by what they fear. Children fill the void with a fear-based view of themselves and of the world. Neglect always produces a fear-based identity. In children this can produce strange results.

Because no one seemed to notice her as she walked the halls of the boarding school with her dolly, Kitty came to believe she was invisible. When she cried on the plane, no one saw. When she called for Mommy, no one heard. No one noticed when she came and went. This happened so often that she concluded no one even knew she was there.

In time Kitty found she could walk out of church crying and no one would notice, just as her teachers had not noticed, just as her parents had not noticed, just as her friends had not noticed. Kitty saw that others were noticed and held and comforted when they cried. People talked to other children and even hugged them. Sometimes people would run over to see someone near her, and it would frighten Kitty to think she had been seen—but it always proved to be a near-miss.

Kitty did not like being invisible and knew her identity was illogical, so she never mentioned it to anyone. She never thought to look for help. When people waved her way, she turned around to see who they were waving at. Usually someone else stood nearby. At other times she could not see who they were waving at because when she looked behind her there was no one there. Still she never thought they were waving at her.

It is hard to go to college and believe you are invisible without feeling distress, so Kitty had to drop out before she fell apart. Being invisible was not much of an identity but it was all she had. She held tenaciously to her view of herself, and became angry and withdrawn if people tried to make her speak in front of a group or have her picture taken. To act as if she were visible when she was not caused her intense anxiety. Fear ruled her life, but she was just considered shy by others. Desperate for attention, she could tolerate it only in the dark where being unseen did not produce conflict. This made her vulnerable to the boys she most feared. Her brain's alarm centers kept her eyes on the dragon's boys and they saw her watching them.

Invisible people are susceptible to anyone who sees them. Other unnoticed people become despondent. Frequently they become involved in fringe groups as a cry for attention. It is an adult version of "I'll just eat worms and die!" Neglected children and adults are at the mercy of their communities because, for whatever reasons, their families have not responded to their needs.

The Community Role in Identity Formation

Neglect is not just a family issue because communities also bear responsibility in raising children. Neglect by the community is a factor for children who are abused as well as for those who are neglected by their individual families.

Storytellers

A community is like a library of stories, except that these are the stories of *us*. Community stories tell why we are here, what we are worth, what we like, what is funny or serious and how we should act.

My community taught me how to think about men and women, Norwegians and Swedes, Native Americans, blacks, Asian motorists, vagrants, Texans, spotted owls, Iranians, Jews, the FBI and the IRS, used car salesmen and going to Sunday school. My community let me know that I am not worth much if I am fat, I am worth a lot if I am cool, I am terminally immature if I am male and I can do anything if I am female. These stories are subject to change from time to time without notice.

These community stories come to us through church, school, television, radio, newspapers, magazines and, especially for children, neighbors. Their power comes from community consensus, not the truth of the tale. Community silence means something is not important, jokes mean a subject is no longer sacred and uncontested stories mean something is undeniably true. These community stories have a large influence on identity formation.

Historians

An intact community tells the history of its own place and people. Who names the streets and who sweeps them, who can speak and who causes all the trouble are in these stories. Communities keep the histories of individual families and the degree of honor each deserves. They also keep track of history in a general sense by telling what teenagers are like and what old women or men do.

Watchers

The community keeps watch over its members to be sure they act like themselves. They ensure that boys don't hit girls, that no one hits someone with glasses on, that you don't tell nothin' to cops, that children don't talk back to their mothers and that girls don't sit like that.

Communities also keep formal track of the limits of freedom granted members. Often adults and those in power have much more freedom than others. Movie and music stars (as well as cool presidents) can act out sexually and win approval, whereas other politicians or preachers acting the same way receive censure. Communities decide it is bad to be a Communist sympathizer, punk-rocker, skateboard rider, abolitionist or anti-abortionist. They also decide

repair. Even then the pause is temporary, and unless the community intervenes, they will soon rebuild the old identity. Many recovery groups work along these principles.

When people's identities disintegrate, they are at the mercy of those around them to know who they really are. A life-giving community will see them through the eyes of heaven. If they are surrounded by Satanists, by contrast, they will be told who they are in a way that combines both their value and their evil nature but that is still far from the truth. In this way future breakdowns are guaranteed, for which the same "help" will be provided. Brainwashing, some call it.

The less prone someone is to disintegration, the harder it is to brainwash him or her. The more closely we were trained to see ourselves as we truly are, the less prone we are to personality disintegration. The truth will make us solid. When the truth about us changes, we make the transition smoothly with the help of our life-giving communities.

Fear-Based Identities and Satanism

Abuse and neglect by parents and communities produce fear-based identities. Pain helps people focus their attention enough to avoid seeing alternatives. The combination of pain and fear produces a kind of hopeless desperation that makes teenagers do crazy things. Controlling people often gives them their final push into cult life.

Abuse prepares children to think as the dragon does. Eventually abused children find ways to run their own lives. For many the teen years are a time of sweet rebellion. Teenagers and victims are likely to form reactive identities. That is to say, they do not know who they are but they know what they are not! This is the simplest way to separate from people they do not like or trust. Teenage Satanism frequently fits this pattern. Young people simply identify with the opposite of whatever they are rejecting.

The more people respond to fear and threats, the better prepared they are for the world of Satanism. They fit in because they understand fear. Fear is their major motivator. Fear maps their world. Little wonder, then, that many Satanists come from abusive families and systems.[9] To really understand and respond to threats without looking for options, you see, requires a bit of training.

Neglect pushes children toward the dragon. We can point to evil from parents, in the form of child abuse, as a cause for children to reject the God of their fathers. This is a major source of the anger that fuels teenage Satanism. But there is nothing like neglect and indifference to produce hopeless, desperate children. Almost any cult provides community, reaches out to the hurting and accepts young, lonely dropouts, but Satanism takes the angry, hopeless ones.[10]

Without hopeless feelings most people would seek help or find alternate solutions when in pain. This requires hope, however, that people will respond to one's pain and fear. This hope for comfort from others is eroded more by neglect, abandonment and indifference than by abuse. In abusive situations, after all, someone is at least interested enough to invest energy and attention. Neglect provides no such hope. An uninvolved, absent or permissive parent thus becomes the typical parent of the teenage Satanist.[11]

As Satanism becomes more acceptable within the youth subculture, these generalizations become less true. If the peer group favors heavy metal music or the gang is involved in Satanism, this will inevitably attract some outgoing, friendly people. The tamer versions appeal to the excitement-seekers with a flair toward rebellion. These hedonists do not take Satan very seriously.

Just as the effects of parental abuse can be reduced with community involvement, so can the effects of neglect. It is unlikely that families will solve these problems on their own. For youngsters who are abused and neglected, the greatest deterrent to destructiveness lies in the hope of relating to another human being. These hopes often run toward the romantic end of things, whether heterosexual or homosexual. Occult practices from love spells to divination offer help with romance. Those who hope for lovers are deterred from entering criminal cults unless those cults are using romance as a lure to obtain members.

The final push toward the dragon is often given by good people. It is my contention that when good people use the *sark* to justify their traffic in fear, intimidation, control, authoritarian dominance, control-centered childrearing and abusive religion, they cut off hope. Under these conditions people are unable to escape fear and discover who they are in the eyes of heaven. They cannot find a community not run by fear. Since fear rules, they feel the push to get good at it. We continue our plunge into fear and evil in the next chapter, where we discover how ordinary evil can produce extraordinary results.

THE RED DRAGON'S LAIR

ORDINARY EVIL

THE ROCKET attack on the Supreme Court building was the highlight of the evening news on November 6, 1985. I watched as the Colombian drug lords, men about my age, attempted to intimidate or destroy their government. United States authorities had asked for the extradition of Colombian criminals to stand trial in United States courts. The drug cartel responded with a terrorist attack on the judges who cooperated with the U.S. What a dangerous country! Drug cartel money ruled, threatening even the nation's highest court. It was hard to believe!

The year after the rocket attack, eleven thousand people were murdered in Colombia, making homicide the leading cause of death for males from 15 to 44.[1] Yet this seemingly faraway violence holds some surprising hints about human evil that we need to understand. Did you ever wonder how people could kill their neighbors like that?

We need to understand how fear and a desire for power can grip a community of ordinary men, women and children in ways that make them kill. It will help us finish answering the questions raised in chapter 1 about the kind of evil reported in satanic rituals. Studying evil is ugly, but if a redemptive community plans to face dragon fire, it must understand the kind of evil we will explore in this chapter. Anyone helping people from a destructive cult will hear worse stories than these. We need to understand how people can act with such depravity.

Few people remembered that forty years before the rockets landed on their courthouse, the children of Colombia were being reared amid terror, ritualized mass murder and pacts with the devil for protection and power. The best estimates suggest that about 135,000 people were killed between 1949 and 1959.[2] The drug lords of Medellín and Cali were children then. Colombia was a violent place to live. I know. I was growing up there, too.

Hardly a child in the whole country, it seemed, did not have some intimate knowledge of horror and death. Many children were eyewitnesses of and participants in violence carried out primarily by Christian farmers. In an orgy of killing, neighbor turned on neighbor, threat answered threat, murder followed murder. Masters of terror emerged from the competition and ascended in prominence to become national idols. People knew them by name. Tiro Fijo, Sangre Negra and other killers were household words.

In this tender cradle the Colombian drug lords and drug runners of today were reared. They learned the power of fear, pain and death. Children saw that fear was how the world really worked; pain made a way to get ahead. A boy who became one of the most notorious drug lords often stopped to visit on Sunday afternoons in the home of one of my friends. My friend's family, like mine, had come to Colombia representing the redemptive community. "Jesus," Colombians said, "came to show us how to suffer and die." But for some the devil taught the way to live and win. Victory, it appeared, went to the most ruthless.

Could it be that a generation of children raised on ritualized abuse would engender the kind of disrespect for authority and justice that brought about the attack on the Colombian Supreme Court building? Information suggests that as children, most of the well-known Colombian mass murderers witnessed acts of violence toward their own relatives or neighbors. Others were forced to flee their homes to avoid being killed by their neighbors. That is to say, they lived in violent communities where life-giving was not the major motive.

Violence was everywhere. A few months after I was born, my parents replaced a missionary who had a nervous breakdown when his chapel was dynamited and shooting broke out in town. Two weeks before our arrival, his temporary replacement narrowly missed a bullet fired at his head through the chapel door. Shortly after our arrival, my dad found a note that ended, "Be notified that a volley of shots and dynamite leaves nothing but spoils and ruins. You have eight days to leave."

My dad writes, "My thoughts turned immediately to six-month-old Jimmy asleep in the next room. If I put his crib by the front wall, he would be in danger from dynamite; if he were by the inside wall, shots through the wooden shutters would reach him there." Dad sent for my mother, who was speaking in another town. The church where she was speaking had been dynamited the night before, so she left the conference and came home. We had a joyful reunion.

Many other families were not so blessed. Some suffered violence from their communities, but many children received it from their parents.

Dr. Carlos León, a Colombian psychiatrist, studied the violence in that nation extensively.[3] He looked for causes as well as results. Most famous Colombian killers, he found, had rigid, tyrannical fathers who used brutal punishment to maintain their dominance. (These are the authoritarian personalities we studied in chapter 2.) Their home life, like their community life, was ruled by fear. In fact, fear was the motivator for all levels of existence, from child-rearing to politics.

Violence in Colombia

Ritualistic Abuse of Children

Children in Colombia were exposed continuously to all sorts of graphic reports of violence. There is no form of cruelty that they were not familiar with in detail. Just as the American West had its necktie parties, so Colombia sported its killing rituals. The different procedures for killing included dismemberment, crucifixion, burning and many forms of wounding or beheading. Each ritual had a name, and children knew both names and methods. They knew it could happen to them. Nor was their knowledge of the violence all cleaned up, the way this book has been.

101

Looking up from a child's-eye level, I could see belts of ammunition and hand grenades under the poncho of the man chatting with my parents. I moved slightly closer to my mom's leg. He was one of the ten thousand Colombian *bandoleros*, but my parents could not see, could not tell. He saw me looking. He knew. I knew. My parents did not know. I stood very still.

He doffed his hat. "Buenas tardes."

"Stop by and visit our chapel," they said.

Maybe he had; maybe he would.

Many children were exposed to violence directly and personally. Dr. León recounts that one ten-year-year-old boy amused himself by trying to match heads with bodies after an entire village was decapitated. Children were often chosen for hideous jobs. Guerrilla leaders found youngsters, who could be forced to do tedious tasks, especially suited to cut hundreds of small, deep cuts in victims. The design left on the skin by these cuts looked like fish scales. This torture made victims bleed to death slowly and painfully. Children were used extensively in these murders and received intensive training in torture, weapons and methods of attack.

At times children were taken into the groups that had murdered their parents and trained as killers. Often teenagers became outlaws to avoid the fate of other family members or to get revenge.

Abisai Londoño was one teen who sought to protect himself this way. When he was ten, a group of masked men rode into his farmyard. They asked his father, Jose, what political party he belonged to, then shot him to death in front of his family. Abisai felt a deep hatred grow inside as he stood over his father's body swearing to get revenge.

After a narrow escape at age seventeen, Abisai joined a rebel group of about fifty men who lived in caves by day and killed by night. For the next seven years it was kill or be killed. Leaving the group was punishable by death.

"I was a prisoner in the group where I thought I'd find safety and freedom," he said. "I didn't know how much longer I could continue to kill and watch others be killed."

After successfully killing Red Devil, the leader of another group, Abisai had to make a run for it and get out of state. He moved in next door to where I lived and we became friends. Abisai learned the ways of Jesus and found that large hurts, hates and evils could be removed by the love and forgiveness of the Lord. Eventually he became a pastor but then left the pulpit to look for those people who felt too guilty to go to church. There was no shortage of guilty-feeling people in Colombia.

Sex and Death Together

Not just murder accompanied this anarchy. Murders were frequently connected with atrocious sexual crimes. New recruits to gangs were required to hack bodies with knives until they reached some sort of sexual exhilaration or climax. (You may recall that Karla Faye Tucker had orgasms while committing the pickax murders for which she was executed in Texas in 1998.) Gang rape was combined with torture and murder while family members were forced to watch. This happened frequently. These sexual crimes often included impaling, dismemberment, emasculation, mutilation of breasts and fetuses, and vampirism. Keep in mind that most of these mass murderers and serial rapists started as simple Christian farmers.

Most of the guerrilla leaders had reputations as great lovers. They were certainly great rapists, often matching the hundreds of murders to their credit with equal numbers of rapes or illegitimate children. In a twisted way, even these killers could not resist the pull toward life-giving.

Women as Perpetrators and Leaders of Violence

One of the most alarming aspects of the stories from cult survivors involves cruelty by women and children. Jurors in ritual-abuse trials have rendered "not guilty" verdicts or lesser sentences because the defendants were women. Yet women were deeply involved with the reign of terror in Colombia. Some cared for the gangs while others were informers and seduced the "enemy" sexually to their deaths. A few women gained reputations as killers and dismemberers in their own right. Murder, torture and sexual crimes with adults and children were practiced and perfected by both men and women. You are not reading "recovered" memories here.

Law Enforcement, Military, Clergy and Political Leaders

Some of the savagery in Colombia was carried out by the police and army as well as by the criminal element. Part of the violence

103

was even incited by clergy and politicians. Portions of the brutality received social support from citizens who erected shrines commemorating well-known killers. All levels of society participated in these abominable practices—political and religious leaders, police and military personnel, men and women, ordinary townsfolk and farmers, wealthy and poor, children and adults.

Torches gathered in the black tropical night. Five more came down the road, always moving around. We could hear voices through the front window of the same grade school where Linda had left a puddle in Miss Clarabelle's room the year before. For more than an hour, shadowy forms gathered down by the gate that faced the town of Llanito. Out that gate and down that road was the Llanito church; past the church was the main road; many miles down that road were Mom and Dad. Torches were now coming up the road to the gate.

My brother and the other kids kept silent vigil at the window. A similar mob had surrounded a church nearby and set it on fire with everyone inside. Stay in the fire or die by machete outside? I tried to decide. It seemed that something bad had happened at the Llanito church, but I did not want to ask about it just now. Maybe my brother could run away out the back and hide in the canefield.

Suddenly all the torches headed up the road. I wondered who was leading them. The local cleric had called for the end of our presence there—we had a school, campground, retreat center and small church—and I was afraid it might be he. I hoped the police did not arrive, because the town's only policeman took his orders from that same cleric and served as his chauffeur.

No sooner had they gone out of sight than the torches came rushing back down the hill and milled around our gate again. For another hour we watched silently from the dark inside the window, until slowly they scattered up and down the road.

"They're gone. Go to bed." A sudden adult voice spoke. We felt our way to our dorm rooms, but sleep was hard to find.

Years later, in 1989, two missionaries were kidnaped from the Llanito school. Libby and Grover were released 68 days later when the cartel concluded they were not agents of the U.S. Drug Enforcement Administration. In the summer of 1998 rockets landed on Llanito as they had on the Supreme Court. There, during a battle between the army and the cocaine lords, Llanito ceased being an outpost of redemption.

where in the world, even here. To become uncommon and powerful, people start bending and breaking rules.

Becoming Uncommon—Personal Power

A sense of personal power accompanies rule-breaking—a certain sense of freedom. Many people measure this freedom by the size of the mess in their rooms or on their desks. The immediate sensation is one of escaping control or domination. Superior at last to those who restrict and command, one is able to create worlds—as Jim Jones did in his utopia.

I discovered the thrill of breaking rules myself. The exhilaration of freedom was there when, at seventeen, I buried the speedometer of my dad's Chevy at 135 miles per hour. I was free from my father, superior to the elements and smarter than the highway patrol! Even in everyday driving today, I sense that the more powerful people are all driving over 65. A high number of police officers exceed the speed limit when they are on their way not to a crime scene but to lunch.

As Russell Miller recounts, it was the lure of this uncommon or "exceptional" personal power that led John Whiteside (Jack) Parsons to invite L. Ron Hubbard's help in creating a "moonchild" for the whore of Babylon. Jack Parsons was a member of the OTO (Ordo Templi Orientis), one of the better-known satanic orders. He was a financial supporter of its founder, Crowley; one of America's leading experts on explosives and rocket fuels; and a respected scientist at the California Institute of Technology during the second World War. During the day he sought power through physics and chemistry. At night he reversed the rules and looked for power from Satan, evil spirits and spells. Parsons believed that Hubbard and Crowley could help him obtain the power he wanted from the elemental spirit of the whore of Babylon.[6] They produced no moonchild. Parsons lost Crowley's respect. He also lost ten thousand dollars plus a girlfriend to Hubbard. He died in an explosion in 1952 a few blocks from the beginning point of the Rose Parade in Pasadena.

Becoming Uncommon—Social Power

Social power, particularly personal importance, is also derived from breaking laws. Importance is ascertained quickly by watch-

107

ing who is allowed to violate rules. A college professor's importance can be measured by how far he or she may go in breaking the rules regarding the time class begins. A professor arrives fifteen minutes late without censure one day and penalizes a student for sitting down after the bell rings the next day.

"He makes his own rules" can be said of powerful people, not of the weak. "Rules exist for the common person" seems true to young adults who have been excluded until now from power. We saw in chapter 2 that achieving social power is a major concern for young adults.

We are all attracted in varying degrees to rule-breakers. Television shows feature people doing incredible things with the warning "Never try this at home." Many entertainers have made a name for themselves by breaking societal rules by the way they dress or behave. Cher does not choose her clothes or tattoos to be conventional. Numerous heavy metal bands have turned to Satanism to provide a stylized way to break rules and have found a large following.

People frequently consider ways to break rules and prevent the IRS from succeeding in their task of tax collection. Many citizens sustain a certain admiration for those who can fool the government's pocket inspectors. These tendencies can be found among people who might otherwise be associated with law and order. Powerless feelings created every April 15 fuel this interest in regaining power.

It has been widely speculated that the interest of Anton LaVey, author of *The Satanic Bible* and founder of the Church of Satan, in Jayne Mansfield was related to the ways in which she broke societal rules requiring undergarments. There seems to be little doubt that breaking these rules contributed greatly to the influence she had with press photographers.

As we continue finding evidence that ordinary people will violate rules and laws in exchange for power, Americans and Satanists among them, it does not automatically mean the culprits will be Satan-worshipers. Many evil people, I am certain, never think of themselves as Satanists and worship no one. But is there any reason to believe the many claims that Satanists in particular might be motivated to the kind of actions their alleged victims ascribe to them?

I think so. Satanists would have both religious and emotional motivation toward evil, as we shall see.

Becoming Uncommon—Spiritual Power

Not only does rule-breaking give a sense of power, but it is a way to impress others with our badness. By occult logic, which we will study later in this chapter, if evil spirits have power, then doing bad things should impress them and gain their favor. Impressing demons by breaking rules releases spiritual power to the adept, although it may bring disaster on the inept. Extending this logic a short ways allows one to believe that the more powerful the demon, the worse sort of activity it would take to release its power. The serious magus must be prepared to be bad.

At this point breaking rules seems far less appealing to most people than when we were talking about shaving the IRS or watching Cher. This area is reserved for the serious power-seekers, be they bandit or priest. What would one need to do to release the power of a really big evil spirit? Something really bad, something unnatural.

This is dangerous. First, because if one gets caught by human authorities doing something really bad, there will be trouble. Second, and perhaps more important to the adept, because really powerful forces, if not handled correctly, can do the magus great harm.

Becoming Uncommon—Freedom

The freedom of rule-breaking is credited with drawing Jack Parsons, the expert on explosives and rocket fuels, into black magick while he was still a student at the University of Southern California. "Parsons was intrigued by the heady concept of a creed that encouraged indulgence in forbidden pleasures,"[7] according to Miller.

It is rare that freedom is associated in our minds with following the rules, although in the expressive arts, freedom and following the rules are seen together. A great musician is said to express the music freely because he or she follows the rules more closely for musical expression. We admire those who follow the rules effortlessly.

There is a difference in learning to follow the rules in an uncommon way, as the virtuoso does, and breaking the rules skillfully to achieve power, as the outlaw does. When the measure of success equals the power to make things happen, outlaws lead virtuosos for most people.

Becoming Uncommon—Identity

Rule-breaking has a marked effect on personality. The identity of the rule-breaker changes regardless of the motivation for break-

109

ing the law. The once-ordinary person will now be either bad or superior, a common criminal or an uncommon magus, a sinner or a god. When we do the reverse of what is expected, we become set apart and different in some way. Those who deliberately break the rules set themselves above the law. To them reversals bring the golden dawn of enlightenment about their true selves.

There are several rewards for people who consider breaking rules: freedom, power, admiration or fear from others and a competitive advantage. We tend to view those who succeed at breaking rules as somehow uncommon. Jesse James, Al Capone and other outlaws have their following. Famous killers in Colombia jammed the dedication lines on radio shows with requests for special songs from the women who longed for someone that powerful. One murderer even had a shrine built on the spot where he was killed. People came there seeking healing and miracles from his power. "The villain becomes the hero, eventually," Anton LaVey once told Lawrence Wright.[8]

Going from Ordinary to Evil

Now we have looked at the behaviors generally reported to be a part of satanic ritual and found them among Christians, governments and common people. Many different kinds of people do what Satanists are accused of doing—children and adults, farmers and military officers, males and females. The range of people committing crimes against humanity fits the range of people accused of involvement with Satanism. We have found evidence of devil worship in other parts of the world leading to the same kind of destructive behavior. In Pasadena we found one brilliant scientist invoking the devil on American soil.

Still, our stomachs and minds cannot believe this is happening. How do ordinary people become evil? What happens to them? What are they thinking? Let us examine the process of identity change, the damage and how people justify the evil they do.

The Identity Transformation of a Satanist

What happens as an ordinary person is transformed into a member of a destructive cult?[9] Obviously it makes a great deal of difference what age one joins and how involved one becomes. Nevertheless young adults I have met, along with their families, have

110

reported remarkably swift changes in identity. A look at their experiences will expose the mechanisms for disintegrating and remodeling identities in abusive cults.

These mechanisms for identity change are central to all discussions of brainwashing, religious conversion, therapy and mind control. All these processes claim some influence on identity. Brainwashing and mind control in particular change the identity to such a degree that people act in ways they would previously have rejected. To achieve this level of change, the original personality must be disintegrated so that a new one may be created.

In chapter 1 I pointed out that there must be a match between the source of damage and the kind of damage produced. Each effect must have its own cause. Bullet holes result from bullets, bee stings from bees, dog bites from dogs and microwave burns from microwaves. The question remains: Would a Satanist's activities produce the results we are observing? That is to say, does that kind of cause produce this kind of effect? Would the Satanist's reversal of good and evil produce mind control, mental illnesses like post-traumatic stress disorder or borderline and multiple personalities, depression, confusion, anxiety and personality disintegration?

Our identities are usually solid and not very open to new ideas, but there are moments when our sense of self disintegrates and we can be made to see ourselves differently. At these times our identities can be changed profoundly. Personalities can be disintegrated if they are incompletely formed (as is the case for children), or if they have weaknesses caused by deprivations (type-A trauma), injuries (type-B trauma) or deceptions about the self (lies). When these weaknesses are combined with a disintegrating stressor, the identity is open to change.

Here are some of the ways identities can be disintegrated. The first three conditions, which block left hemisphere memory functions, match with the three ways the hippocampus (memory librarian) can be overwhelmed (as we saw in chapter 1):

1. Severe or prolonged pain (high cortisol levels)
2. Hypnosis and trance states (split attention)
3. Panic or terror (massive discharge of the amygdala)
4. Sensory deprivation and mind-emptying meditation or monotonous chanting

5. Psychoactive drugs and hallucinogens
6. Near-death experiences
7. Sleep deprivation
8. Sexual climax (orgasm produces temporary disintegration of the self)

Some will recognize in this list many of the entry points for demonization. Others will recognize the ingredients for brainwashing. Others will recognize standard experiences in Satanism and destructive cults. The central event is one of personality disintegration, which allows whoever is in the vicinity great power to change people's ideas of who they are. This is generally called brainwashing or mind control.

Our identities shape and control what we do, think and feel. Changing our identities changes our mind. Controlling our identities can control our mind. A life-giving community will tell us the truth about our identity, while people who want control will shape our sense of self to suit their goals.

It is phenomenal how quickly identity change can take place if the personality structure is not complete and strong. Personalities can be altered in two or three weeks through disintegration. The road into Satanism can be very fast if the people along the way are good at this sort of thing.

Teenage experimenters, on the other hand, will take months or years to spiral down on their own. This is because they do not have anyone evil to define their identities and no one to disintegrate their identities knowingly. People do not brainwash themselves with the fervor they apply to controlling the minds of others.

One exception to this is when a spirit guide is involved. Spirit guides can greatly speed the disintegration. It appears to me from watching Satanists that once they become dependent on their spirit masters to put them back together, their spirits desert them and let them plunge into insanity. Those who maintain their identities by disintegrating others seem to die violent or painful deaths.

Now why would someone allow his or her identity to be disintegrated? He or she would have to be fooled. Here is the simple, diabolical plan: Make people feel powerless and then tell them that the very things that disintegrate them will bring them power. The harder they try, the more they disintegrate. The more they disintegrate, the harder they try.

Organized cults can be methodical about their efforts to transform their power-seeking followers. One of the ways to make people believe they are powerful is to let them have all the pleasure they want—especially forbidden pleasure. In this way a leader can make many people feel powerful at the same time. Sex and drugs are good for that because they produce a personality disintegration while people are not looking. This is the value of much of the gratuitous sex in Satanism.

The sexual magick developed by Aleister Crowley for Satanists and by Gerald Gardner for witches allows many forms of personality disintegration to be combined. When the goal becomes power rather than pleasure, sex can be combined with all forms of torture. Let me give some brief, horrifying and, unbelievable as it seems, still sanitized examples of life inside the red dragon's lair.

A Survivor's Story

The following story illustrates the techniques of traumatic personality disintegration. It is included here to demonstrate the powerful effect that mind-altering, sadistic torture can have on an adult personality. From it we can infer even greater effects on child or weakened personalities. This story should not be read by children or those with weakened personalities.

Dave got involved with Satanism as a young man.[10] He was looking for pleasure and power. His mentors helped prepare him for what he was told would be the thrill of his life. They kept the young man up several nights by leaving him alone in a totally dark room where it was too cold to sleep. This, he was told, would purify him. Next they gave him a mind-altering drug. Then he found himself in a warm room, surrounded by chanting people. Next they blindfolded him and forced him to participate in a horrific ritual that involved sexual pleasure and torture. What he thought initially would lead to sexual pleasure turned into pain, horror and torture. Dave was afraid he would be killed.

The leader praised Dave for finding what he really liked. They tortured him if he showed signs of disliking the party. They told him how much power he would receive and how he belonged to

113

Satan and the group now. By combining pain, sexual climax, sensory deprivation, trance states, sleep deprivation, drugs, panic and the sense of a near-death experience, Dave's personality showed all its cracks. He became very confused. Thinking about it later would not change what he had done under this degree of personality disintegration.

To change such messages and confusion, it is necessary to disintegrate the personality to the same level, then reassemble the self with new messages. This, as you can see, is a terrifying prospect, and few people wish to endure the pain of the projected reconstruction. It is this unwillingness to face the pain that destructive cults are banking on to keep the person returning to them for identity repair. "We know who you are," they say, "and what you like!"

How can Dave know that what he has been told is not true? He participated in those activities, didn't he? His body had seemed to like it. Who could he ask? Suppose he came to your church. Could Dave ask if you or your God thought he was someone who liked this kind of perversion? If no one in your church talks about these things, it would seem that the Satanists are right: Only they know who Dave is.

Meanwhile the telltale signs that Dave's identity had not been assembled correctly began to show. He fell apart in rages and terrors. He felt alternately homicidal and suicidal. He felt hopeless about relationships. His sexual thoughts were a twisted mixture of pain and pleasure, arousal and fear. When his mind told him he really liked this stuff, he began to panic. He could feel himself falling apart, and that was more terrifying yet.

It was time to seek out those who knew how to put him back together—the people who really helped him. There was a ritual that night. It was time to go to the place where he belonged.

One great contradiction about Satanism, incidentally, is found in the level of involvement among Satanists. They are the most isolated of people. They trust no one and seek power and fear over love and nurture. Yet because they are people they seek closeness. They get together constantly and have sexual contact with everybody. I think Satanists spend so much time together because their way of relating to each other is dissatisfying. Rituals are time-consuming and tiring, but much time is needed to meet any real needs.

With time it became more and more important for Dave to get in control. The more he fell apart, the more control appealed to him. Obviously the people in control had power. To gain more power Dave participated in more rituals. The better he did at the rituals, the more power he needed. Each time Dave went back, it was harder to believe he did not like what happened there. In addition, to get more power it was necessary to do even worse things. Becoming aroused while planning rituals made Dave sure he liked this sort of thing. That thought alone pushed him toward disintegration.

In the cult, however, Dave faced a problem. Rituals break down quickly into those doing and those being done to. Satanists are not known for accepting bad things graciously. Revenge is common.[11] You do not want to do something to someone who will pay you back later. Doing unnatural things, therefore, requires victims. The long and short of it was, Dave had to be careful whom he victimized.

Children provided the perfect solution to his problem. Not only were they unable to resist, escape or get revenge, but it is unnatural to abuse them, which pleases truly strong spirits. Besides, God loves children, so it is strong magick to humiliate and destroy them. Children were the perfect victims. In addition, since no one believes children, they could not get him into real trouble.

His cult required church attendance. Churches, schools and clubs were potential sources for children, or else Dave could produce his own. As an alternative, he usually used animals in his rituals. This is the choice of most beginning and teenage Satanists. Torturing the animals produced large amounts of adrenaline in their blood. By drinking the charged blood, the cult could become intoxicated. This added to the high produced in the ritual.

Dave almost passed out at his first human sacrifice but was told that the disintegration he experienced was a spiritual high. Thus he stayed on a search for more highs. He needed them to offset the anger and misery that keep sneaking up on him.

By now Dave was almost used to intrusive thoughts when he tried to rest or drive. Pictures and fears flashed into his mind whenever he let down his defenses. Drugs or compulsive sex helped him sleep at times but his body seemed to have a life of its own. Headaches, chills, pains and sexual feelings seemed to come and go at will. Dave controlled them by making small cuts in himself or by putting his finger into a flame. He was jumpy and ill at ease when he was not in control of a situation. He flew into a rage at anyone who crossed him—unless that person was too powerful for him.

Dave wanted to rest, but if he let down, one of the more powerful Satanists or spirits was likely to select him as a target. Leaving the group was out of the question. There is only one way out and that led directly to hell. His mind played back horrible images. Strange how ruling could lose its appeal so quickly. He felt like throwing up. He felt he was totally repulsive. Who but Satan would want him?

In church Dave could barely cover his disdain for the blind people next to him quietly taking Communion. These fools could never manage his rituals with real blood and flesh.

"Whoever partakes of the body of the Lord unworthily eats and drinks damnation to himself," the minister said as they ate.

Sure, Dave thought to himself. *Even here they agree I am fit only for hell. Well, at least I'll kick butt when I get there.*

But nothing happened when he took Communion.

I guess this god doesn't keep his threats, he thought. *Maybe he's too weak.*

Certainly he did not have a "spiritual" experience to match the human sacrifice.

The more alienated Dave became, the more he was reduced to trying to impress Satan. Like everyone else, Satanists need to be connected to someone who will tell them who they really are when they need it.

It Would Work

Dave showed signs of depression, anxiety, post-traumatic stress, drug addiction, sleep disorders, sexual disorders, dissociation, social isolation, confusion and paranoia. If this degree of damage had been done to his personality when he was an adult, children raised as Satan's victims will do worse. There is enough trauma here to produce severe damage to young identities: multiple and borderline personalities and realities too terrible to be able to remember. It would be enough to match the damage I see.

The stories of children in Satanism have been told in several books. These are divided into stories of children raised in Satanist families and those of children who encountered Satanism through preschools, Sunday schools, babysitters or professional people like pediatricians and dentists.

I would recommend that interested readers examine several of the books listed in the bibliography. Some stories, such as *Unspeakable Acts*, are told by journalists, others by adult survivors of satanic ritual abuse.

But our stomachs say again, How? How could they do that? What are they thinking? It is time for one last trip into the red dragon's lair to see how ordinary people think about the extraordinary evil they do—an answer found in the twisted logic of occult thought.

Earlier in this chapter we saw that breaking rules can make ordinary people feel uncommon. We saw how doing this might be used to impress or intimidate others, even evil spirits. But let's take it further. If we use the logic of fear, then laws are for scaring people. Laws exist to protect powerful people and to keep common people common. The hidden (occult) secret for locating power is to do the opposite of what a common law says. This reversal will reveal what is hidden from frightened, ordinary, common people.

Reversals, Laws and Power

Central to all reversals is the belief that you get more by breaking laws than by following them. This is the occult worldview. Within this view, laws and rules exist to prevent the common person from obtaining power. The same mindset applies to laws restricting minors from driving, drinking, marrying and possessing nuclear warheads for resale. Rules are for common, immature, weak and stupid people.

Religious or moral laws are viewed in the same way. Religion, according to its detractors, keeps people from taking power or having pleasure. Religion is the opiate of the masses because religious rules prevent people from obtaining power. It should not surprise us to find that the founders of Communism, Marx and Lenin, were deeply influenced by occult thought and practice.

Laws reduce our power and freedom. Violating laws, therefore, should make us free, uncommon and, if done correctly, powerful. This is an alchemy approach to life. By following strict "secret laws," the occultist violates natural laws in the same way that alchemists sought to make gold from lead or bring life from dead matter. This approach can be tried with physical, judicial, social and even moral laws. The occultist works to become an uncommon person who knows "higher" laws than those issued to common people. Uncommon people have power so they do not need common rules.

Mystery and secrecy surround this systematic attempt to gain influence by violating the "common" rules. Only those properly initiated are permitted to know and use "higher" principles. This is a world of codes, symbols, secrets, rituals and their guardians.

The secrecy and effort needed to master these hidden principles increase the feeling of finding something special. After all, places with alarms, armed guards, strong walls and locks and careful surveillance make us assume that something valuable resides there. Most of us are sure Fort Knox has more gold in it than our neighbor's trash, although few of us have been in either spot.

There are precautions that must be taken by the occultist. If laws are violated carelessly, one can end up hurt, dead or in a great deal of trouble with law enforcement. Secrecy is needed to protect the users of these "higher" laws from the enforcers of the common laws. Evading human authority is aided by disbelief because, as we saw in chapter 1, what juror is prepared to believe that his or her neighbors—grandmothers, doctors, teachers or parents—are intentionally doing things so revolting in the good old U.S.A.?

Occultists believe that if one takes the right precautions, and then carefully breaks a law, one may obtain the power which that law keeps away from common people. The more natural laws one breaks in this way, the greater the power obtained.

To talk about this reversal another way, we could say that the Satanists' objective is to act in the most unnatural way possible. Only in this context do their actions make sense. Simply ask yourself: What are the most unnatural things I could do? It will not be long until you compile a list of the standard fare for Satanism. This is also the reason the reports of cult activities are so unbelievable: They are so unnatural.

This helps to explain some of the generally degrading treatment of children in Satanism. They are forced to be covered with blood, feces, vomit, urine, dead and decomposed bodies or parts of bodies. They are often forced to eat these same substances. Satanists do not think they are doing anything amiss. The argument starts with the premise that power is power. How then can we call a power source evil? In fact, power is good, provided that it serves man, so this process is good, provided that the power does what one wants. If doing something gains the power you need, then it is good to be unnatural. There you have it: The most disgusting thing you can think of has just become good.

Such logic may help some Satanists, but I doubt it. This sort of thinking is reserved for conversations with outsiders. Satanists are not moralists who have cleverly decided to exchange the definitions of good and evil so as to be able to call themselves good while they do abhorrent things. Rather, they choose to do abhorrent things because they, as much as we, are convinced that these things are unnatural.

Is it natural to love your children, sleep at night and seek life? Is it natural to avoid dead things, pain, eating waste or keeping the company of dangerous people? Survivors report that Satanists eat what is not food. They kill animals but not for food. The list of revolting substances Satanists have forced their children to consume is long.

Some "experts" in the media debate have claimed, however, that children make up these stories because all children secretly desire to eat blood, urine, feces and semen. This, they claim, is a hidden urge of our unconscious minds. If that is the case, then no doubt you found yourself as a child frequently sneaking a meal of feces. You probably still get the urge from time to time or dream of those glorious days of childhood. Since these same experts tell us that if something happened we would remember, we will not swallow one explanation without the other.

Survivors in every book I have read charge Satanists with eating human flesh. This practice strikes me as the most unnatural act of all. There are ways to make it even more revoltingly unnatural, but none worse than eating one's own children. This violates every law given by God, so it is the greatest success of Satanism. This particular expression of incest is the extreme of depravity; consequently it should provide the most occult power.

The anguish created by the very discussion of this activity is difficult to bear, yet such is the mindset of many cult members that incestuous cannibalism is highly desirable. If you must be unnatural, then this is the greatest success because it violates almost every natural standard known to humankind. Human beings were given the power to give life and commissioned to use it generously. This practice precisely reverses all we are meant to be.

Perhaps the greatest area of overlap between the occult and Satanism is in their predilection to choose the company of the dead over that of the living. This unnatural turn of events often finds different motivations within these two groups, although their methods borrow largely from the same sources.

Many subscribers to occult practices are interested in the dead in order to feel connected to dead loved ones. Many spiritist séances or mediums seek a word from the dearly departed. Perhaps it can be said that they are all seeking the living among the dead. (This heartwarming motivation is missing in the New Age movement, which is more interested in seeking information and novelty through mediums and channelers. In this group, the need to be connected to something or someone out there is far more vague.)

Satanists maintain an interest in killing the living and bringing the dead back to life. These two unnatural interests and activities lie at the heart of most horror stories we hear from ex-Satanists.

You have probably noticed that these two are among the list of activities restricted to God alone. Indeed, the majority of restrictions on human behavior in a biblical worldview are intended to prevent human beings from doing those things that only God has the right to accomplish. Revenge, taking someone's life for one's own, raising the dead, receiving worship, possessing and enjoying everything and everyone—all these belong to the Almighty. But the occultist wants the power God is hoarding.

This look at Satanism and occult thought has shown that within their worldview exist both the rationale and the incentives to motivate Satanists toward totally depraved behavior. There are in the Satanist ideology and worldview, therefore, the necessary elements for participants to behave unnaturally and to break every moral and natural law. Satanists possess the motive to do what they are accused of doing—behaving unnaturally and violating all law. Satanists have both psychological and theoretical motivation to violate law in the most unnatural way possible. Some people report that cultists have also had ample opportunity—an opening provided by community confidence that such acts "could never happen here."

A Flick of the Dragon's Tail

Excitement was soaring higher than the thermometer on June 22, 1994, as Rami and I sat in the Rose Bowl and watched Colombia play the U.S. in World Cup soccer. Andrés Escobar, who had not been expected to make the team, was playing defense for Colombia when he scored a goal against his own country.

Before the ball was out of the net, I told Rami, "He'd better ask for asylum, because if he goes back, he's dead."

"It's just a game," the man next to me scoffed.

A few days later Rami caught me in the hall at home. His eyes were big.

"Guess what!" he said. "Escobar is dead."

He had been shot by a woman and two men outside a bar near Medellín three days after his return. The killers were said to work for the drug cartel.

Learn how the dragon thinks, because denial can kill. But don't believe him. Don't fear him. Don't teach your children to fear him, because he has met his match. There is a better way—a power greater than fear. We are about to see how fear and Love compete for us.

5

Dragon Love

FEAR BONDS, LOVE BONDS AND WEAK BONDS

WHAT IS stronger, fear or love? What will motivate, bond, get results, make people understand, make them move, get through to them, keep kids out of trouble, teach them a lesson, get their attention, make them mind, stop the racket, keep the family together, stop the nagging or the screaming or the drinking and keep them home nights? What cuts through anger, rebellion, laziness and indifference? What do you do when everything else has failed?

Our bonds with other people are emotional connections that help us meet our own and other's needs. We connect through fear, joy, hate, love, lust, excitement, guilt, shame and other feelings. Although there are many different emotions, they may all be reduced to either fear or love. Fear bonds cause us to avoid painful experiences while love bonds attract us to others. Our bonds, or connections, allow us to interact based on one or both of these motivations. People respond to us because they love or fear us. Conversely they ignore us because they do not love or fear us. The emotions we exchange through our bonds become our relational dynamic.

These connections can be weak or strong. But we have our own "bottom line" bonds—the emotions we rely on when everything else fails. We expect these emotions to provide the strongest bonds with others. Each family prefers certain bonds or emotions more than others. Each community depends on some bonds more than others. Each church and denomination relies on some bonds more than others. Each culture develops some bonds more than others.

When we combine the values of a particular group and its bonding style, we see patterns known as group dynamics. We often believe, mistakenly, that we are motivated by our values when we are actually *guided* by our values and *motivated* by our bonds and emotions. As American Christians we usually analyze values carefully for truth. But we are not nearly so thorough about the relational quality or power of a bond. Thus we are always shocked when teaching good values fails to be enough. Cults grow when people leave their values in search of stronger bonds.

Fear and Love Bonds—Weak and Intense Bonds

The values of love cannot be implemented by the motives of fear. Instead we get a corrupted system in which one thing is spoken but another is practiced. Young adults are sensitive to these blends and call them hypocrisy. Satanists have noticed this duplicity among certain Christians and accuse us of hypocrisy as well.

Family or church dynamics might be based on guilt bonds, hope bonds, denial bonds or some combination. Members of groups understand that meeting needs in their groups depends on producing these feelings in one another. People seek out others who use the same dynamics—people who bond as they do. Just as drug users and square dancers and heavy metal fans find each other, so, too, bonders over lust, shame, guilt or rejection find one another. Together they form families, communities, churches, schools, cultures and countries.

Even people who reject feelings must bond this way. Bob was a father who rejected all feelings as weak and irrational. He mentioned this frequently to his children. He wrote an article on the subject in his church bulletin. Bob decried emotional preaching.

Every time his children had a feeling of some sort, he repeated the message that it was bad to feel and good to be rational. As a result Bob has developed a shame bond with his children. They are motivated to be afraid of shame and carry huge amounts of that emotion. They are motivated by their father's fear of emotions.

Fear Dynamics

Fear is avoidance-based thinking and behavior. Fear causes us to train the spotlight of our awareness on things that can hurt us. This is a life of worry. The emotional effect of fear is only temporary although it produces long-lasting changes in our thoughts. Diminishing returns from fear demand greater threats to achieve the same response. As fear fades, so does its ability to motivate action, thus requiring constant renewal to be effective. This is why people who try to diet by keeping themselves afraid of being fat can never succeed. Fears fade while hungers grow.

What we avoid most depends on what emotion we most fear. This emotion is usually the one most dreaded by our group. Some of us avoid shame—the fear that someone will not want to be with us. In a shame-based dynamic you had better have a good reason to take off your shirt. Shame is a right hemispheric emotion. Guilt, however, is a left hemisphere emotion—the fear of being bad. In a guilt-based system you need a good reason to disappoint your mother. There are other negative feelings as well. Anger is the fear of being hurt; rejection is the fear of abandonment. Then there is fear itself. In a fear-based dynamic you need a good reason to bother the boss.

When these fear dynamics are strong, the strong fear causes the brain's alarm centers (amygdala) to dominate the brains of all those who lack a strong, joyful identity center in their prefrontal cortexes. When this happens, their wills can no longer control what their minds do. They are easily controlled by whomever they fear. They can think of nothing else.

Even within this fear dynamic there is hope, because God is the most frightening power we know. Wisdom (the way out of fear) begins with fearing God. The first words out of His mouth, however, are usually, "Fear not!"

Love Dynamics

Love, like hunger, is a desire. Love grows rather than fades. Love becomes more motivating with time. Love bonds produce a different dynamic than fear bonds do. Love's dynamic is based on joy. Joy means, *Someone is glad to be with me.* Joy means, *Someone will share my good and bad times because that person wants me.* Joy is the spontaneous response on both ends of a love bond each time they meet.

Joy, as we saw in chapter 3, is the only emotion that infants seek on their own during the first year of life. Joy stimulates brain growth for the prefrontal cortex—the only part of the brain that can override the fear centers. As the prophet said, "The joy of the Lord is your strength" (Nehemiah 8:10). We experience joy when someone loves us. Positive feelings like hope, trust or joy are grown through love. We tend to seek more of these feelings.

Weak Bonds

It is hard to overstate the problems caused by weak bonds. There are weak bonds of both love and fear. Weak bonds of either kind produce:

- Weak identities
- Immaturity
- Anxious attachment[1]
- Poor motivation
- Fragile relationships
- Inability to handle power appropriately
- Emotionally dominated behavior
- Detachment and inability to keep commitments

These are just a few of the problems created by weak bonds. Because humans cannot stand life with weak bonds, they readily focus on anything stronger. To people with weak bonds, any intense emotional experience appears strong. Learned values alone will not keep them from seeking something strong.

Intense Bonds

I use the word *intense* because intense emotional experiences form strong bonds, but not all strong bonds form strong identities. In the last chapter we saw that intense emotional experiences bonded Dave to the cult. These intense negative bonds are also called trauma bonds.

When people are desperate, they intensify their group's bonding emotions to try to get a response. If the strongest bond is an anger bond, they get very angry; or if it is guilt, they blame forcefully; or if it is fear, they make dire threats. Someone who believes bonds are based on guilt and fear, for instance, might threaten suicide to get results. This is common in homes where guilt and fear of punishment are used to motivate children.

Intensifying fear bonds draw people into Satanism. The typical recruit comes from a home with weak fear bonds. Weak bonds, rather than family values, seem to be the key factor. These teens are seeking the most intense music, experience, high or rush.

The spiral into intensity is typical of dysfunctional and abusive systems, whether they are family or religious systems. This increasing intensity is characteristic of religious abuse generally—including "Christian" religious abuse. This is the spiral that finally got Jim Jones, the Colombian farmers and Dave. Bonding through intense and overwhelming emotions is dragon-style love. Satanism is intense.

Family Dynamics in America

Comfort and greed are the two leading values in the American family dynamic. These two values contribute directly to weak bonds and greatly to the neglect of children, control of others, hoarding of power and rampant immaturity. This cultural version of comfort means avoiding all pain for ourselves so we can live comfortably. I do not mean the kind of comfort we should give to those in distress. Comfort has brought us political correctness, apathy and passivity. This is the "primal soup" for cult growth, abuse and dysfunction.

Weak Bonds in American Culture

Even American politicians have come to the conclusion that as a culture we have weak family bonds. We conceive children and kill them by the millions before they are born, calling them tissue or fetuses. It sounds like a weak bond to me. Of those who survive, seventy percent of children live in homes where the father is absent. Much of that is due to divorce—a weak marriage bond.

Our churches have weak bonds with their members, communities and denominations. It is no big deal to change churches or even religions. Our jobs have weak bonds, too. We change employers and locations readily. And we have weak bonds to the land. We sell our homes and move for little more than money.

Apathy and Passivity

As a society we are so busy seeking comfortable lives that we have little room for demanding relationships. We reserve our intense emotions for movies, sports, television, video games and amusement parks. We hire talk show hosts to express our opinions and moderate our debates. We watch the news. We observe sitcoms and dramas to experience emotions without risking any relationship. Many children would pick their televisions over their fathers.

A look at the Presidents we have elected recently reflects our vote for apathy. Who has strong conviction, integrity and character? What percentage of us even vote or go to parent's night at school? What would an average American die for or face social humiliation to uphold? If we overcome our passivity at all, it is only to acquire possessions.

Doing nothing is often the worst thing we can do. This apathetic lack of life, as much as any other factor I could mention, pushes people toward intensity. Maybe they will find life over there.

Escapism and Denial

The culture of our young country has been dominated by new arrivals. Most of these immigrants came or stayed because they thought their lives would be better here. Did you ever hear an American question someone's sanity for wanting to live here? From the Mayflower to the Cuban boat lift, people immigrated here to get away. North America is populated by people who generally want to believe that their problems, once they arrive, will be over. Our country is founded on the belief that things are better here. We have quite a bit of economic evidence, moreover, to back our case.

So we dream of escaping all discomfort. Our dream vacations are getaways. We came to America in the first place to leave evil behind; who wants to admit it came over with us? Believing that evil has followed us here exceeds our tolerance for discomfort. We want comfort at all costs, which has become a seedbed for denial and escapism. We live in denial.

It is the certainty that things are better in the U.S.A. that contributes to denying problems such as poverty, abuse, evil spirits and depravity in the hearts and actions of our citizens. (We saw in the last chapter that we tend to relegate wickedness to hemispheres and social classes not our own.) We are fairly sure that, despite acknowledged problems with congressional compromise and public servants who serve themselves, we have escaped the world's problems like corrupt government and tyranny. We even tend to deny the very existence of evil.

One must admire the extent of the North American denial of malevolence—a denial as insane as our cocaine and marijuana habit that provides the money to fuel the violence-crazed minds of the Colombian drug lords and keeps this violence going strong. We can scarcely believe in human evil, far less cosmic evil. Anything more intelligent than we are would have to be kindly disposed toward us. Extraterrestrial visitors like ET must have good things to offer. Spirit guides and ascended masters must have our best interests at heart.

Is it true on earth that the more intelligent the life form, the kinder it becomes? Are people the kindest creatures we know? Not at all. We do not treat all lesser life forms kindly. Look at how we treat anchovies. Intelligence does not make us kinder than anchovies are. Isn't it reasonable to expect that if an intelligent life form came along that made *our* minds appear as small as anchovies look to us, we might end up on *their* pizzas? Or perhaps we might receive the same kindness we give cows. After being fed and housed, we might be milked, bred and then barbecued. Even affection might not save us. Often the farmer's daughter's pet pig becomes pork chops.

Can we make the case that even among humans, intelligence predicts kindness? Hardly. If I had to judge by the sample we have been given on earth, I would judge kindness and benevolence to be hindered, not helped, by intelligence.[2] There are no grounds for the belief that increased intelligence increases benevolence. Yet we deny that we can be evil because we claim to be intelligent.

The extent of our denial of evil is most obvious when cases of ritual abuse come into the court system. There a peculiar thing takes place. It is necessary to prove not only the guilt of the parties involved but the very existence of the crime. When we have a murder trial, we start with the belief that people kill each other, and in this case we have a dead body, so we need only prove that this one killed that one. When we have a robbery trial, we need not prove that people will rob, only that this person did. In cases involving satanic ritual abuse, however, it is the existence of the crime that must be proven to the jury. We observed in chapter 1 that a jury is unlikely to believe in crimes they have not heard of. After one trial the jurors commented that they could not believe this sort of crime existed, so they voted the accused innocent. Denial is a powerful ally for evil.

Because our lust for comfort breeds passivity, apathy and denial, our bonds are not strong enough to face real evil. In fact, our community bonds crumble in the face of evil because we will not accept that it exists or that we should do something about it.

Greed

A young couple in my office sobbed desperately about their living situation. They were unable to meet minimal expenses. In spite of frugal living they had not been able to take a day off in over three years. Both were exhausted and close to emotional collapse. What was wrong with them, they wondered, that they could not make it?

Their families had abused both husband and wife. Both sets of parents were hopelessly in debt. As a result the young couple had emotional wounds and no resources to help them.

"There isn't anything wrong with you," I told them. "You can't make it because you don't have the resources."

They were what the Bible would call *strangers*. They had insufficient income, no sustaining relationships, no community to surround and help them when she was laid off or when he suddenly became sick. They had no one to help with expenses or emotional support. Their bonds with the community were weak, and they were sinking because they lived at the mercy of a greedy Los Angeles community with opportunistic rental prices that said, "Pay us what you owe or get out."

Poor people are just as apt to be greedy as the rich. It is probably the amount of attention given to greedy endeavors that makes an individual or society greedy. Judging by the influence of advertising, Americans spend much time on greedy endeavors.

Greed causes parents and communities to overlook the needs of their children. Our devastating abortion rate is a tribute to the relative value of life and prosperity. "You want something which you cannot have, and so you are bent on murder," James 4:2 tells us. Most abortion is traceable to the cost of having and rearing children, particularly when one considers the loss of time from work. Greed weakens the bond to children.

Perhaps those in the most unfair position are those who have been abandoned by greedy spouses in communities in which they must raise their children without any family support.

Still, as bad as those situations are, I see little evidence of these children turning to Satanism. The ones who present the greatest risk are those who have no one in home, church or community who cares what evil happens to them. They have weak bonds and they want strong ones. Neglected children are on the lookout for some way to be heard. The appeal of the occult lies in being connected to something out there—something that listens and talks to you, something that responds. Greed breeds the abandonment and neglect that make young adults desperate enough to try bonding with anything, even dragons. This is a community concern as much as a parental one.

At a conference of mental health workers, a discussion broke out about how to help children who have almost no resources. Illegal alien children, for example, might live with twenty people in a garage. Some of these children might be abused by transient residents of their "home." What could be done without funds, parents and with only a few hours of professional help available per child?

The response from knowledgeable workers at the conference: Devote time to help representatives of the community—usually the teacher at school—to recognize the existence of the child. If the youngster learns at school that someone is interested in whether he or she is prospering, there is hope. Having felt concern from the community, he or she may seek to bond later in life.

A community that cares even a little bit is a great deterrent to despair.

Abusive Family Dynamics

There are exceptions within American culture to the passive, weakly bonded family. One is the abusive family. Strong fear and trauma bonds unite abusive families. Strong fears are the family dynamic. Fear does business. You may recall from chapter 3 that Christie and her mother—who terrorized Christie with a broom handle—lived just this kind of life.

Family power dynamics have deep and lasting effects on the identities of family members. By acting in ways that mimic the person with the power, people can also achieve a sense of identity that lets them feel powerful. When children feel powerless, they imitate the behavior of powerful parents. Many children attach to their parents anxiously by imitation. Often this imitation continues well into adult life in spite of the person's conscious wishes. Adult children find themselves duplicating the precise behaviors—the most abusive ones—that gave their parents the most power.

Abusive family systems employ emotional intensity and call it love. Fear, excitement, arousal, even pain, signal closeness and involvement. Dragon love is a strong fear bond, isn't it? Those who believe they need this intensity become distressed if they go very long without it. In the absence of intensity, their identities start to disintegrate. They soon become afraid they are losing their minds or souls. As a result victimized people seek out intensity as a way to repair their disintegrating selves.

Intensity does not meet needs and is a substitute for intimacy. It is only afterward, however, that the emptiness shows up. Most people surmise that they need more intensity than they received. "I guess I didn't get high enough," they conclude. They live with the belief that intensity will fix anything. Homes like this can be very noisy and dangerous.[3]

Family Dynamics and Cults

Cults are known for their intense bonds. Weak bonds prepare people for cults by creating a sense of isolation and vulnerability. Broken family ties, neglect, disinterest and distraction by greed all produce weak bonds and the need for something stronger.

Intense fear bonds prepare people for violent cults. Those who solve family problems by increasing the intensity of what they do understand how quickly cults can get out of hand. Destructive cults can be viewed as extended families of an intense sort. Satanism maintains strong fear bonds with its members. In a culture known for weak bonds, there is something appealing about this strength.

Satanists maintain high levels of involvement with their constituents. They are dedicated in their own way. Their level of involvement, from what I can tell, is quite intense. The dragon's forces, it seems, have been that way for some time.

The night Jesus was betrayed, the forces of evil were more dedicated to their master than the "good guys" were to Jesus. The disciples had been blessed that day. They took a walk, had a meal, drank some wine, had their feet washed and then showed their dedication by going to sleep.

There is no indication that Satan treated his forces to any such good times. His forces may have had a bad day, but they were still present and alert by the hundreds. They stayed up all night, although they had an important hearing with the king and governor the next day. Their side even had guards ready to stay up the next two nights watching Jesus' tomb.

I suppose I admire their dedication. Take, for instance, the way a Satanist community gathers to celebrate a child's birthday. Birthdays are often major ritual days. Involvement is intense. Men participate actively even when the birthday being celebrated is not their child's. Sexual magick cults use intense sexual activity to bond. Men are involved in all the wrong ways, of course, but they are involved, which is more than can be said for some fathers.

Many a "good" dad would not consider attending his child's birthday party, staying up all night with the youngster or bonding with a friend's child who needed extra involvement. Evidence of weak bonds, perhaps?

Why aren't more good men forming strong joy bonds with children? Do Christian men avoid involvement with youngsters because they would do the same thing with them that Satanists do? That is what their victims think. Satanists say so, too. The only difference, they say, between "good" people and themselves is that they are honest about what they want. In their view Christians hypocritically condemn Satanists for the pleasures that religious people are too afraid to seize for themselves—at least publicly.

Let us examine ourselves and answer the Satanist charges. First of all, we *could* do the same thing. We are not beyond bad motives.

"The spirit which God implanted in man turns towards envious desires. And yet the grace he gives is stronger" (James 4:5). What matters, according to St. James, is which of the two is stronger. Those who are full of love want to fill children with joy. If we have strong love bonds with God and our community, we will be full of life and not need to suck it out of children. Men and women who lack life and want to get joy and pleasure from others should stay away from children until they are mature enough to give without needing to receive in return. Which is stronger, love or fear?

Let's go a step further. Where are we and what are we doing when evil strikes? Are we asleep like the original eleven disciples? That can hardly be right. We need to make a stand without fearing the intensity of the conflict. The prophet Elijah faced off with some ritual-abuse-prone Baal worshipers who cut themselves and got intense all day, but in the end Elijah's strong relationship with God prevailed over intensity. Which is stronger?

Satanists are looking for power and control, but not just control over children. Where control is important, fear bonds are the family dynamic. Cults rely on fear bonds because fear gets quick results. Since occultists are intent on controlling spirits, fear bonds become their spiritual dynamic. Satanists extend their fear bonds to the spirit world as a way to do business with evil spirits.

Family Dynamics and Evil Spirits

Families form the model used by most religions for interacting with spirits. Since spirits are a personified source of power, it is little wonder that people use their relational rules to help them figure out how to get spiritual power. Given this outlook and the perception of dealing with a male deity or spirit, most people expect spirits to act like men they know, particularly Dad. What kind of power did Dad have? More importantly, what got him to use it? What did women, men, friends, enemies and children have to do to get his reaction? What induced him to share his power? Christians often use the same logic with God. God the Father is expected to react the way Dad did.

The inverse can also seem true. Since we know from the Bible what God likes, we may speculate that Satan will favor just the opposite. If God seeks goodness, then badness must impress his enemy. People whose fathers could not be pleased or induced to share their power may feel they are doing better with the devil than they did with Dad.

Evil spirits, it seems, want to have certain things done. They appear willing to help a person who will give what they want. It is a sort of bargaining that resembles family dynamics in dysfunctional families: "If you give me what I want, you can have what you want—but don't cross me."

The means of controlling spirits in occult rituals is peculiar. Consider eating feces or causing the death of an animal in a way calculated to be painful. Why should doing painful things control the actions of spirit beings? This ritual behavior resembles family dynamics. Children impress their parents, and later their friends, by what they do. It amounts to gaining power by obtaining approval from the person in power. The use of family dynamics to control spirits suggests that family patterns contribute more to the occult than physics does. There is nothing about physics that particularly resembles the logic for obtaining power from powerful spirits. An even more peculiar logic is needed if these forces are, as some suggest, impersonal.

For women in Satanism the same dynamic holds true. They are brides for Satan; they act the part of the mother in birthing rituals and carry on these "family" sorts of activities that are supposed to release power. But what kind of superior intelligence wants women to pretend to give birth as a way to be compelled to give power? Do such activities induce spirits to release power? No, these rituals look like the manipulations of fear-based families. The family theme is deeply entrenched in satanic ritual.

The discussion of patterns does not answer the question as to whether these manipulations will work. Rather, they explain some people's motives in trying Satanism. These manipulations may work because they are the lure that people bite on. It seems reasonable that any spirit wishing to control an individual would take these factors into account. This is true for God as well, who as Creator is fully aware of the motivations within us humans.

It is not true, of course, that God grants favors in return for goodness, and Satan may not always care for the opposite. When trying to figure out this problem, family dynamics will suggest ideas to participants about ways to motivate their deity (power source) to share power with them.

Family Dynamics in Churches

Family dynamics decide the way needs will be met in families. These dynamics precondition people to interaction patterns in their jobs, schools, churches and communities. Churches form using either fear or love bonds, which produce either fear or love dynamics in the congregation. Churches and cults can have a mixture of fear and love bonds; cults, however, have fear bonds as the stronger ties. Cults almost always have more intense fear bonds than churches.

Weak Bonds

To "cult-proof" their members, churches must meet the needs that cults address. Churches that cannot face needs fearlessly will be in trouble because cults show great confidence on this point. Cultists give answers and often appear far less fearful than church folk. Because cults do not avoid emotional intensity, they often show more openness to intense needs.

In many traditional and modern Christian gatherings, there is little to meet intense spiritual needs. These Christians would not know how to talk about the existence and power of spirits. Their church, community and denominational bonds are weak. Most avoid anything to do with Satan or evil. They show no joy when damaged people arrive with their needs. They have no power or relationship strong enough to challenge the dragon's love. They lack the vitality necessary to stop fearing the dark.

Nevertheless churches are to be leaders of their communities. When a church is committed to its own comfort rather than to comforting, we can expect trouble. When a church is full of greed, or lacks grace toward those who cannot take care of themselves, we can expect trouble. That church has weak bonds. It is an evil community that believes its members can all take care of themselves and their children. Such a community denies our need for one another, and in so doing denies our need for Christ, for it was Christ who, when He ascended, gave us as gifts to one another (see Ephesians 4:10–11).

Fear of Needs

Avoiding the appearance of having needs is tied more closely to cultural values and weak bonds than to doctrine. We would rather be cool than Christian. Denial of needs falsely sanctifies Western independence and individuality. It is rebellion against God that denies our nature as dependent creatures who continuously need one breath at a time. Denial of needs is not denying ourselves and taking up our crosses daily (see Luke 9:23), as Jesus commands, but sanctifying a cultural definition of what is cool. Hiding needs denies God's interest in our intensely felt human condition.

But freedom from needs is what many people believe makes them fit for Christian society and, by consequence, for God as well. When Christians deny their need for one another, they encourage a fear-based church dynamic. Their needs, they fear, will bring them rejection. Thus they hide from others and refuse to admit problems. If we hide common needs, such as our need for encouragement after failure, comfort during loss and even simple requirements like our need for rest, how much more likely are we to hide our deep needs? Being "cool" becomes a cultural trap that prevents our Christian community from touching our deep identity and maturity needs.

A community without needs is a community without bonds. Our bonds are built on our needs, particularly our identity and maturity needs. While our identities must be built on truth, the truth must be held in love bonds or it is no good. No amount of correct knowledge can compensate for weak bonds or fear bonds. Authentic Christianity is truth with power in loving relationships. We do not face intense needs just by being right. Love responds to needy people with joy: "I'm glad you're here with me!" Growing churches attract people with problems because these churches believe they have solutions for needs and are not afraid to say so.

Lack of Faith

Many devout Christians think that having needs displays a real lack of faith. One man said, "I grew up in a fundamentalist church where having emotional problems was not accepted. Needs didn't count except when turning them over to God. Then I went to a Pentecostal church where it was O.K. at first to have problems, but when I wasn't healed immediately, they claimed I didn't have enough faith."

Family Dynamics in the Redemptive Community

Will people find what they need by knowing us, or should they look elsewhere? All too often I have seen Christians run away when they see lonely, upset or intense people. Satanists seek out lonely, hurting or hurtful people. If action represents our faith in our solution, who has an answer here?

People have needs left by the dynamics of their families. People who traffic in fear need love; those with weak bonds need strong bonds; those whose identities have been misassembled need new ones. Cults seem ready to meet these family needs while many churches hold back.

Cults meet needs by becoming family to their members. Jack Parsons called Aleister Crowley "Most Beloved Father" and signed his letters "Thy son, John."[4] Adoptions and other family-altering rituals exist in both multigenerational and child abduction cults. (What I mean by *child abduction* is the ritual abuse of children without parental knowledge, such as happens in childcare centers.) The level of adult involvement with these adopted children, compared to most parent-child relationships, is intense.

Spiritual Adoption

Nowhere are family needs more starkly apparent than for new Christians whose families are all cult members. These converts must lose both their spiritual and their biological families to follow God. Like Ruth the Moabitess, they must leave their gods and family behind and become aliens and strangers in church land.

Looking for another Christian to become family for a lonely woman with a background in Satanism earned me a poem from which the following excerpt is taken. Her indictment is well-placed—if not of me alone, then certainly of the part of the Body of Christ I represent. My church was not ready to be the family of God for her.

Wendy needed human contact, even by phone, with someone. She wanted to share prayer concerns, and I knew she needed someone who would notice if she disappeared or got sick. Three years went by as I asked one person after another if they knew anyone willing to pray with her each day. Thinking that retired people might have the time and maturity to help a young woman, I went to my church, which had more than five hundred people in the senior department. Both of our senior adult pastors told me they did not know any older person who could pray with her, and suggested I try another church, saying, "They know how to pray over there."

Each week Wendy asked, "Have you found a lady who will pray with me? I just need to share with someone before I can go to work."

Each week I said, "No, but I'm still looking."

Each week she would cry and say, "Couldn't you call just for a minute, then? Mornings are so hard and I feel so sad and alone."

Each week I would say, "I don't think that would work. I'll keep looking."

Finally Wendy wrote these words:

> Take your plate
>   and go
> Away, you kindly say.
>   My boundaries are strong.
>   I draw the line.
>
> For my face
>   I want to obey
> Take my plate
>   and go away.
>
> Take your plate
>   and go away.
> You will not eat
>   No, not
>   today.
> In a year
>   or three
>   you may
> But then again
>   there is a chance
> They may all
>   reach down your pants
> After they prepare you
>   for a feast.

> Why have you led me
> to the table
> and forbidden me to eat?

© 1989, used by permission

Every morning Wendy prayed alone. It shocks me how little I was willing to do about it. Equally shocking is how hard it was to find an elder to help me find a spiritual family.

"It can't really be that bad," one said—in denial.

"I'm not very good at that sort of thing," said another—lacking power.

"It makes me uncomfortable, so it can't be God's will," said a third—liking comfort.

While Christians compiled reasons they should not get involved, my poet was well aware of people who would stay up all night looking for her. She knew people who would go out of their way to be with her, so why didn't the Christians want her? She knew it was not cool to be needy at church, but she was.

Even at church it could not be said that no one took an interest in her. Wendy was a petite blonde who attracted lascivious responses from men in every church she attended. Because of her abuse history, she had experience only with fear and intensity bonds. She was a stranger in the biblical sense who did not know how to grow her own community or attach through love, but she formed an anxious attachment to me. The only problem was, each time I sent her out with the assignment to try connecting with others, she got retraumatized.

We exhausted every possibility of finding natural family ties. We bombed out in churches and therapy groups. One day she came and asked if I would be mad that she had put my name down as the one to call if she had an accident. She wanted someone to know or care if she was hurt or died. I started working harder to find a family for her. There must be one in the church somewhere.

Every family I approached, however, had the same response: The woman was threatened by the thought of a single woman entering the family. The few we tried quickly blew apart, except for one.

I was so relieved when a woman volunteered her home that I never asked any questions. One family member in the home proved to have an extensive trauma history and problems severe enough to merit mention in a book by her therapist. The interactions stirred

139

up more feelings than there was time or ability to clear up. The results, for Wendy and the family, were disastrous. However merciful their intentions, the family members were not yet ready to be elders. As a result the relationship was severed after more than a year, with hurt feelings on all sides and great disappointment that their caring had not been enough.

Surprisingly, for all my mistakes, Wendy continued her anxious attachment to me. I consulted weekly with experts and a whole treatment team, until after more than five years of counseling, all available options had been tried. We concluded that without a community-of-the-self holding her, no real improvement would be possible. "Breaking even" was the best outcome under the circumstances that I could hope for.

I gave Wendy the news and she did not take it well. She pointed out emphatically how hard she had worked on every assignment. She reviewed her efforts to find support. Finally she said, "I'm going to pray that you will be my father."

"I *refuse* to be your father!" I answered.

My boundaries were staying very clear.

Again, it shocks me how little I was willing to help her.

A Redemptive Community's Response to Satanism

The pivotal questions in a confrontation with Satanism are these: *Do we have the right answers? Do we believe they will work? Do we care?* These questions correspond to *truth, power* and *relationship*—the three needs of young adults and the building blocks of Christianity. Doesn't it seem that the group with the correct answers to human needs should be motivated and willing to meet those needs?

Humans most want to know who we are and what will meet our real needs. The answers, delivered through strong bonds of love, allow us to mature into the persons we are in the hearts Jesus gave us. The context for our growth is the family of God, which we must enter through spiritual adoption. This becomes the only family for strangers, widows and orphans—the disconnected people we find most coming out of destructive cults.

Who can address the family-bond needs of those who lack a community-of-the-self? Elders can. By elders I mean those who have raised their own families and are ready to nurture those who are strangers, widows and orphans. Elders can serve a meal without, as Wendy wrote, reaching down someone's pants. Elders need not have an empty nest if they are willing to be the family of God.

What is missing in America is elders—those who, having raised their own families successfully, adopt their communities. Elders provide parents for those who lack them, distributing resources to those who need them. Elders established in their own lives can avoid greed and love those who have no one to care about them. Elders have experience and the vision that sees beyond their own walls.

We need elders to view us through the eyes of heaven and tell us who we are. Only in this way will we know what we really need. If we had elders, who would need cult leaders? But that is not what most of us think we need. We think we need independence, power, comfort, intensity and more stuff. When we lack elders, however, there will always be room for evil to deceive us.

A redemptive community looks at the pain, hurt and ugliness caused by evil and says to someone, "You have come to the right place. We know what to do. You can be part of a family that never ends. That bond can start with me. If you will have my God to be your God, then my people will be your people. Together we will fear no evil, for God is with us."

"Lord, to whom shall we go?" Peter said to Jesus in John 6:68. "Your words are words of eternal life."

If we say we know this life but do not love those in need, we are deceived. In God's heart, truth and life go together. They are greater than the powers of Satan. They must be the central dynamic of our community life and worship. Wherever there is need, we must demonstrate strong, fearless love.

CHRISTMAS SAVINGS BONDS

SYMBOLS OF ETERNAL BONDS

CHRISTMAS changes everything. The December holiday is universally recognized by Christians as a symbol that God bonds with humans. The Baby in the manger signifies that God bonds with human bodies and through human relationships. Mother, father, sister, brother, child and friend mean more because of Christmas. It is a time when we remember to exchange life with our spiritual and natural families.

Christmas Day is a peculiar symbol because it is nowhere mentioned in Scripture. Christmas is held on the date of a pagan festival that was semi-Christianized and owes more to Constantine than to Christ. It is unlikely to be the actual birthday of Jesus. We celebrate the day, in spite of its pagan origins, because the meaning of the day has changed through the stories we tell.

Symbols mean nothing if we do not know the stories that go with them. Changing the story changes the meaning of the symbol. Christmas is a symbol that still has many different stories. There are personal, family, cultural and religious stories about this day, many with their own symbols. Family and childhood memories make up most of our Christmas stories. These stories make Christmas a family-oriented, gift-giving time. Cultural and religious stories also change the meaning of Christmas. For some Jewish children it is the time their non-Jewish friends get lucky and receive presents.

Symbols of Eternal Bonds

Christmas must be our culture's favorite time for symbols. The tree, the ornaments, the lights, the food, the gifts, the people or places we visit, the music, the entertainment—all are carefully chosen. The day and the season are themselves symbolic, although the meaning of the symbols varies from place to place—proof that symbols and stories must always go together.

There are many kinds of Christmas symbols. Symbolic objects like the crèche, the Christmas stocking, mistletoe or the Advent wreath have special meaning for those who know their stories. Abstract symbols like geometric stars, melodies and snowflakes presuppose a common language. Symbolic events or acts like Christmas Eve, Christmas dinner, giving a gift or a kiss point clearly toward bonds with others. Even relationships can be symbolic; the Madonna and Child remind us of God's love toward us.

Some symbols are private, known only to one person. Yet to that individual they can be powerful. One Vietnam veteran always carried a little piece of shrapnel but would never speak about it. Friends would sometimes see him staring at it on Christmas, but he put the little piece of metal away if people came around. We know there is a story there somewhere.

Two people can share a symbol. Often Christmas gifts have a meaning known only to the giver and recipient. This is like a private language for two and is a sign of love. When lovers say, "They're playing our song," it is a symbol for two.

Some symbols are family-wide because the whole close group knows the story. Last Christmas Kathy Dillman, whose family has celebrated Christmas with ours for many years, gift-wrapped plastic trash can liners for her husband, John. When John opened his gift, the family smiled approvingly and John giggled. Everyone knew John's frugal character drew the line at garbage can liners when deciding which purchases were a luxury. To her family Kathy's gift meant, "I want John to live the good life."

Some symbols are culture-wide, like figgy pudding, Santa and Frosty. These symbols come from the stories of the culture.

Global symbols, like a mother with her child, depict love to all people groups. These stories are universal enough to span differences between cultural styles of expression. So whether an African or Swedish mother is nursing her child, we all understand the bond and the story.

Identities, Bonds, Stories and Symbols

A group's dynamics and values are communicated from one generation to the next in their bonds, stories and symbols. These are the means of transmitting cultural and family values. They are the ways of establishing identity. This is true for individual, family, community-of-the-self, spiritual and cultural identities.

Symbols change meaning if you change their stories. Stories change meaning if you change their bonds. Identities are formed and maintained by the arrangement of these bonds, stories and symbols.

Rainbows convey a different meaning with the Noah story, the New Age story and the lesbian story. Gestures have different meanings in different cultures because they go with different stories. When my missionary family traveled from one country to another, my mother cautioned me against making certain gestures with my fingers, saying, "You don't know what that means around here." A rhythm pattern interpreted *Shave and a haircut, two bits* in the U.S. is an obscene phrase in Mexico. The story shapes the understanding of the symbol.

Symbols are also used to remind us of our bonds. Cultures, rituals and traditions are built around bonds and their stories. Weddings, birthdays, anniversaries, retirement parties, feast days like Passover, the sacrament of the Lord's Supper, funerals, Valentine's Day, Mother's Day and Thanksgiving—each celebration has its own symbols to remind us of the bonds we celebrate, bonds that give us our identities and through which we give others their identities.

Bonds, as we saw in chapter 5, can be either fear- or love-based. These bonds leave us with either fear- or love-based identities. Fear

144

or love will then color the way we hear stories and understand symbols. If you love your father, you will run to find him when you hear his car in the driveway, and you will be glad to hear his footsteps coming toward your room. You are anticipating the beginning of another wonderful story in your life. If you fear him, those same signals indicate that you are about to be humiliated, hurt, ignored or molested. For Christie, whom we met in chapter 3, a mother and broom symbolized not a clean house but torture. Christie had fear bonds and a terrifying story.

Symbolic Objects

Symbols remind us of our stories, stories remind us of our bonds and our bonds remind us of our identities. By changing the symbol, story or bond, we affect our identities. The extent of the impact depends on the strength of each part of the chain. When bonds are weak, symbols and stories do not mean much. When the stories are vague, symbols do not maintain our bonds or identities. If our identities are in shambles, it takes good bonds to create good stories and meaningful symbols.

Occultists are very interested in symbols. Did you ever wonder what need they meet? God is fastidious about His symbols. Did you ever wonder why? Advertisers spend huge amounts developing symbols for products. Businesses protect their logos fiercely. Most of us would flatly refuse to wear a wedding nose ring. Why does it matter?

Because symbols contain our stories, stories explain our bonds and bonds define our identities.

CHRISTMAS SYMBOLS

Many objects connote Christmas to us and we are particular about them, right down to the trees. Some people must buy their trees on Christmas Eve while others must cut their own. My grandfather would have only a balsam tree. After Christmas Grandpa would take some branches and keep them under his pillow to enjoy the fragrance as long as possible.

Every year Rami and I go looking for our tree, which must be a seven-foot, full-bodied Douglas fir, or else we will not buy it. Kitty and I have one of our two annual fights when we put it into the tree stand. I always put on the lights, all sixteen strings of them, then synchronize the lights to the music on our stereo. Kitty keeps the tree watered and Kitty and Rami hang the decorations. Every ornament has special meaning and memories. One special ornament always contains Christmas savings bonds from grandparents to help with college.

Angels, Advent calendars, Nativity scenes, yule logs, Santa, reindeer, camels and stars add to our list of symbols. We always keep eggnog in the refrigerator, where it always goes bad. Many different objects symbolize Christmas so long as we know the story.

OTHER SYMBOLS

Our culture has many symbols not related directly to Christmas. One Christmas Jamie flew up to San Jose to surprise Stacey. With him he carried a small, velvet-covered box. Inside was a round gold symbol with a heart-shaped diamond, which he presented to Stacey. Down on one knee he asked her a well-rehearsed question: "Stacey, will you marry me?"

It was a Christmas gift but it symbolized much more.

BIBLE SYMBOLS

Many children learn Psalm 23 as one of their first symbolic stories. The Lord is my Shepherd. He makes me lie down in *green pastures.* His *rod* and *staff* comfort me. He anoints my head with *oil.* Green pastures represent good places to thrive. His rod and staff represent guidance and correction. Oil embodies comfort, honor and protection for our heads—the ruling part of us. Many children never learn any of God's symbolism beyond this psalm.

Houses are another symbol used in Scripture. Each family's house symbolizes the earth, which is our house as a people. Our bodies, homes, churches, temples, earth and sky symbolize heaven, which is God's house. How we clean our houses teaches others about God. It is our job to keep our houses clean so they will provide protection for us. God guards a clean house with His blessing.

Scripture is full of symbols and so is nature. God is most often called a *rock,* yet few people think of God when they see a rock. God's people are *sand.* Wise people build on rock while foolish people build on sand, yet God boasts that He can forever hold back the greatest ocean and the highest waves using nothing but sand. *Ocean* is a symbol for the heathen nations. Objects in nature are symbolic but we need to know the stories.

The righteous are also called *trees* and the unrighteous *shrubs* or *thistles.* Few people remember these meanings, however, when they look at vegetation, seashores or rocky mountains. We have forgotten the stories so the symbols mean nothing and do not touch our identities.

Abstract Symbols

Not all symbols are objects; some are ideas, patterns, groupings or even movements. These are abstract symbols.

CHRISTMAS SYMBOLS

Music is one abstract symbol of Christmas. The first four notes of *Silent Night* make almost everyone think of Christmas without hearing a single word. Jamie will not permit the playing of Handel's *Messiah* before Thanksgiving or after Epiphany. Kitty wears red and green outfits around the holiday—colors that are an abstract symbol for Christmas.

OTHER SYMBOLS

The fish many people stick onto the bumpers of their cars does not mean *aggressive driver*, as Kitty's office partner claims. The fish is an abstract Christian symbol from a Greek acronym. The first letters of the Greek words for *Jesus Christ, God's Son, Savior* spell *ichthus* (or fish). It was an abstract symbol developed by the early Church.

BIBLE SYMBOLS

In the Bible many numbers are symbolic. Seven means perfection; six is the number of man. The number four can represent several objects that have four corners or parts. Houses and altars each have four corners. The earth is our house *and* God's altar. A cross is an altar with four points and represents both destruction and salvation. Each time we hear about the four corners of the earth, we can visualize the cross, which will clean our houses. An altar represents destruction for the unclean and salvation to the clean. Death and life are the two outcomes of the great cosmic cleanup of evil.

Blood is another biblical symbol. As a scriptural symbol blood means life. Our existence is about receiving and giving life. As our blood flows through us, it takes life wherever it goes. Life is distributed by our hearts, which are responsible for the quality of our lives. Blood belongs in our veins, where it gives life. When we read in the Bible about Jesus' blood, we can substitute the phrase *Jesus' life* and keep the meaning largely intact. In the Christian story Jesus gives us His life that we might also live. The blood of Jesus is further symbolized in the wine of the Last Supper. This creates a symbol within a symbol.

Blood is an abstract symbol to theologians and a symbolic substance to people who see blood in rituals. Christ teaches that His blood means life—a life that unites us with those we love. This story can be understood through love bonds. Those who fear blood cannot see this symbol the same way. Satanic ritual teaches that blood means death, and that death unites us with others.

FEAR BONDS AND BAD STORIES

Many survivors of Satanism describe blood from the dead and dying pouring over them. For them the story has been changed so that blood symbolizes horror and destruction. They confuse the phrase *There is power in the blood* to mean that there is power in bloodletting or blood-drinking. They are in no mood to "plead the blood" or to ask to be covered again in death and dismemberment. Fear bonds and gory stories make these Christian beliefs sound like a glorification of death. How different the way of Christ actually is! Death is an enemy whose defeat is certain. Blood means life in a love bond.

Some Christians invoke the blood of Jesus against all spirits and sicknesses. But the phrase *the blood of Jesus* has no power in itself. Symbols have no power in themselves. Believing that symbols possess power is magick and converts words into incantations. Symbols are powerful because they are the way God talks to us and represent how He thinks. When we think, talk and move symbolically, we abide in our bond with God. Being part of that greater Kingdom story is made possible by symbols.

Symbolic Events and Acts

Activities can also become symbols. These symbolic events and acts have their own stories, yet they may also combine many other symbols within them.

CHRISTMAS SYMBOLS

The celebration of Christmas is an event that symbolizes God's gifts to humans. Giving and receiving gifts on Christmas Day are symbolic acts reminding us that we are God's gifts to each other.

Gifts on Epiphany remind us of the gifts the three wise men gave the Christ Child.

Other symbolic acts are less lofty. Throughout the entire season, guests at our house receive oranges with peppermint sticks for straws. Sipping the juice out of the orange through the peppermint stick appeals to young and old while they watch the lights on the tree. This Wilder tradition goes back more than eighty years and symbolizes a blessing on our community: health and happiness to all who enter.

OTHER SYMBOLS

Many acts have symbolic significance, but perhaps few are more common than eating. Meals are a global symbol for life-giving. People of every culture eat regardless of menu or methods. But we do not often think of meals as a symbolic activity. In fact, the stronger symbols are understood so universally that no thought is required to use them. Meals are symbolic times together. Only the people most important to us are invited to Christmas dinner, but all meals have significance. Thanksgiving repasts, birthday suppers, Sunday dinners and "let's do lunch" are all meals. Meals supply the relational context in which food and other messages are exchanged.

Food is a symbolic language for us. Turkey and pumpkin pie represent Thanksgiving. Hot dogs remind us of ballgames and the Fourth of July. Doughnuts make some people think of the police. Cereal reminds us of breakfast, while hush puppies make us think of the South. Soul food and lutefisk remind us of different ethnic groups. Some foods are meaningful to only one individual.

As a child I remember my grandmother as an affectionate person. Sometimes when life was hard, or for no apparent reason, she would invite me into the bedroom, where she kept her candy. Reaching into a long, narrow box of thin mints, she would produce one and give it to me with a large, almost smothering hug and kiss. Days that I am feeling unloved, I crave one thin mint to remember that my grandmother loved me. A thin mint says *love* to me in my own private vocabulary.

We know someone cares when that person fixes our favorite meal because he or she knows our language. This is how we like to be remembered on special days like birthdays. Food (a symbolic object) provides a meal (a symbolic activity), which reminds us of home (a symbolic place) and parents (a symbolic relationship.) So one symbol becomes tied to another in an endless progression.

BIBLE SYMBOLS

The twenty-third psalm has many symbolic acts. The Lord *anoints* my head with oil. He *leads* me beside still waters. He *prepares* a table before me. Since the title *Christ* means "anointed," so our ruling member (our head) is made like Christ (being anointed), making us little christs. Leading us shows God's care, while preparing a table points to the importance of our needs. How can so many Christians deny their needs when their God prepares tables?

Eating in Scripture stories is symbolic. Original sin was a food not fit for a meal. When angels visited Abram, he fixed a meal, as did Gideon. Temple sacrifices were meals, as were feasts like Passover. Communion is a meal, too. The Bible is full of food symbolism. To understand the sacrament of holy Communion, we need to understand food. In fact, most churches are very fussy about the food "vocabulary" used for the Eucharist. It is important to keep the symbols clear because the Lord's Supper is the most intensely compacted symbol in the Christian vocabulary.

Understanding God sometimes depends on food symbolism. Dr. Kenneth E. Bailey once told his seminary class a story that hinged on this point. As well as I recall it went like this:

There was once a missionary named Dr. John Haugg, who traveled through southern Egypt bringing good news to the villages. He encountered hardships but won the hearts and souls of many through his persistence and wisdom. On one occasion he was received in a village by the Coptic Orthodox reader, who put him to a test. As they were seated, his host asked the doctor about his adherence to Scripture.

"The Scriptures say that one who travels as an evangelist should always eat whatever is set before him. Do you believe this?" asked the host.

"This is true," the missionary affirmed.

At that Dr. Haugg was brought a plate of camel dung. As it was set before him, everyone watched to see if he would really follow Scripture.

But he said to them, "This is not food for people; it is food for the fire. If you bring me food for people I shall eat it."

If you visit that town today you will find a church.

150

The point of this story is not food but choosing between traditions and Scripture. Yet if we do not understand food symbolism, we will not understand Scripture. The Coptic reader had not understood the symbol of food in what he read. Dr. Haugg needed to know that eating food really meant receiving life. Thankfully for his palette, he did.

FEAR BONDS AND BAD STORIES

I avoid eating breakfast.

The first year of my boarding school experience in Llanito, breakfast usually meant watching two little girls get fed. The twins would have their oatmeal spooned into their mouths, throw it up, then be taken out and spanked. After listening to the blows, the rest of us children would hear, "Be quiet! Do you want me to spank you again?" which could turn out two ways. Eventually the sniffling girls were returned to their high chairs and refed the very oatmeal they had vomited onto the table. Then the cycle would repeat itself. When one twin gagged, the other did, too.

The sounds, sights, smells and feelings of breakfast did not sit well with me. Not wishing to be spanked or to throw up, my rear end often held discussions with my stomach about joining breakfast activities. Breakfast became a symbol to me of children staring at their plates, eating vomit, listening to spankings and wails while learning a morning Scripture verse. Breakfast connected Scripture memorization with vomit and beatings and made oatmeal a bad word. Thus was breakfast tied to me with strong fear bonds.

What would be the effect of changing the Communion meal from a loving relationship with Jesus to a fear-bonded horror? This is a common story from Satanism. Consider the following differences in food stories between Christianity and Satanism:

Eating is how we receive and give life: Jesus
Eating is a way to take life and humiliate others: Satanism

Eat nutritious foods and prosper: Jesus
Eat nonfoods (feces, urine, etc.) and vomit: Satanism

Feed your babies to help them be strong: Christianity
Eat your babies to make yourself strong: Satanism

151

One survivor of my acquaintance tore off his skin and ate it whenever he felt afraid. This man literally ate himself when he needed to prosper. Survivors often have eating disorders. Some cannot eat while others eat compulsively. Many eat nonfood items or are drawn to drinking their own blood.

Considering how the twins put me off my breakfast, what could a deliberate distortion like a satanic black mass do to the meaning of Communion? This kind of contamination, either unintended or deliberate, is continuously changing the stories that go with symbols. We must retell the true stories ceaselessly, affirm our needs and remember the Shepherd who prepares our meal in the presence of our enemies.

Symbolic Relationships

Symbolic relationships tell us something of what is happening between people even if we do not know the individuals. When we say *boss*, we know who gives the orders. These are our most important symbols because they are tied so closely to our bonds and stories.

CHRISTMAS SYMBOLS

The relationship between mother and child comes at Christmas to symbolize aspects of the relationship between people and God. This relationship celebrates God's life-giving nature. We see how God entrusted His nature and being into the care of people.

Visits to parents or phone calls on Christmas celebrate the same parent-child relationship that symbolizes God's life-giving ways. If parent bonds are strong and loving, it is not hard to understand God's identity. If those bonds are weak or based on fear, we will have trouble understanding God. We will see His identity through strange bonds and strange stories and fail to understand. Our life stories, then, color our understanding of God.

Our own feelings and bonds with babies determine how we feel about Baby Jesus. Those who love babies will love Him and bond. Those who withdraw from babies will have the same response to the Baby Jesus as they do to the babies near their tree on Christmas morning.

The relationships with the three kings in the Christmas story also illustrate our relationships. The Child-King Jesus, the evil king Herod and the wise kings interact very differently with those around them. Jesus receives; Herod takes and kills; the wise men give.

My mother will never forget Christmas dinner in Colombia the year I was two. All the missionaries gathered for a communal meal in the middle of the violence-torn country. During the meal her little boy became paralyzed by what later proved to be a stroke. In hours I was deathly ill from viral meningitis. The other missionaries, who formed the basis of our community, brought their Christmas money and paid to have me flown to the United States for medical treatment. Our neighbors were like the wise kings with their gifts. These neighborly Christmas bonds may have saved my life.

The twenty-third psalm begins with, "The Lord is *my shepherd*," a symbolic relationship. Ordinary shepherds with their care for flocks come to represent God's style and character. God refers to His people as *His bride*, making wives and marriage symbolic relationships. Jesus calls God *His Father*, making father and child a symbolic bond.

How we understand these bonds depends on the stories we know and believe about the bonds. Satanism has its own stories about fathers, so we will examine this symbolic relationship later in this chapter. What shepherds, brides, mothers, judges and fathers do in our stories will, rightly or wrongly, interpret these symbols for us.

Eve, like Mary, symbolizes both bride and mother. A bride is a helpmate, and that is what Adam got with Eve. She helped by enjoying, serving and protecting the earth as Adam did. She helped bring life. Eve also helped bring death. Helpers come in two kinds, and these are often housed in the same person. Nonetheless, when Adam and Eve lost the rights to the planet, God established a *bride* as one symbol that help was on the way. Not only would the helper be the mother of the new Adam (very helpful indeed!), but when the new Adam regained the rights to the planet, anyone who became His bride would inherit the Kingdom. They would become the new Adam's helper.

The Church is the bride of Christ. This is why we pray in Jesus' name. As His bride we also have the right to run His defeated enemies out of our inheritance in order to keep it clean. We help clean the four corners of our house. We also bring life. Isn't it good to be adopted back into the Kingdom we lost?

There are other symbolic relationships as well that mean *helper*. A bride is not the only symbol of the Church. Helpers come in many forms. Jesus the Conqueror has His army for a helper. Jesus the High Priest has His nation of priests. Jesus the Servant has His slaves. And so it goes. Consequently we learn, by contemplating these symbols, about helping and being helped. This is no abstract assignment. We contemplate by noticing how well we help others to enjoy, serve and protect the earth.

FEAR BONDS AND BAD STORIES

Satanists use the same symbols. Satan has brides. He tells his followers that to be his bride is better because he will not make them clean their house. "God does not want contaminated brides like you," he says.

That is almost correct. God does not want His bride contaminated and He refuses to the utmost to share His bride. That is why we cannot eat from the table of God and of demons (see 1 Corinthians 10:21).

Occult Symbols

Occultists have vast numbers of symbols. It is doubtful that they have all been catalogued, but thousands have been. More important to us here, however, is the role of reversal in occult thinking, particularly in Satanism. Occultists, keeping in mind that one ostensibly gains power by doing the reverse of what a rule requires, use symbols in reverse ways as well. The story, bond and identity that accompany each symbol become the opposite of what a Christian expects. In this way Christian symbols can be used, unless the bonds and stories are changed, to *maintain* the identities of Satanists.

Like Satanists, pagans tell changed stories about symbolic objects like rocks and trees. When pagans conduct a ceremony around a tree or use colored sand for healing, most Christians are oblivious. Trees and sand—both symbols, as we have seen, for righteous people—are altered by pagans to produce power, just as Christian symbols are reversed by Satanists. We can see a reversal of symbols involving the sacraments, Jesus' blood, the cross or baptism because we recognize these symbols and know these stories. But because we do not recognize symbols from creation, Christians are not bothered by pagan reversals the way they are about the black mass.

The Battle for Bonds, Symbols and Identities

Bonds tell us who we are. Symbols *remind* us who we are. Symbols also direct us, when forming new bonds, by reminding us of our stories. This way each new bond produces a correct identity on both sides of the bond, ensuring that life, and not death, gets passed through the bond. The faithful interpreter of symbols tells stories that build bonds to God and to the storyteller. Yet in the end it is the strength and character of the bond that give the story its importance. In a land of weak bonds, no stories or symbols are important.

Family dynamics based on fear or love, weak or strong bonds, have profound effects on our interpretation of culture and theology. People with weak love bonds cannot understand the reactions to symbols (such as pagan religious artifacts) for people with strong bonds, especially strong fear bonds. Calling such reactions superstitious hardly solves the problem. Even knowing the story does not help greatly because the importance always comes from the strength of the bond, not from the story. The power of the Gospel is no greater than the strength of its bonds.

When our youth pastor, Mike Schoonover, was confronted by a man with a gun who told him to renounce Jesus or die, it was the strength of the bond, not his theological accuracy, that was being tested. Mike answered quietly that he could not renounce his Lord. Seeing that Mike's love was greater than his fear, the man asked to know this same Jesus. Like Pastor Mike, Christians often find their bonds tested by pain, suffering and death, silence from God, confusion and doubt. The apostle Paul could test the spiritual health of his churches through the intensity of their affection or bond with him (see, for example, 1 Thessalonians 3:5–6).

Spiritual Bonds and the Gender of God

We understand the symbolic meanings of spiritual bonds through the reality of our family bonds. Both Christians and Satanists traditionally see their deities as male—as either fathers or bridegrooms. This is true of other cults as well. Consequently whether one loves, fears, hates, trusts or avoids one's father has a formative effect on spiritual bonds.

Since both God and Satan are generally seen as male, Christianity and Satanism are, in the common consciousness, male

155

deity religions. As a result the emotional attachments, expectations and interactions with either deity often fit family dynamics with males.

Witchcraft is generally both a female and a male deity religion. This is one of the major differences between Satanism and much of witchcraft. Most witches have room for masculine gods, but their understanding of cycles in nature does not center on male deities. Hatred between the sexes is a dynamic in witchcraft, however, and some feminist witches are devoted entirely to goddess worship. Indeed, feminist witches have been known to help women escape from Satanism. This action can be traced, in large part, to the antipathy of feminist witches to male deities, particularly those whose followers abuse women and children.

It is my observation that the worst abuse of children is linked to sexual magick. Witches from the traditions of Gerald Gardner, who originated modern witchcraft based on sexual magick, actually have more in common with the sexual magick of Crowley and his Satanists. This does not automatically indict Gardnerian witches, nor does it safeguard them from the sexual abuse of children.

Occultists, Satanists and Cabalists have long tended toward some androgenization of Satan. In recent history some Christians have proffered God the same treatment. Theologically symbolism is not static. Theologians may speak of God as male and female, and Baphomet may have both male and female features, but in common thought androgens quickly deteriorate into bisexuals.

Another way out of the sexual typing of deities has been depersonification. God and Satan, in the minds of some proponents for both sides, are not actual beings. But regardless of whether these theologians believe in the literal or figurative existence of their gods, both gods have stayed male in the minds of the faithful. It has long been the lament of finer theological minds that their insights have so little impact, but then theologians have not developed a reputation for strong bonds.

God and Satan as Fathers

Of all the members of the holy Trinity, it is "God the Father" who is most often interpreted by the family context in which people were formed. *Father* represents a symbolic relationship. The power of the symbol *father* comes from the associations we have formed to the word starting long before we ever reflected on their accuracy. The similarity between our feelings about God and the bonds we experienced with our own fathers has been noticed by most observers. This is part of the reason the interpretation of the father symbol has become so contested.

Practically speaking, few pastors are encouraged by the idea that people in the pews associate God with their biological fathers. This problem has been worsened by systematic theologians and preachers themselves. Much more is made of God as Father by the preachers of the last two centuries than the Scriptures might suggest is prudent. It was not until the nineteenth century that systematic theologians began to use the names of God to organize their thoughts. This may have contributed to the increased attention paid to "God the Father" as a Father. Another cause may be the dearth of good human fathers, which sends people searching for substitutes. Ministers and priests tend to be their mothers' favorite sons, which suggests a third cause: Clergy members may have weak father bonds, which increases their own interest in a strong father.

With God as Father, Satan becomes the opposite of one's father. In fact, the two conflict. A comparison of father dynamics with people's views of God and Satan will help illustrate the effects of family stories on metaphysics. Typically the claims made for Satan as a superior father or parent are these: more power, more acceptance, more fairness to followers, more involvement, greater respect for his followers, more intelligence and more consistency. It is easy to see how people with human fathers who were weak, rejecting, unfair, uninvolved, disrespectful of their children, foolish and inconsistent would find this appealing. This is especially true if one's father or parents claimed to follow the Lord God.

THE EFFECTS OF WEAK FATHER BONDS
ON A CHILD'S CHOICE OF DEITY

Weak father bonds are most often caused by absent or ineffectual fathers. Emotional and physical absence tend to produce one of two effects: deep hostility or idealization from their children.

God, like all fathers, can survive anger and hostility far better than idealization. Idealization closes the mind toward exploring

157

reality. If examined, God will fail abysmally to reach our ideals. This is the category into which I see God squeezed most often.

1. Ideal protection. While most Christians find it easy to think that hostility toward God is unwarranted, few would object to the idealization of God. After all, He is perfect, isn't He? Yet it is clear, on a moment's reflection, that God falls far short of our ideals. Anton LaVey makes this point on behalf of many thoughtful people when he reacts to the death of a child. What kind of loving, all-powerful God would allow this? God is clearly not the ideal, protective, nice father of our dreams. Little wonder that whenever life is found to be unfair, not nice or not accepting, people with weak father bonds experience God as distant and uninvolved.

2. Ideal acceptance. Unconditional acceptance is another fondly held ideal that God fails to meet. God is the Judge. He has a judgmental approach toward the contamination of His creation.

Provided we overlook Satan's destructive plans toward good, he appears accepting because he accepts what God seeks to destroy. For people hounded by parents because of their "badness," God's decontamination does not seem like acceptance; rather, it seems like waiting for Dad to get home.

The inverse is also true: God accepts what Satan seeks to destroy. Those who feel that Satan is out to destroy them cling to this hope.

3. Fairness. Another ideal God fails to reach is fairness. He is not fair and introduces such unfair concepts as mercy, grace and forgiveness. All three of these clearly reduce the fairness of life, as we can see in the parable Jesus told about the farm laborers (see Matthew 20:1–16). If our experience of father lacked these three ingredients, however, we will neither appreciate nor miss them. Without these virtues fairness is a much better choice.

I have yet to meet anyone who completely believed life is fair. It is hard to match an idealized God to less-than-fair experiences. Life experience, coupled with childhood unfairness by either parent, produces a growing chance of resentment toward Father God.

As regards fairness, Satan promises to reward people exactly according to their performance. The worse you are, the higher you rise on the inverted power structure of hell, with power and goodies to match. Not only so, but the results are often immediate, as those who have messed up or succeeded in a ritual will testify.

In unfair situations a sense of power comes from getting revenge. This power is available to Satan's followers but not to God's. When Mom and Dad can get revenge on each other or on their children, but the children have no redress for injustice, revenge becomes appealing. Any deity that will help becomes more attractive. Revenge equalizes weak and strong, big and little.

Four-year-old Billy used to follow me around when I mowed his father's lawn telling stories about "when I was big."

"When I was big," he would say, "I drived a big tractor. Brrrroooom-mmm-pa-pa-pa-pa-pa. If somebody hit me, I could plow them."

When he was big was, by far, Billy's favorite topic. He already had an appreciation, at age four, of how more power would help him even the score—that is, if being plowed and being hit are equivalent.

4. Involvement. Weak father bonds cause people to idealize God's involvement, yet God is notorious for His absences and silence. Job, David, Mary, Martha, Jesus and Dietrich Bonhoeffer were but a few to say so.

Many people perceive the devil as far more likely to whisper in their ears, offer them something nice, show up when they are in trouble, want to touch them and know what they are thinking. This reflects these people's expectations of what a father would do.

The fact is, we expect bad boys and girls to whisper in our ears, give us nice things, be close when we are getting into trouble, want to touch us and know what we think secretly. Satan is the ultimate "bad boy" for those who do not think of fathers as involved or for those whose fathers' involvement is, in fact, evil.

The level of paternal involvement in cults and aberrant groups appears to be much higher than in church communities.[1] This is not altogether good news, particularly when one counts rape and physical and sexual abuse as forms of involvement. Intensity in these groups, as we saw in the last chapter, substitutes for love.

5. Respect. The need for respect follows closely on the need for involvement. Satan's proponents can be proud and command respect, which they measure in the form of obedience. Do things correctly and you give the orders to spirits, elements and people. Satan is not, we are told, like the Christian God, who demands that His followers grovel and beg for crumbs.

Since Satan is not so distant and difficult to understand, he responds immediately to those who do things correctly. This is why Satanism is the most appealing form of the occult tradition to teenagers and addictive and dissociative identity disorders. Immediate results appeal most to those who are unable to delay gratification or who have a limited view of time or cause and effect.

Communities that fail to respect the needs and characteristics of subgroups provide an environment that stimulates interest in a father who will respond powerfully without making people humiliate themselves and beg. In fact, it appears that children raised in institutions, which often provide little respect for individual differences, are one of the prime categories of young people who develop an interest in Satanism.[2]

6. Intelligence. Since it appears that God has not understood how to get results from people the way Satan has, the Satanist concludes that the devil is smarter than God. It can be argued that Satan has the better grasp on human nature and existence. The fact that Satanists can visit Christian churches without fear of discovery further enhances the view that God is stupid. Obviously no Christian would manage to go unnoticed in a gathering of Satanists. The conclusion is unavoidable: God can be fooled but Satan cannot.

THE EFFECTS OF FEARFUL FATHER BONDS ON A CHILD'S CHOICE OF DEITY

Those who experienced their fathers as angry and dangerous have even more problems with bad parts of life than those whose fathers were absent. Angry and dangerous fathers have this feature in common: Neither will accept problems as their own responsibility.

1. Blame, shame and rejection. As a result of blaming others, fathers create an impression that children deserve all the anger or pain sent their way. With this as a background for all bad things in life, children tend to believe that the angry parent was sent by God because of their "badness." Badness becomes the children's identity; then the dragon takes over.

Many children rejected by such a "good" angry father long to be taken in by a "bad" father. Not uncommonly a child molester or pimp will accommodate them. Many "bad" children are taken in just this way. Satan can be a welcoming bad father.

2. Inconsistency. Perhaps the father most conducive for creating an emotional desire for Satanism is the two-faced father. Alternating from good to bad creates the impression in a child's mind of having two different fathers. It is a battle for control between good and bad—a battle that will be won by whichever side is stronger. Since these two natures are clearly in opposition to each other, and since the good side is viewed as the more desirable, the failure of good to retain consistent control seems to validate the superior power of evil. While such an argument fails to compel intellectually, it is hard to escape emotionally. If a child has witnessed the repeated switching from good to evil in a parent who makes a pretense or effort to be good, the most natural conclusion is that evil is stronger than good.

It is worth recalling, in this regard, the effects on Anton LaVey of watching alternations in the character of churchmen. Evil must be stronger, he concluded, if "good" men showed up to see strippers. (This highlights Paul's mandate in 1 Timothy 3:2 that leaders be "above reproach.")

Interestingly, the alternation from good to bad in parents can produce the opposite result on children in multigenerational Satanist families. Under these conditions the inability of parents to stamp out goodness convinces the child of the inherent superiority of goodness.

It is my view that both good and evil resist being removed from people completely. Since good and evil are tenacious, there is a tendency for a person to attribute superior power to whichever side he or she is trying to eradicate. This could explain some of Crowley's reactions to his mother, a woman bent on the removal of his evil. As the founder of modern Satanism, he went on to be known throughout England as "the wickedest man on earth."

Satan can be seen as more consistent than God because he makes no effort to be meek and gentle. God claims to be both loving and destroying. His complexity makes theology a difficult endeavor. To those whose fathers went from nice to enraged, this reality is far less appealing than a consistent God. One woman with an abusive father said, "I can't stand it when people are angry and still treat me nicely. I know how to handle it when they are angry and violent. I like to be hit."

If you are anxious enough, any sort of consistency becomes appealing.

THE EFFECTS OF LOVING FATHER BONDS
ON A CHILD'S CHOICE OF DEITY

Love has only the credibility it earns through suffering. Christ said, "I have the right to lay [my life] down, and I have the right to receive it back again" (John 10:18). His bond of love was to be tested by death. This is either a great example or absolute nonsense.

Strong love bonds with one's father reveal a parent eager to share the good and bad of life with his child. Joy is this dad's standard, and the return to joy his daily goal. These bonds do not break due to pain or fear. He demonstrates love through availability and interest in his child's identity, whether he is there at the moment or not. Healthy love bonds grow stronger by sharing both positive and negative emotions. Love bonds grow stronger both by getting closer and by moving apart. These bonds help everyone feel stable and act like himself or herself. Love bonds provide both freedom and connection. If this kind of bond is real with father and God, then Satan's appeal drops.

Is it any surprise to find that young adults attracted to Satanism do not understand love to be positive or real? Bob Larson quotes an interview with a young Satanist named David:

> I had asked David, "Why are you so angry?"
>
> "This world has no love," David responded. "Hate is better than love. I can see the effects of hatred and what it does to people. I can't see love."[3]

This is how the battle between the two fathers is being fought. Our values, symbols and stories are credible only when bonds are strong and loving. Let me ask you: Is *father* a symbol of strong love in your family?

The Proper Defense of Bonds and Symbols

Here is my version of a short history of the world:

> God is good and eternal. God creates good things. Some of the beings He made were given choices. Quite a few of them had a choice about staying good and decided to be bad. It was like a bad virus infect-

162

ing what God had made, so He decided to do a complete decontamination, because only good should be eternal. At our point in history the decontamination is not finished.

God is complex, so the history of the world is far more interesting than the one just told. In fact, this process is so complex that
we would have great trouble figuring it out if we did not possess
symbols and stories and songs and pictures to help us. God has
given us symbols for good like *clean, high, light, restful* and *alive.*
He has also established symbolic meanings for objects like rocks
and trees and for activities like kissing or anointing with oil.

In his book *Peace Child,* missionary Don Richardson tells of his
struggle to explain forgiveness without a symbol that the people
of Papua New Guinea could understand. If our symbols are incom-
prehensible, our message will not get through. The current problem with symbols can be traced to our failure to meditate on them,
the deliberate perversion of symbols, the loss of God's stories in
our culture, and weak or fear-based family bonds. As a result our
symbols no longer transmit or maintain Christian values.

James B. Jordan helped me understand why symbolism is important by pointing out that God speaks in symbols.[4] Understanding
these symbols teaches us to speak in God's vocabulary. He places
His symbols in stories, pictures and songs and in creation itself. To
experience God's symbols is to receive a message from Him, provided we can recognize and understand what these symbols say.

Once I received a tour of a church full of pictures and symbols.
The colors all had meanings—some biblical, others traditional—
and conveyed many different ideas. The presence of colors in the
world told something about their Creator. "Our God is beautiful"
was one meaning I had never before contemplated.

This contemplation takes time, and symbols require study to be
appreciated. It helps to start simple. Consider a rock. We observed
earlier in this chapter that in Scripture God is often called a rock.
In fact, He is characterized this way far more often in the Old Testament than He is as Father. By meditating on rocks and on what
the Bible says about them, we can better understand our God.

Just as people enter the occult to find explanations for the spirits they sense around them, they also need to know what the world
about them is saying. Many people sense some meaning to storms,
earthquakes, trees, rocks, caves and animals. This is part of our

fascination with Indian lore, magick potions, talking to plants and astrology. Even though it is irrational to the Western mind, the longing remains in us to be told the story of the brook or the coyote. There are many sources of interpretation in which we can find answers. Spirits and their channels, our subconscious minds, our culture, ancient cultures, Church history, scholarship, biblical texts, dreams, logic, experts, the Holy Spirit, teachers, cosmic consciousness—each of these provides answers to the meaning we seek. The options range, however, from helpful to harmful.

Occultists are deeply interested in these symbols for power and control. The interactions of symbols and the results of symbolic actions are noted carefully in grimories, records of the outcomes of sorcery, by students of the dark arts. The average Christian takes no similar interest in his or her prayers or study. But the people we believe least capable of this effort—bright, antisocial, adolescent males—often spend the longest time learning about dragons, spells and symbolic lore.[5]

A major struggle is taking place over the ownership and meaning of symbols. Christians are greatly at odds with occultists everywhere about what symbols mean. The more symbols are changed from their original meanings, the harder it is to understand God's message. Witches and pagan storytellers simply give symbols their own meanings without regard to the Lord God. But no group of occultists is more determined to change the meaning of each symbol God uses than Satanists. Their reversals require them first to understand, and then to reverse, God's symbols.

Should we abandon the cross as a symbol because Satanists use it? Should we give up the rainbow to New Agers? Should we refuse to visualize our symbols in prayer because humanists do it? Should we decline to bless because *Blessed be* is a witches' greeting? Should we give Christmas back to the pagans? Perhaps we should let them have the unicorn (since God did not create such a creature), but does that give away our imaginations as well? Which is the leading force here, the contamination or the cleanup?

The bride of Christ must reclaim boldly what belongs to us and free it from the contamination it has suffered. To do that we must learn our own songs, stories and pictures. Once these are ours, we must teach them to our children, our neighbors and our spiritual families so that the bonds in our communities-of-the-self will form correctly.

Symbols and the values associated with them are learned best from experience and stories. Research on methods for teaching values indicates that the best way to teach values is through stories.[6] Symbols are very short stories. Woven together, *symbols, stories* and *bonds* become a three-stranded rope that is not easily broken (see Ecclesiastes 4:12).

"Obviously!" we say. "Jesus taught in parables."

But the evident lack of knowledge about God's symbols and the lack of teaching about them in Christian circles suggests that *Obviously!* does not translate into common practice. Who sits down at *your* feet to hear you read, tell or sing the stories of the Kingdom?[7] Does your house have pictures and symbols on the walls to tell stories of value? Do you work to make your house smell good and look pretty so people will know of a God who is beautiful and fragrant? Would you think to mention, when someone tells you your house looks nice, the source of your inspiration?

I hope this minuscule introduction to symbols will open our eyes more to some of the messages available to us from our world. The message is in the Bible, creation, church and family life as well. We can learn from them about God and His ways. We can find their life-giving message by loving the Lord God with all our hearts, souls, minds and strength. Whatever helps us bond with God will teach us how He speaks. But how many of us see the symbols, tell the stories and love the listeners?

At Christmas time we bring out the symbols of Christmas. We play the music, serve the foods, wear the colors and tell the stories. We are careful to get every relationship bond right, if we possibly can, because each one matters. How much more should we care about the bonds that save us and their symbols and stories?

On that Christmas Day, Jamie gave a ring to Stacey. She agreed to be his bride. A girl's dream come true—a boy's dream, too. Jamie had to fly home later that day, but returned for New Year's Day. When Stacey picked him up at the airport, she was not wearing her ring. It was the first thing he noticed. His symbol was missing! In her excitement to see him, Stacey had put on hand lotion and left the ring in the bathroom. She was on her way to the airport and running late before she noticed. She hoped Jamie would not notice.

Brides should be careful with their symbols. Someone is likely to notice.

GIFTS OF PREVENTION

GIVING LIFE TO CHILDREN IN OUR HOMES AND COMMUNITIES

> "If ye then, being evil, know how to give good gifts unto your children; how much more shall your heavenly Father give the Holy Spirit to them that ask him?"
>
> Luke 11:13, KJV

STRONG love bonds, familiar stories and clear symbols help form and maintain our identities. In this chapter and the next three we will examine practical ways to create these life-giving conditions. This chapter will focus on preventing problems by bonding well with the children in our homes and community. Chapter 8 will address the corrective process of redemption with ex-Satanists. Chapters 9 and 10 will outline principles of restoration within the redemptive church family that apply to many cults and abusive situations.

Concern for the children in our homes and communities has two major parts: preventing victimization and preventing our children from intentionally turning to evil as they grow up. Some parents are trying to keep their children from being abused, while others are trying to keep their children from going "bad" in a variety of ways, including Satanism and other cults. Many parents are trying a bit belatedly to catch up with the situation.

Preventing victimization involves social, economic, political and judicial changes in our society—topics that lie outside the discussion of this book. Preventing victimization is also a mandate for the redemptive community, and a subject we will discuss briefly later in this chapter.

First let's examine the parents' role in preventing their children from developing an attraction to destructive cults like Satanism. By giving our children the necessary gifts, we can make them much stronger. To give these gifts we must examine our own identities and correct any cracks in our own defenses against evil. These gifts help develop strong love bonds and clear stories and symbols to explain the good and withstand the evil in ourselves and the world. As a result our family identities will leave fewer ways for the dragon to reach our children.

An important period of a child's life for building his or her defenses against Satanism is, as we saw in chapter 3, while the child is learning identity repair, beginning at six months of age. If the period from six to eighteen months goes well, there is far less need to be concerned about occult attractions when the child is a teen or young adult. The infant whose needs are recognized and met comes to understand that need, discomfort and pain mean that comfort and provision are on the way. He or she knows the way back to joy. Someone knows him and loves him in ways he cannot begin to understand. What an image of God!

As children grow up, more aspects of their identities must be established. Love bonds must encompass all aspects of the child's identity and world. We create these strong love bonds through meeting needs, accepting pain and returning children to joy. Love bonds must have the strength to meet needs and address the failures of life.

As families we must live with everything we have done. Parents and children do good things. Parents and children also do bad things. As a result our love bonds must be strong enough to face the evil within us and in our world. Confessing both the good and bad in our identities challenges both parent and child. Our love

167

must "fear no evil," as we learned from the symbolic story of the Good Shepherd.

Confessing both the good and bad in and around us summarizes a process that leads us toward God, the only hope of our decontamination. All the rest of this chapter can be seen as teaching children to live with the good and bad that we and they have done. When we come to terms with both, God can correct our errors. Then our bonds will produce strong identities and redeemed stories.

Eight Gifts to Protect Children in Our Homes and Community

Here are eight gifts you can give your child to make him or her a difficult target for Satanism. These gifts provide a defense against the weaknesses exploited by Satanism and cults. By avoiding the temptation to let the major beliefs (or worldview), family dynamics and lifestyle of the occult seep into your home, you will better be able to build strong, moral children who find the occult far less appealing than those who are unsure who they are.[1]

1. The Gift of Power

Power attracts those entering Satanism. Providing your children with power and teaching them how to use it well is a major form of Satan-proofing your children. Powerful children can do hard things. Powerful love bonds build powerful children.

Parents are the powerbrokers of the home. Some get into trouble by giving out too much or too little power. Other parents time the transfer of power to their children in ways that increase the children's growth and satisfaction.

Parents always have lots of power, although many do not feel that way. The felt lack of power among parents is usually related to either a lack of necessary resources or to difficulty in controlling the children.

Lack of resources is generally caused by a major failure in the support network around the parent that leaves him or her attempting more than is possible. Divorces, absent fathers, addictions, debt, natural disasters, cults and deaths can all destroy the community-of-the-self.

The second source of feeling powerless is produced by attempting the impossible task of trying to control children. Children, like all humans, cannot be controlled, and attempting this will end in failure that produces the powerless feelings. People who understand this will try rather to guide them toward careful choices.

GIVING CHILDREN TOO LITTLE POWER

Reversals, which we studied in chapter 4, appeal to children who received too little power. It seems to these youngsters that rules exist to keep them away from power. If they break rules they think they can get more power. In this way, then, giving children too little power actually prepares them for occult thinking.

Fear and anger are two major symptoms of people who feel a lack of power. It is common to find both symptoms in abundance in homes with too few resources or with too much desire to control. Fear and anger frequently become the main means of doing family business. These are fear motives and fear bonds. Yelling and breaking things become ways to say, "Do what I want!"

Life becomes a series of manipulations when fear and anger motivate choices. The cost of each action is determined by how frightening it is. The cost of each reaction is calculated by how angry it makes others. Using fear and anger to get children to act or obey takes away their power rather than giving them power.

Using fear or anger to motivate children encourages them to search for power that does not come from their parents. They steal power through reversals like disobedience, rebellion, not remembering what was said and answering most questions with, "I don't know." That is why we are taught, "Fathers, do not exasperate your children" (Colossians 3:21). Do not leave them feeling powerless.

Satanism teaches people to get power from any source available. This is very appealing to exasperated children. Adolescents learn that while parents have power, they are not the only source of power. Exasperated children do not see their parents as a source of power at all. In fact, they view parents as taking away power. The "father below" becomes very appealing when he promises to treat children differently than their parents do. He is happy to dish out some power—so he says.

This produces a convoluted problem involving power. Children who need power are left with two spirit fathers from whom to choose. The choice will be decided in part by how the children understand a father's use of power. Start with these questions: "Why are people allowed to hurt others?" or "Why doesn't God stop them?" Examined from the point of view of power, the heavenly Father's actions can be understood in two ways. Which way makes sense depends on whether one believes fathers give power or take it away.

If it is true that fathers give out power, then God has given people enough power to hurt others if they choose to do so. If fathers take away power, then clearly God the Father does not stop people from hurting others because He is a wimp and cannot get power away from Satan. If *you* need power, your prediction about how fathers act will help determine which father you seek.

Do you view parents as a good place to go to get power you can use, or good people to avoid? This question goes for spouses and children. Must you "not tell Dad" in order to get things done? If so, then Father is a power-stealer, not a power source.

If Father is effectively absent or passive while Mother gives out the power, then children will be inclined to believe the world runs the way Wicca says it does. Wicca (witchcraft is a Mother Earth–centered, polytheistic system) prefers to ask the goddess for what needs to be done. If neither parent gives out power and children must take it where they can, then the world runs the way Satanism says it does. Satanism prefers to grab the power wherever possible because power goes to those who take it. What are you teaching in your home?

Stories of families in which parents do not give power are always sad and sometimes tragic. People who were raised in Satanist families recount, not surprisingly, that this is how it was for them. Satanists' parents tend to hoard power and look at their children in terms of what power the children can give them, rather than the other way around. Children are useful for rituals, parental sexual gratification, pornography and prostitution. They are also a convenient place to vent frustration and anger.

GIVING CHILDREN TOO MUCH POWER

Giving children too much power is almost as bad as giving them no power. It produces the same powerless feelings in children because they cannot handle the power they are given. This is a favorite pattern in Satanism as well. By giving people more power

170

than they can handle, cult leaders produce out-of-control, power-less feelings and the desire for more power.

A simple version of this happens when we disagree politely with people and they respond, "Oh, I'm just stupid. You're always right. I'm always wrong." These people have suddenly given us power to decide their intelligence and future course. This produces in us a powerless and angry feeling.

Children whose "weak" parents give them excessive power usu-ally become codependent and overly responsible adults. They are good candidates for religious abuse and make good cult members if they are tricked and traumatized into it. They end up working to please cult leaders out of fear. They feel responsible for everything that goes wrong and are easy to blackmail because they feel it is their fault they are in trouble. People like this often go back to the cult even when they are given a chance to get out. We say they have been brainwashed if they keep going back to the cult, but we say they have been converted if fear keeps them going back to prayer meetings!

Children who are given too much power by powerful parents are more likely to seek Satanism than those who see their parents as weak. When powerful parents consistently give too much power, it is usually as a substitute for love. Unloved children are angry and often find hateful reasons to use power any way they want. Doing so generally means using power in ways other people dislike. This sometimes leads to intentional cruelty, humiliation and control of others. If these children who have been given too much power are attracted to Satanism, they are more prone to be leaders.

Rebellion is this kind of power. It is a negative force that holds one's identity together primarily by opposing something. Rebellion is characterized by having power without knowing how to create with it. In this way rebellion always tries to derive power from what-ever it opposes. How much better when power is given freely and wisely!

GIVING TIMELY POWER TO CHILDREN

How do we give power to our children? A major way is helping them achieve their goals. When Jamie wanted to get to know a cer-tain girl, for instance, I would give him items that needed to be delivered to her parents and he would take them over. "I enjoy help-ing you," he would say, feeling an extra boost of confidence.

When Rami wanted his room remodeled, we helped him plan the job. His mother helped him paint and then decorate it. That gave him some power over his own environment. Later he could get a job that called for painting because he had the skill. That, too, gave him power. The money from the job gave him another form of power. He smiled as he told us he was now a skilled painter. Self-esteem was yet another form of power that had flowed in part from his mother. This makes her a desirable person in his eyes and is part of her joy from giving Rami power and watching him grow.

Another way to give power is teaching your children to think wisely. The simplest form of this is teaching them to solve problems on their own. Planning is another way to think wisely. Even helping children plan and prepare a meal or pack their clothes for a trip can help. How the world can open up for the wise! Thinking well can help, but thinking well is no substitute for wisdom. We need to receive power when we are learning to think wisely. This is why Scripture speaks of our need to receive power in order to understand God's love (see Ephesians 3:16–19).

Sometimes wisdom tells us we must live with limitations in our thinking. Trying to be certain about everything we think can make us feel powerless. Exact answers are not always available. As a wise priest told me once as I pressured him for the truth, "Perhaps I have less of a need to be certain than you do."

Thinking people can be attracted to the occult if they cannot live with their own limitations in knowing. Sometimes they need to make odd jumps into the irrational to feel connected meaningfully to their world. The New Age movement, with its crystals and past lives, is like that. Satanism attracts bright people as well. The occult in general is likely to attract thinkers who cannot live with the limitations they experience.

So is it a tricky proposition being a parent? Not really. First, get comfortable with the reality that we will fail. Self-evaluation should help us realize that failure in life is commonplace. Some failures are large. Look at what happened to God's two kids in the Garden. But most failures do not amount to much. If we do not get the food hot enough in the microwave, we simply give it another shot. Failures will occur.

Second, most kids turn out unbelievably well considering the way they were reared. Most people seem to get through life with a moderately clear and consistent idea of who they are. Many manage to do well enough at meeting their own needs to live to old age. And most manage to be kind in spite of the evil in the world. It really is amazing!

2. The Gift of Affection

Affection builds strong love bonds because affection brings closeness, emotional contact, comfort, availability, responsiveness and interest. Affection meets many important needs at once. Affection in physical contact, words, voice tones and movement is a big part of bonding.

Affirm your children's value with regular affection. Someone used to protective affection from his or her parents will not be in a hurry to be raped in return for infernal power. They would rather pet a kitten than cut it open. They would prefer to give and receive comfort than to give pain.

It is good to hold and caress our children in a protective way. Affection surrounds and covers our children with safety, dignity and worth. Patting their heads, stroking their hair, giving them hugs and rocking them mean they are worth keeping safe.

AFFECTION IS NOT SEXUAL

To understand affection it is necessary to know how it is different from sex. Some people skip affection and molest their children. Others avoid all touch in order to avoid sex. In either case there is confusion about sex and affection. This confusion is often passed on to children. Children who cannot tell the difference often look for sex as teens. When they become parents the cycle starts again.

Affection covers while sex uncovers. Affection calms while sex arouses. Affection is indifferent to age or gender while sex has definite preferences. Affection is for everyone while sex is for marriage partners. Everyone needs affection to grow while sex is strictly optional.

TEENS NEED AFFECTION

Picture yourself as the average teenage boy. You feel insecure about your changing appearance. You might like to be a man but you shave only once a week, and even then you do not really need

173

to. You have immense needs for affection. What do you do to meet them?

Can a teenage boy take a direct approach? It might go like this. The boy walks up to his male friends and says, "I feel insecure and need some affection. Would you hold me and stroke my hair awhile?"

That won't work? O.K., suppose he tries the same thing with the girls. This is much harder, of course, because girls are different from him and far more threatening than boys. Not every boy could find the courage to walk up to a girl and ask her for affection. Most boys have trouble asking for a date.

"Don't be ridiculous!" you say. "The boy should ask his dad for affection . . . or is it his mom?"

The truth is, few teenagers have the courage to ask anyone, particularly at the times they feel most insecure and need affection the most.

The plight of the teenage girl is often no better. She has body parts that good people are afraid they might touch and bad people are too eager to touch. If she asks for affection, she is likely to get mauled. Girls are often left to conclude that touching and comforting are all sexual. A young couple who work with teenage pregnancies said they would like to write a book called *I Only Wanted to Be Held*.

Due to the great need for affection in the teenage economy, sex becomes a form of power. This is one source of power available to the teenage girl who has not been empowered by her parents. Treating sex as a source of social power fits nicely with the sexual magick that people like Aleister Crowley introduced into Satanism. In both cases sexual activity is used to obtain power. It still makes a poor substitute for affection.

Free sex is used as bait for people entering Satanism. Guilt-free sex. Any kind of sex. This sort of sex is captivating if we need affection and personal power, and repulsive if we are sated with protective affection. Proverbs 27:7 tells us that starving people will eat bitter food, but one who is full will turn away honey.

3. The Gift of Connection

Strong love bonds will stay connected even when the children are in pain. It is important to tell the truth about pain—both that it hurts and that sharing our children's pain is a sign of their great value.

174

Good parents share their children's pain: "Let me kiss that boo-boo and make it better." We know that love can mean suffering so that someone else does not have to suffer. Sometimes love means suffering with someone so that he or she will not have to suffer alone.

When my son Rami has needed surgery, I have been there to hold his hand when he got the anesthesia and as he came out of it. Rami squeezed my hand tightly when it hurt. As he has gotten older and stronger, I share more pain. He is worth it.

CHILDREN SHARE THEIR PARENTS' PAIN

Children also share in their parents' pain. There is evidence to suggest that it is more damaging for children to see a parent hit than to be hit themselves. It is painful and scary to see the people you depend on for survival get hurt.

I recall crossing the Andes Mountains one night when I was four. When our train was stopped by an avalanche, we had to leave the train and walk in the dark, across the buried tracks, to a train waiting on the other side. It was rainy, cold and stormy. One passenger was carrying a sheet of glass and in the dark my father got cut. For a small cut it bled profusely. Seeing my father bleed upset me far more than getting cut myself. I shared his pain but added my own terror because Dad was my strong tower out there in the stormy night. My fortress was bleeding.

When the parent is able to act like himself or herself again, in spite of the pain, and eventually return to a sense of well-being, children learn the way back from painful feelings. They will follow this path back to joy themselves when they encounter pain later in life.

STAYING CONNECTED

Most days in a family are not that dramatic. Most pain is best described as unpleasantness or irritation, at best. Even simple tasks like mowing the grass, however, allowed me to share my sons' unhappy feelings. Every other Saturday I said to them, "Today you need to mow the lawn." They hated that. I hated it, too, as a boy, and still do.

More than once we went outside and talked together about how miserable it is to mow the lawn in the heat. There were always fun things to do instead.

"Yes," I said, my arms around their shoulders, "you hate this job! It isn't much fun. It's hot and unpleasant and there are lots of things you'd rather be doing. This is a hard part of being in our family."

Sometimes I told them about the unpleasant job I would do while they were mowing; at other times the focus stayed on them. "It's time to do our unpleasant duty," I said, and we were off.

After the yard was done, I put my arm around each one and we took a "pride tour" of the yard. I pointed out where they did good work. The first few tours required some creative looking to find a place where the grass was cut evenly, but that soon changed.

"Did you enjoy it?" I asked.

"No" was always the answer.

"Well, I'm proud of you men for doing good work, even when you don't enjoy it."

After sharing the difficulty, we could share the satisfaction and return to joy.

LEARNING FROM SHARED PAIN

One value derived from sharing pain comes from teaching children that, when necessary, pain can be endured. Adults need to take their share.

Parents who escape pain at every opportunity open their children to the call of Satanism. In the dragon's house, suffering belongs to the weak, not the strong. In many families the powerful do not suffer. Dad gets his choice of chair and TV show. The strongest is always right and everyone else is stupid.

Now, to be clear about tough love and codependency, I need to say that taking away suffering that belongs to someone else is not love if it keeps that person from learning from his or her mistakes. Parents who use pain to control their children, on the other hand, and who are not interested in sharing that pain should not be surprised when their children use pain to control their parents in return.

Learning to think of pain as a form of power also clears the way to Satanism. Causing pain is clearly equated with power in many forms of black magick, juju, Palo Mayombe and Santeria. Satanism and some witchcraft have "pain-equals-power" formulations. The objective in these practices is not to share the pain but to obtain power. That way of thinking begins to make sense to children who cry themselves to sleep alone. If you have power, you do not need to have pain.

176

Sharing pain with others changes all that. If our intention is to share any pain felt by others, then "pain-equals-power" will strike us as nonsense. Pain is an invitation to draw close and heal. We want to kiss the boo-boo. Pain is lifted when it is shared willingly by another. This is joy.

In one way parents who were themselves abused as children can be the best equipped to share their children's pain. First they must learn that the pain of others is to be shared. Pain is not the best way to control others. Causing pain is not a parent's secret weapon. With this in mind their own hurts will help them stay connected.

4. The Gift of Self-Control

Those who give timely power and affection and share their children's pain build love bonds. Still, thistles can grow with wheat and fear can be mixed with love. The gift of self-control comes when parents refuse to build fear bonds they could use to control their children. What parents forfeit in control becomes self-control for their children.

It might not be apparent at first, but people who blame and control others think about all interactions and relationships in terms of power equations or vectors. This means they live in a world based on manipulations. In this family dynamic, whoever is wrong has to give in to the one who is right. Blaming others ensures that the one doing the blaming is always right. They always get their own way.

Paradoxically those who blame others actually lose power, whereas those who blame themselves gain power. This is because the person at fault has the power, by implication, to make things turn out differently. If a father tells his son, "It's your fault the lawn is brown," he implies that the son has the power to change the color of the grass. This makes blaming an inherently unsatisfying practice.

One principle in rape counseling is to let the victim carry a bit of the blame. Now, before I have to duck incoming rocks and bricks hurled by irate victims' advocates, let me explain. If a person bears no responsibility in a situation, then he or she has no power to prevent or change the outcome. Perhaps the victim's responsibility is to be more self-protective next time and avoid parking in a dark parking lot. Never, never, never is the victim to blame for the exis-

177

tence of evil or the actions of rapists. But she often contributes to some aspect of leaving herself at risk.

Fear bonds of blame are basic to understanding magick. The magus, sorcerer, witch, alchemist and spellmaker all want to gain control. The shaman, witch doctor and diviner all want to know whose fault this problem or sickness really is. Ascribing blame helps them control the forces involved. Those who believe in control and blame need such answers. And families that work on these principles create a thirst for magick.

SELF-CONTROL IS NOT TYRANNY

Let us review a basic truth: People cannot ultimately be controlled. Children, as we have said, cannot be controlled. The mentally impaired cannot be controlled. The mentally ill cannot be controlled. Spouses cannot be controlled. The elderly cannot be controlled. Ask or watch anyone who is trying to control others, and you will see frustration and powerless exasperation.

Even the self cannot ultimately be controlled. Influenced and directed, yes, but not controlled. Self-control does not mean tyranny over the self. Further, self-domination is not a worthy goal because the self can never achieve God's will and follow His laws, especially not through dominating itself. True self-control is living in harmony with who God is creating you to become. Self-control is a truthful expression of the identity you receive from the heart Jesus gives you. You guide your being into its new and greater expression through the life you receive (see Ephesians 2:10).

Did you ever see someone trying to control his or her drinking or eating or feelings of love or anger? With real effort this person manages to control himself or herself for a while; then the "beast" breaks loose again. Not many of us have escaped the temptation to try to control ourselves. Consequently we know how powerless we feel when we try.

Here is a strange truth: It is usually the people who feel most out of control who try to control a situation. They attempt to correct a lack of power by taking control of others. They extend their fear bonds and try to do "fear business" with others to quiet their own fears. Attempts to control grow out of feeling powerless and fearful. When we avoid the temptation to control our children through these fear-based manipulations, we give them a real gift of self-control.

5. The Gift of Integrity

Integrity is central to strong bonds and a strong identity. You cannot disintegrate an identity that has integrity, as Satan learned with Job. It takes integrity to give this gift.

THE LACK OF INTEGRITY AND BAD SECRETS

There are two sorts of lies. Some are the untrue things we say. Others are the untrue things we do. Both kinds of lies cover over bad secrets. Bad secrets are the kind we keep because we feel ashamed or frightened of the truth. They represent fear in our lives and identities. Bad secrets reveal a lack of integrity.

It is an emotionally compelling truth that hidden things wield more power than open things. To study this we need only look at the effects that bad secrets have on our lives. The impact is powerful and creates strong fear bonds.

Adultery is one such secret. There is a regular flow of families through my office who are being torn apart by this secret and its power. Children who are in on the secret lives of their mothers or fathers are always in trouble emotionally. Families who guard secrets know how powerful they are because of the tight security around them. Intense fear often results from the very thought of mentioning the secret to certain family members. People often fear for their lives or those of others if the secret were to come out in the open. These are powerful secrets. Explosions and angry disintegration of family life can often be found a generation or more after an adultery secret enters a family.

Sexual faithfulness is a gift of integrity to our children.

Other secrets are powerful as well. Bob's grandfather is also his father. His mother's husband pretends to be Bob's father but Bob knows he is not. Do you think this secret has any effect on this family? Incest victims often show more damage from having lived with secrets than from the molestation itself. Inside themselves victims feel that secrets are very powerful.

Sexual faithfulness is a gift of integrity to our children and to our children's children.

We have already seen the power of secrets in the story of Anton LaVey, author of *The Satanic Bible,* but we need to examine the consequences more closely. He observed that the same men he saw in church were sneaking into girlie shows and concluded that the

179

secret life was stronger. What else could he surmise? If the open truth were stronger, men would not be paying to peek at women.

I wonder what those men would think if they knew the contribution their secrets made to all those who eventually read the works of LaVey? We are parents to others besides our own children, you see, whether we choose to be or not. How much better to choose to be good parents!

Sexual faithfulness is a gift of integrity to our children and to our neighbors' children.

Anton chose truth as he saw it. Satanism and the secrets of occult magick were, to him, more powerful than God. But the man still did not like secrets, so he went public with his Church of Satan and books of secret knowledge. Did he escape the power of secrets and find the truth? He was trying to have integrity without sexual faithfulness.

Both adultery and incest secrets convey to children that sex and sexual secrets are powerful indeed. They have great control over people's behavior. People with sexual secrets can be controlled if it is done right, or else they will control others who handle it wrong. The parallels to sexual magick are more than obvious.

Sexual faithfulness is a gift of integrity to our children and to those who seek the truth.

Alcoholism is another common cause of family secret-keeping. The truth is often held hostage to control and blame issues. Alcoholism teaches the value and power of secrets. Since drugs are illegal, they are automatically secrets. Do you have any doubt about the power of the drug "secret" in our country or in countries like Colombia? Bad secrets have power to destroy.

Sobriety is a gift of integrity to our children and to the world.

Greed is another secret that, along with theft, wields power in homes, schools and businesses. Duplicity describes the person who carries these bad secrets, these lies in action. Such people are attracted to power and are often the first and fastest to jump for any position of power. We often see these sorts of people in leadership roles for just that reason. The book of Jude describes them well. Look at visible positions of leadership and power and you will usually find a few people trying to cover their greedy activity.

Satisfaction and *honesty* are gifts of integrity to our children and to our fellow workers.

The truth about the truth is this: Bad secrets have destructive power. Truth has creative power. If your family uses pain and destruction to get results, then the power of secrets will be the power for you.

Truthfulness is a gift of integrity.

Mystery religions—which cover most of the occult to New Age groups, including Satanism—are based on the power of secrets. Parents with powerful secrets hidden in their lives teach their children that real power lies in the secrets. Real knowledge lies in the secrets. Real truth lies in the secrets. What a wide-open invitation to occult thinking!

Openness is a gift of integrity.

It should not surprise us, then, that people go into Satanism because they can get some relief from these dreadful secrets. Satanism promises that no secret is too evil for them. Bad secrets contain power and people with power are welcome.

When I met Susie, she was a mess. Susie's mother carried around secrets like molestation, family alcoholism, embezzlement and several affairs. Her mother's secret rage nearly killed Susie. Mom was attracted to a group of Crowley's followers who knew what to do with secrets and their power.

"Secrets," they said, "are real and the rest is an illusion." They had room for a woman with secrets. "Unlike the church," they said, "you can be honest here." Too bad that each time she left their company, she carried another bad secret with her to impel her to return.

This matches the recruiting strategy for teens by some Satanist groups. They have parties where drugs (bad secrets) and free sex (bad secrets) are available to youth. They take pictures of participants in compromising positions; then these secrets begin to show their power. Children who have been taught that secrets control the family destiny give in easily to this pressure. What can they use to fight it? Those who have been shown that the truth, however ugly, clears the way to forgiveness and healing will be far less compelled by the power of secrets and their threats.

Confession is a gift of integrity.

We must ask, then: Is there a way for our bad secrets to be unloaded in churches and within families? Does the truth set us free? Is freedom better than power and control? Answers are easier to give than they are to practice. Integrity is expensive.

Forgiveness is a gift of integrity.

6. The Gift of Acceptance

Acceptance builds strong bonds and strong identities. Acceptance strives to find the truth and use it as a starting point. Work to accept everything about your children—but that does not mean you have to like everything they do. Acceptance is not approval. Nor is it encouragement or indifference to what we find in our children's lives. Acceptance is knowing where our children stand at any moment so we can move on from there.

Acceptance is closely related to the old word *grace*. I don't hear *grace* used in many English sentences and almost never on TV. If it is, *grace* usually refers to walking or running: "The impalas on the Serengeti leap with such grace. . . ." Grace does help us avoid careless collisions, which is why it is used to describe the way we get around.

I think of grace as being like grease. It is a lubricant to smooth rough spots and reduce friction between people. Grace is what helps us accept our children rather than grate against them. Grace is like touch-up paint. It covers a multitude of sins with love. This does not mean making sins into secrets. Grace is the force that moves to find forgiveness. Grace extends forgiveness.

To many people forgiveness is a bad word, an ugly word that means accepting any evil done against them as just fine. When it is not fine by them—and sin should never be fine—they cannot lie about it and pretend it is no problem. If we distort forgiveness in this way, we lie about the evil and pain involved. We cannot base forgiveness on lies. Grace helps us want to forgive truly ugly and evil sins rather than seek revenge.

I have seen beautiful examples of grace at work forgiving and healing such ugly things as murder, cannibalism, incest, drug abuse. Often I am the sole witness.

The problem is, grace would not talk about these things to others. Those who have been forgiven hesitate to mention their glorious forgiveness because they do not expect to receive more grace from the Church. Perhaps as a group we can demonstrate more grace to accept each other's faults.

Practice grace. This is the best way to live with the good and bad we all have committed. Learning to live with our good and bad natures is, as you recall, the key to protecting our children from Satanism. Grace in practice is what that requires. This is the gift of acceptance.

7. The Gift of Community

No child has much of a chance to grow up well if he or she has only two parents. Take my son Jamie. One day he said to me, "Dad, I want to get an earring." That caught me off-guard.

I was not sure I knew what it meant to wear an earring, but it did not seem very manly. On top of that came the overwhelming feeling that I would be embarrassed to be seen in public with my son. Not that I was totally conventional as a teenager, mind you; at one time I wore bell bottoms, somewhat long hair, a beard and even sunglasses when they were not needed. But never did I dream of an earring.

"Jamie," I said, "I can't think of any moral reason you can't wear an earring, but there is one problem. I'm not sure how I'll feel about you in public. Could you take it if your dad was embarrassed to be seen with you?"

"I could handle that," he said.

Rats! I thought. *Wrong answer.*

It is hard to express how little I liked the idea. My feelings made it hard to think. It was time to call in some other dads for my boy.

"As a courtesy to my feelings," I told Jamie, "I will ask you not to get an earring for now until we can figure this out. Since you're becoming a man, I'll let you decide for yourself after you seek the wisdom of two other fathers."

We talked it over and selected two mature men whom he knew and trusted. These men were in his life already. Jamie needed other fathers who were not so deeply involved in their feelings that they had lost perspective.

Perhaps I should add that if we expect our children to have extra parents, we should be prepared to parent other people's children. Some churches have formalized this need by providing godparents for babies. Often this amounts to little more than an additional source of baby gifts, but it is meant to go much deeper. We give the gift of community by seeking such relationships for our children and by responding to the godparent needs of others. A wise father will help his children locate other fathers when they need them.

Gary and Dick were there for Jamie when he needed to decide about the earring.

Gary said, "Go for it! Your dad should be there with you to enjoy the moment."

183

Thanks a lot, Gary, I thought, feeling really mad at him for a moment. Then it dawned on me: Gary was getting me involved with my son again when I was stuck. I felt grateful for that.

Dick said, "There are small things and important things in life. Don't spend all your energy fighting small things. Come back next week and tell me what really matters."

Jamie did. He learned wisdom. So did I.

The next week Jamie said, "Dad, I still want my ear pierced."

So, taking Gary's advice, I went with him to the mall. It was not that embarrassing after all, so we went for a malt and talked about the things that really matter in life. *Thanks, Gary and Dick.*

A wise mother will seek other mothers for her children. This helps teach children how to take their needs to people and have them met.

My wife, Kitty, was afraid of the water as a girl. So when she saw Emily's reluctance to go into the pool, she understood. Kitty became Emily's "pool mom" for the summer, carrying her about until she learned to swim. Emily's mom was a working, single mother who lacked the hours it took to teach her little girl to overcome her fears. Two moms were better.

And, lest we forget, parents are privileged to help their children meet God, their heavenly Parent. What greater proof can be found that children with only two parents need more? But finding human parents for one's children helps them expect to find a place to go if they become stuck in a conflict with their own parents. It also shows them a vision of how to act when one day they become elders of their own communities. A community with elders will never be short on the loving relationships needed to deter Satanism.

8. The Gift of Spirituality

Nowhere do our bonds, stories and symbols become more important than in the gift of spirituality. Like all the gifts we give, spiritual life does not originate with us. We can give only the gifts we have received. To give our kids the gift of sports, we take them to sporting activities. To give them the gift of music, we take them to concerts. To give them the gift of nature, we take them on trips. And to give them the gift of spirituality, we must take them on a tour of the spiritual world.

Most people I know start to become uncomfortable with anyone who takes personal interest in supernatural beings. This is particularly true if we are talking about demons and spirits. It feels silly to take spirits seriously.

Most cultures have guidelines for talking to spirit forces. Most of these cultures are clearly pagan. Paganism is beginning to fill this need for many Americans as well. Satanism is full of such guidelines and, frankly, I do not like them. People want answers to the things that scare them, and darkness is answering this void in our culture.

Our children's travel into the supernatural world begins before they are born, as various spiritual powers take an interest in what is happening deep inside Mommy's body. On the positive side, John the Baptist did his jumping in there when God's Spirit touched him. He is the youngest on record to demonstrate the emotion of joy in Scripture. On the negative side, many deliverance workers tell of evil spirits that claim entry into children before they are born. In general we ignore such claims or believe they belong with some "primitive" people group. Still, many cultures spend considerable effort and time arranging with the spirit world for the arrival of their children.

Not only do we fail to prepare a way for our children, but we often do nothing more about the supernatural after they are born. We act as though these spirits can be safely ignored. Our children probably learn more about the supernatural from movies than from their parents. Yet the fact remains: Our children need a guide to the spirit world.

Our family had gone to visit a friend's church when ten-year-old Jamie reached up and pulled my sleeve. His voice was frightened.

"I can't feel any love, Dad!" he said in a shaky voice. He was reacting as though he had suddenly gone blind. "Help me, Dad! I can't feel any love. It's all cold!"

This was new and alarming. Jamie had never talked like this before. We had never talked about feeling love—in church or anywhere else, for that matter. I did not know what was happening, so I did what a father would do. I gathered the family together in the parking lot, put my arms around my boy, held him and prayed until he felt better.

It was a year before I learned what had happened and how to heal the damage done to my son.

Clients coming out of Satanism frequently talk about not feeling love around or in them. They describe feeling cold. Usually they say, "I don't feel God's love," or, "I don't feel loved." In most cases they also report the presence of an evil spirit at the time of the distress. Could these things, I wondered, be related?

After putting two and two together, I went to find Jamie. Although we had not talked about it all year, he immediately remembered the incident and reported that he still felt coldness inside. Only when I prayed for him to be healed of any damage done by an evil spirit did he feel better. His joyful smile afterward was gratifying.

I had not been a good tour guide to the supernatural. I did not understand it very well. Yet all parents, if they take parenthood seriously, will end up being tour guides to places they have never been.

Is this getting a little weird? Protecting your children from getting strange may mean doing strange things yourself. To many of us, spiritual subjects are unfamiliar. Can you explain what you really believe about ghosts, Ouija boards, waterwitching, the filling of the Holy Spirit, demon possession, prophetic dreams, UFOs, psychokinesis or ESP?

Here are two simple examples. My aunt in Minnesota claimed that if she sat and thought about her sister in California, her sister would call in minutes. A third aunt talks about driving through an intersection with my uncle once and becoming distressed by an image of two cars colliding. In a panic she described what she saw to my uncle. On their way back home about an hour later, they came to the same intersection. This time it was full of emergency equipment and the two crashed cars.

Have you ever heard such stories growing up? What do you make of them? What is the correct explanation? Is it a good thing for your child to be like my aunts? A majority of people report having extrasensory experiences during childhood. Although many of us feel awkward talking seriously about such experiences, they are invitations for explanations.

OCCULT TOURS

If your child has any such questions and you do not answer, he or she may find occult answers. If you avoid the subject or dismiss it, the dragon may gift-wrap some spiritual tour for your child. The New Age gives beautiful, mysterious and fascinating tours. Wicca gives tours on order, harmony and influence. Satanism gives wild tours of power and fear. Each tour offers its "benefits."

Satanists appear bold, confident and powerful in this realm. They are prepared to give the secret answers to control spirit forces. They welcome clients to the Silver Star Supernatural Tour Service. As a special benefit, frequent fliers can become rulers of hell—but it will cost.

What is worth visiting in the spirit world? What should be avoided, and how do you tell where you are? What kind of protection should you take along? If you encounter an unfriendly force, do you draw a circle? Hold up a cross? Do you keep one around your neck just in case? These are simple touring questions that each parent should be able to answer to guide young travelers.

Church Tours

For the answers to these important questions, most people turn to their churches. A church should be a doorway to the supernatural world. Going to church should offer a tour of the spirit world. At times, however, it is more like a doorway to the choir, offering plate and pews.

The average Sunday school's child tour seems to include the following:

1. Be good.
2. Say your prayers.
3. Go to church.
4. Learn your catechism or Bible.
5. Remember, Jesus loves you.
6. Obey your parents.

These steps look suspiciously like the recommendations in the back of several books on how to keep your child out of Satanism. As foundational as these Sunday school lessons are, they are no substitute for strong love bonds.

Tours of the supernatural should leave from church regularly to show members into God's presence and catch the view from there. That is the place of forgiveness and healing. That is the place to give thanks and worship the God who is behind the cleanup of our planet and our lives.

187

LOVE BOND TOURS

We may give our children the wrong answers to every question I have asked about the supernatural world and still come out of our errors alive if we maintain the quality of our relationships. Love bonds are our guideposts to the spirit world. The tests of where we are and whether that is a good place to be are relational. We ask, "Is there life here?" and, "How does each spirit or response relate to the Creator of the universe?"

People not used to testing their relationships for signs of life, or to checking how they connect to the Creator of the universe, will find these ideas hard to grasp. A book is a poor way to learn about relationships, however, so it becomes almost impossible to explain adequately what I mean. The way to learn is to join a seasoned traveler and take tours together until you get the knack.

Love bonds are essential to life. While we tour the supernatural world, we need to keep an eye on both our spiritual and our human relationships. Never travel alone for long. Find companions sensitive to the life-giving elements of relationships. They see things through the eyes of heaven. This is the best advice for parents shaky about giving tours themselves. It will not get you out of your job; it just makes you more successful.

People who are full of life have their own unique styles. By understanding these styles, we can see how different people can all give wonderful tours for their children.

TOURING STYLES FOR VISITING THE SUPERNATURAL

Many kinds of parents with many kinds of interests can be tour guides to the spirit world. Let touring fit your personality. If you start to think you need to be a shaman, relax. You do not need long hair, a fascinating navel or garlic around your neck. I even recommend that you smell nice while on tour; after all, our God smells wonderful! He likes incense, flowers and other great fragrances.

Nature Lovers. These people, it seems, would be natural tour guides to the spirit world. Well, no one is natural at it, but people who like hiking and the outdoors can learn to be guides to the spirit world. Nature walks to mountains, tide pools, deserts and areas with trees and rocks explore the beauty that surrounds and sustains us. Nature lovers know how to point out beauty, even in snakes and poison oak, while staying out of harm's way. They know the interrelatedness of ecosystems. Nature lovers judge what they see, not only for its own beauty but for its effect on the rest of the system. They look for the long-term consequence of each plant, animal, mineral or geographic aspect of a given environment in relationship to the rest, and are not fooled by what seems pretty or convenient.

These are the characteristics needed to judge what we find in the spirit world as well. Often the fastest way to get results will, in the end, ruin the balance of life. The tour Guidebook says there is a way that seems right to a man but the end is death (see Proverbs 14:12). Nature lovers understand this principle, and it helps them give safe tours.

Artists. Music, art and literature lovers can make good guides of the supernatural. They can spot patterns in relationships that other people miss or take much longer to find. They know how patterns are created, repeated and changed. They know the awe of beauty and how long it can take to appreciate complex works. They recognize that symbols, sounds, stories and movement tell us about both greater and lesser things. They know how developing taste can help us avoid junk. The spirit world is a complex place and always in motion, but a good tour guide can find the patterns and the rhythm.

Plain People. People with simple tastes and style can be great guides. They often see through deception and temptation to the bonds that really satisfy. Content with meeting their needs, they do not take fancy bait or forget to seek love. Plain people seek value, not flash. They can give reliable tours.

Fun-Lovers. Lovers of food, fun and fellowship can know about enjoying all that is good and spitting out the bad. For them relationships meet real needs or are discarded. Whatever does not bring joy must be suspect. They test each experience to see if it contributes to life. Follow these guides to see who really delivers the "words of life."

Workers. Lovers of work and craft make fine guide material. Perhaps this is why many occultists refer to their practices as their craft. Each different background and personality style has something to offer. More than one carpenter has become a spiritual guide. Noah, Bezaleel and Jesus were craftsmen, while Paul, Dor-

189

cas and Aquila had trades. Workers take items and improve them to serve useful purposes. Craftsmen take pride in making products right. They disdain cheap materials or workmanship.

Sellers. Sales people get needs and solutions together. They want quality and will search and pay for it. They know how to spot a pearl of great price. What an excellent personality style for a guide!

Preachers and Teachers. This is a group that seems to have trouble with its style. Teachers and preachers are good guide helpers but often poor guides. It does not have to be this way but sometimes it is. Remember that teachers are judged by a stricter standard. A good guide is always close at hand, whereas community leaders are often off somewhere unavailable, especially to their families. Most of the time their children cannot go with them. But when preachers remember that life flows through love bonds, they can really give tours! The symbols and stories come alive; trivia becomes richness of character; and people call the teacher's children blessed.

There really is no way around it: Your children need you to be their tour guide to the spirit world. Whatever your style, there is a way for you to judge the quality of the spiritual relationships you find. The search for life will always lead to Jesus, the Creator of all life. You need only love the Holy Spirit to complete your preparations. The Holy Spirit is our Teacher in the spirit world. Without God's Spirit we are blind. Now find an experienced fellow traveler and take off.

The Gift of Protection: Preventing Victimization

These eight gifts can be given by parents, but they can also be given by brothers and sisters, aunts and uncles and grandparents. Neighbors, teachers, coaches and friends can all become tour guides and change a life.

There are some gifts, however, that cannot be given in full by any parents or family. Protection is one such gift. Viewers of the movie *Schindler's List* saw parents in Nazi concentration camps who were powerless to protect their children from death, while Oskar Schindler, who still had community power, was effective in saving a few children. One need not go to a death camp to realize this point. Many parents must send children to schools they know are unsafe places. And in divorce courts all over the country, parents watch helplessly as rulings are made that they know will be bad for their children.

For a number of years at Christmas I was invited to speak on the subject of holiday grief at the local chapter of Parents of Murdered Children. Afterward the Pasadena Police Department hosted a Christmas party for them. Each parent received an ornament with the name of his or her murdered child to hang on the Christmas tree. Parents were free to say anything they wished about their children. Some just cried. They had not been able to protect their sons or daughters. Often they said the killers were being protected by their communities, which would neither inform nor testify because of their strong fear bonds. The Christmas tree was soon covered with ornaments, but the parents left very sad.

Revolving door justice puts repeat rapists and pedophiles back into our communities. Crime remains one of our largest political issues and national fears. Protection from social evil is the function of the community and its government. No family is big enough to stand against it alone. Parents often move to different communities to obtain more protection for their children from crime, disease and other factors, but they do not always succeed.

Family crime must be addressed by the community as well. Out-of-control families and parents require community involvement and support to stop their abuse. Domestic violence, sexual abuse, religious abuse and physical abuse of children by their parents *require* community participation to correct. We depend on our families and communities for protection.

Protection from ritualistic abuse, more than any other kind of abuse, depends on our communities. Reports continue to surface of satanic rituals in daycare, preschool and church schools. Similar reports about babysitters who involve children in satanic activities or child pornography continue from time to time to appear. It is obvious that any childcare providers involved in such perverted activity are not notifying parents of the nature of their services.

Understanding this whole area is a most disheartening proposal. Facts are hard to obtain. Investigations are often badly handled. The response from law enforcement to one report of ritual abuse in a preschool was to go to the director and ask if they did those things in her school. When she said no, that ended the investigation. In other cases there is insufficient evidence. That is to say, no one contested that a child was abused, but the only evidence of who had done it was the child's own word. A family cannot straighten this out alone.

Perhaps the most troubling part of these reports is that the suspects are women and men, old as well as young. There are no "dirty old men" stereotypes to help select perpetrators. In addition, such incidents represent a coordinated effort by professionals—people who know what they are doing.

We are accustomed to thinking of people planning murders and bank robberies carefully to avoid detection, but we have difficulty believing that a group of people would spend an equal effort planning to abuse children in a way that makes it impossible to detect or for the child to disclose. While the detection and correction of ritual abuse lie outside the scope of this book, let me reiterate that the major way of preventing undesirable people from reaching our communities is to keep healthy people involved in meeting needs. Strong love bonds are our best protection.

The safest way for a parent to protect his or her child is to stay so close to the youngster that changes in mood and behavior are immediately apparent. Again, keeping strong love bonds is our best protection. Remaining sensitive to relationships, both spiritual and human, provides a much better chance of detecting problems early.

Sensitive parents will not be able to prevent all bad things from happening to their children, but they will be able to react quickly and keep these problems from continuing—if they have sufficient community support. This sensitivity to others should lead us to ask questions and seek further information. When we are in doubt, it is always better to be loving to a child than simply to have faith or hope that things will work out. It is better to give a gift than to hope that gift is not needed.

At times our own gifts will not be enough and we will be at the mercy of others. The strength of the love bonds within a community shows up most clearly when there is a problem, as we will see in the next chapter. People coming out of paganism and cults reveal the nature and strength of our bonds. How well our children fare is best seen in how their children are received.

Two of Jesus' ancestors should be an inspiration to us. Naomi may have been a bitter old widow, but her bonds still passed the test. Ruth's "Your God shall be my God and your people my people" has become the standard for love bonds and the doorway to spiritual family.

GIFTS OF RESTORATION

GIVING LIFE TO THE STRANGER AND ORPHAN

SUDDENLY the young man's hand shot up, stopping me in mid-sentence.

"He is here," he said, his eyes closed. "That Guy who gives me a choice."

His hand, still in the air, had authority.

Lord, I prayed silently, *this had better really be You.*

"He says I can come with Him and you can explain to me later about the difference between killing babies and God sending His Son to be killed."

Thanks a lot! I thought.

His eyes stayed closed but he burst into tears.

"I'm sorry," he said to Someone. Then calm descended on him and he actually smiled. "I will go with You," he said and opened his eyes.

"I think I'll like Him," he said to me. "What do we do now?"

Like many of those who have been in Satanism, this young man was terrified at the thought of saying the name *Jesus*. Even though he was a devout Catholic, he used euphemisms like *Mr. Choice* or *that Guy* when he needed to ask questions or pray. Here, in the middle of a discussion on killing children, we both felt God appear. Abraham and Isaac, God the Father and Jesus, the young man's own father and a dead child—all were momentarily eclipsed.

Reclaiming People from Fear

God earned His name Mr. Choice because of His strange decision to allow people to genuinely choose to do bad, destructive things without stopping them. To those who need protection, this God who gives choices to evil people does not appear good or loving. He does not seem powerful enough to stop evil and is not nice. The evil they fear seems stronger.

The God who so loved the world is a childkiller when first seen through fearful eyes. They are afraid God liked killing His Son or that He did it to get power over Satan. This fear of evil interprets God's stories and symbols incorrectly. The fear of being weak, unloved or hated interprets God's allowing people to make evil choices to mean He does not care. Worse yet, He may hate them personally because God hates evildoers. Cults often interpret Scripture this way so their members will avoid God out of fear of being hated. People with fear-based identities begin to know God only by fearing Him.

Not surprisingly people with fear-based identities form fear bonds or intensity (traumatic) bonds with everyone. They believe fear is what motivates others, too, so they create their individual and group identities around shared fears. Fear-based people form fear bonds as their way of maintaining life, self, security and relationships. This means that people whose very selves are based on fear will relate to everyone through fear. They do not understand love, let alone trust and use love as the basis for relationships.

They worry about what will make someone mad, for instance, instead of thinking about how to find comfort. Worse yet, when they really are in need, they turn to the people they *fear* rather than the people who *love* them. Fear and intense emotions delimit their families. In the absence of stronger bonds, they are drawn back into their fear-producing cults every time they feel out of control and need their identities reestablished. Love bonds are simply too weak and inconsequential to matter. The strongest bonds are those that will work anytime, day or night, no matter how intense or bad things get. These night-or-day bonds mark the people we can call family.

When we consider the task of reclaiming people with fear-based identities, we must be aware that love bonds do not mean much to them at first. On top of that, since strong bonds prevail over weak bonds, strong fear bonds overpower weak love bonds. Another way to say this is that people with fear-based identities return to abusive relationships even when they are loved by someone else. In the abuse they find the intensity and fear that bind them together inside and outside. Strong bonds are what they need. They find their identity and family in abuse.

Obviously the farther and longer people have been in abusive, occult or criminal activities, the more "beat up" they will be. In every case we find wounded, scared people.

They are not only frightened; they can also be scary. Their emotions, actions and reactions can be intense and frightening—after all, that is what creates fear bonds. When fear-based people want a relationship, they must eventually scare their partners. For a strong bond they must scare the others as close to death as possible. Terror makes intense family bonds.

Damaged people can also be unpleasant and ugly. Occasionally the wounding is so severe that it is hard to recognize portions of their minds as human. Discarding mutilated, grotesque, evil-appearing people is the human way to clean up. But God prefers decontamination through suffering love. His way is returning to joy from terror, rage, shame, disgust, humiliation and hopeless despair. Since our nervous systems equate joy with "someone and I are glad to be together," traumatized people need someone who is glad to be with them in order to find joy in the presence of the pain. For joy to overcome trauma, someone must share their painful events with glad, suffering love. Those who lack the joyful identity necessary to do so must have the help of others, as we saw in chapter 3.

We are called to witness God's redemption and decontamination. As witnesses we must see what truly occurs and announce it, saying, "This great work was done by God and it is wonderful in our eyes!" (see Psalm 118:23). This great work is nothing other than the undoing of fear, deceit, deception, treachery, ugliness, violence, shame, degradation and similar revolting parts of the history we have created or observed.

Giving Life to Strangers and Orphans

As witnesses we observe firsthand how God does *His* work through the bonds *we* form. These divinely appointed bonds produce our family and friends. These individuals are also God's family and friends. As He adds to His Church, He adds bonds between His people through spiritual adoption. Our God becomes their God and our people their people.

God's family, according to Jesus, commands all loyalty. Pseudo-Christian cults attempt to live this out through fear bonds; mainline churches through baptizing infants. Cults call on members to discard their biological families. Churches call their members to make all their family ties "Christian." If all natural family members are spiritual family members, there will be no need to choose between families.

The cost of discipleship for cultists who come to God includes leaving behind all their fear-based family ties. The cost of discipleship for "church-reared" Christians is to grow stronger family ties to spiritual family than to biological family. This always means accepting fear-based people into our homes as our own kin. Mainstream Christians must eventually choose between families by deciding if they will reject God's children.

God persistently adds widows, orphans, aliens and the powerless to His family. They come making fear bonds, not love bonds. They come seeking intensity, not peace. They come acting abusively or like victims rather than graciously. They come to our tables trying to eat but running back to frightening people when things get tough. Damaged people can be like that. But those who lack loving connections are to be our family. We are here as a community-of-the-self for those who are too repulsive, annoying or afraid to make joyful connections on their own.

Fear-based people bond much more easily with cults than with loving families. Some frightened people get stuck in an endless tug-of-war with fear bonds while others break free. In some ways people have a choice to make before they can be free, but we also have a choice to make before they can get free. Disconnected people lack the capacity to make the necessary choices even when they turn to God. God pulls them free by bonding them to us. This fascinating thought calls for fearless living.

Cult and abuse survivors and all those with fear-based identities require strong family love bonds to change their identities. They require mother and father, sister and brother, grandfather and grandmother bonds in which to learn love. The greater the fear they carry, the greater their need for strong family bonds. No one has more fear than those who have worshiped the red dragon.

The Work of Restoration

Picture yourself as a rescue worker after a major earthquake, seeking signs of human life and remains. Coming across a still form with traces of life, you are no doubt moved immediately to prayer but simultaneously to action. Do you need to get help? Is there still hope?

The best-trained emergency workers will summon help. Not only are they themselves equipped to help, but they bring radios with which to summon the trauma team. A rescuer who cannot call for assistance is not much good, nor is a rescuer who becomes disabled in the rescue process.

God's people work as a team. Those with the gift of mercy find the needy and bring them to those with ministry gifts. They in turn seek help from those with teaching gifts to develop the basics of spiritual maturity. Maturity is developed in a spiritual family, where mature elders and spiritual parents provide structure and babies can grow up. Developing spiritual maturity means becoming who we truly are. This change of identity is accomplished through joy, without coercion or threats, which makes it very different from brainwashing.

Making disciples is different from a simple earthquake rescue because we are not just trying to save a life but to complete our family. Long-term effort takes a different toll than crisis work. Making disciples often starts with a crisis and ends with a test of endurance. Both can cause post-traumatic stress and other problems for the adoptive family. These wounds require healing, as do the many hidden wounds that are sure to surface in the adoptive family. God is working on everyone.

Unfortunately Christians who would not venture to reconnect an arm to an injured person will try to reconnect a wounded soul— a much more difficult and painful procedure. Both victims are equally likely to be healed by prayer, faith or admonition, but Christians who venture into such pain unequipped are likely to hurt someone and be hurt in return. How to help without being destroyed is a difficult challenge for the helper. More about that in the next section.

Twenty Guidelines for Trauma Teams

Here is a summary of more than twenty years' experience I have gained on one of the best-known Christian trauma teams in America. The lessons amount to fewer than one guideline per year. You can learn quickly what I have learned slowly.

1. Learn to Feel Helpless

One summer day when I was twelve, my buddies and I went to swim in a river we had never visited. We had been told there was a good swimming hole below a dam where the water was deep. I had just finished reading a Red Cross lifesaving book and was bragging about my training.

"If anyone needs help, they'll be glad I'm here," I said, strutting down the path.

The river turned out to be quite wide and deep. Near the dam there were two and sometimes three large whirlpools that looked ominous. We agreed to stay far away from them.

Moments later, however, we heard shouting from the far bank of the river. Someone much older and larger than we was being drawn into one of the whirlpools. As he swirled into the vortex, my friends shouted, "Rescue him! Save him!" and pushed me toward the river. But I had grown roots under my feet.

I went home that day in sadness, shame, humiliation and disgrace.

The first lesson in making a disciple of an ex-Satanist is to learn how to feel helpless. We will need to use this skill for hours, weeks and sometimes years. One cannot witness God's great works without feeling helpless.

Nor can one hear about evil without feeling helpless. That is how I felt for those few agonizing seconds before the young man was spun and sucked into silence. It was the feeling I had when the breath I gulped in as he went down began to burn in my lungs, forcing me to draw another. There is nothing anyone with the greatest faith can do to change the outcome.

Take note of what your mind is doing to deal with this small dose of helplessness. Are you angry, thinking of options, playing *what-ifs*, pushing on with the reading—or something else?

2. Come to Terms with Evil

The hardest part of dealing with ex-Satanists is coming to terms with evil. It is not that Satanists have the exclusive rights to evil, nor are they necessarily the most evil, but some are trying to be, and the influence shows. Unless we understand our own evil propensities enough to feel the pull of evil, we will be little help in understanding the struggles of others when we form loving family bonds with them. If we cannot deal effectively with evil, we will be seduced or scared off.

3. Work One Step at a Time

For all of us, bonding with God progresses in stages as we bring Him into one area after another of our lives. For the ex-Satanist this often begins with trying to say the name of Jesus. Just saying *Jesus* can produce immense fear or demonic manifestations.

Survivors of childhood experiences with Satanism often develop many personalities. Fragmentation of the mind is caused by the terror of severe trauma. Frequently these multiple sub-identities of the total person are partially, and sometimes totally, unaware of one another. Often these personalities must be won to Christ one at a time during the conversion process. Because of the amnesia and mental walls between them, it is often possible to find personalities who have yet to hear of Jesus years after other personalities were reborn.[1]

If this unnerves you a bit, think for yourself how Christ is just starting to touch some areas of your life. All of us are changed one stage at a time, although we are entirely justified by faith in Christ in an instant. Christ's progressive victory in one area of life after another stands out more dramatically when it is framed by amnesia.

Amnesia is like the nerve damage caused by an accident that leaves a person paralyzed. One may be able to feel or move one's fingers within days, but moving the toes may take months. The difference with dissociative identities is that the trauma has affected consciousness rather than the muscles. Bits and parts of the mind come out of a coma thinking they are still in the original disaster. Each piece must learn the good news individually.

The Christian should not fear facing and understanding this severe damage to the heart, soul and mind. Do not assume that faith without knowledge will provide restoration to the mind any more readily than faith without knowledge will fix a blown engine on your car. To lead a trauma team, one should be at least familiar with child abuse, terrorism, dissociation, memory function, demonization and the results of all of these. While many leaders are professional counselors, organizations like Elijah House have training programs that help gifted lay people find their own healing and then minister to others.[2]

4. Teach through Example

Often we need to teach these new Christians through our example what Jesus would do or say. For a long time they will see Jesus as being like us. After they have grown in the Lord for a while, they will begin to see us as being like Him in some ways. But it rarely starts that way.

It is the nature of our bonds that gives meaning to the stories we tell. Through our bonds others come to be like us. Let's hope we are becoming like the heart that Jesus gave us.

5. Displace Evil Spirits

Teaching love and displacing evil spirits go hand in hand. These are the basics of the Christian life, so we will not review them here. The good literature available on spiritual warfare will help us if we need review.[3] Do not be surprised by the presence and strength of evil spirits in and around people who have gone out of their way to attract the strongest demons they can find.

6. Reject the Occult

Adult ex-Satanists must go through the process of rejecting all things occult. This should be required as a step of faith. They need to rid themselves of all the ritual and magick collection they have amassed. Be prepared to accompany them with a group of people skilled in discernment and faith.

7. Reclaim Symbols and Stories

Confusion about what symbols mean is rampant with Satanists, cultists and pagans. The systematic programming and corruption

201

of symbols by Satanism is extensive. Correcting this distortion can be a monumental task. Western style evangelism, based on rational conversion and a mutual understanding of symbols, is a poor model to follow. We need to explain and correct the meaning of almost every word and symbol we use to express our beliefs.

Consulting with a missionary experienced with pagan, non-Western people groups can be very helpful. Most Americans tend toward a rational teaching model, rather than a relational bonding model, for conversion. The relational model, also known as incarnational theology, is described by E. Thomas and Elizabeth S. Brewster in the booklet *Bonding and the Missionary Task.*[4] This will prove more important than it might seem to the average reader.

The stories that go with our symbols are very different when told by Satanists. This frequently means that ex-Satanists will have great trouble understanding or tolerating most church services. Starting them in small group worship allows them to question everything and learn the Christian stories. Great healing from fear is possible when the parts of them that originally participated in a black mass can receive Christian Communion with understanding and love.

Attending several different churches helps new believers experience the variety and freedom of Christian expression. Liturgical churches use more visual symbolism and produce more shocks for the ex-Satanist, while praise and worship services tend to trigger tormented reactions and demonic activity.

8. Take Steps to Provide Safety

One of the alarming reports about Satanism concerns the violence and injuries done deliberately and purposefully. Reports of threats on life, family and property are common among cult defectors and their helpers. It is safest to believe that destructive cults will try to reclaim or destroy defectors, if possible. They will also eliminate people who help their members escape, if they can.

STAY IN A GROUP

Reports of actual rapes and murders do exist, but most people who escape by becoming part of another group seem to make it out of cults. Some who are not programmed can move to distant areas successfully and start over. Others who are left behind when cult groups collapse stay in their own communities and build new family bonds. Those who must stay near an active cult need a new group identity with strong bonds in order to reach safety.

RESIST FEAR

Satanists are confident in their mental and spiritual power. They use it to control others. Most are deeply convinced that fear is stronger than love. The strongest fear that God's people can produce is fear of hell, and Satanists are preparing to rule there. Thus we are practically unarmed in a fear shootout with Satanists! Terrorism is not the strength of the Christian.

In addition American Satanists seem to share an eschatology similar to that of Hal Lindsey and Dave Hunt that we are rapidly approaching the great Tribulation and the reign of Satan on earth. Their view of how the end of the world is developing, and who is alive and well on planet earth, are about the same. Consequently the Christian escape is viewed as short-lived. Very soon Satanists expect to be in power and have their revenge on those who bothered them. This arrogance, I believe, allows many people to escape.

CONSULT LAW ENFORCEMENT

Before the end of the age, it is the law that restrains cultists. As long as they do illegal things, they do not want to be found out. Consult your local law enforcement to find out about the possible or known dangers of any given group. But do not be too surprised if law enforcement is reluctant to talk about the situation. Trust needs to be earned.

I have limited exposure to Satanist groups composed exclusively of teenagers, but I expect they would be more impulsive and less restrained by the law than groups concerned to maintain respectability.

PUBLICLY SEEK COMMUNITY SUPPORT

It is helpful to make widely and publicly known that we are helping an ex-Satanist who has been in a local cult. As a caution let me add, Don't make a spectacle of the ex-Satanist as though you had bagged an exotic prize. Nor should you reveal the new Christian's identity publicly. But be sure your support group is well informed on whom to investigate should anything go wrong. Expect to be harassed by the cult.

We have nothing to fear from Satanists who do nothing illegal. Any cults that break laws will be hindered by our holding them to public accountability. Their only recourse becomes secret or spiritual attacks. Alternately they can make us look like idiots if they do nothing. Sometimes it helps to look like an idiot.

INVOLVE EX-SATANISTS IN FINDING SAFETY

We need to enlist our adoptee in this process, as the average ex-Satanist seems to think that he or she should give information to the cult but hide it from the church. That is backwards and leaves him or her open to being threatened and intimidated.

LIVE TOGETHER

Sometimes fearless volunteers must stay with the new Christian around the clock during difficult times, dangerous dates, full moons or whenever necessary. Because the wildebeest who gets separated from the herd becomes dinner for the lions, so the weakest Christians in the church need to keep in the middle of the herd to stay safe. Often, however, they are left on the periphery. It is unlikely that ex-Satanists will survive such exposure without severe harm—if they make it at all.

Instruction on ways the Church can help is available in the *LIFE* Model[5] and through C.A.R.E., a group devoted to helping the Church with survivors.[6]

9. Provide Extended Family as a Spiritual Community

Isolation is the greatest weapon Satan has against the injured. Spiritual parents and their children often feel they are carrying around terrible secrets and wounds that others will not understand. The emotional needs of the ex-Satanist can be extensive. Just as with the issue of safety, no one can bear this burden alone. We cannot be father, mother, sister, brother, friend, counselor, healer, teacher, exorcist and protector for those in our care.

We need to be reminded that the average ex-Satanist is not totally alone. He or she has strong fear bonds to a community that will accept and support his worst propensities. This highlights his need for an accepting family. Young adults need to develop a whole new group identity based on joyful love. Even child victims need community support because they have been victims of multiple perpetrators and will require multiple restorers.

Since spiritual family bonds need a faith community around them, and since the ex-Satanist has no reason to trust others to love and care for him or her, the entire burden of making this work falls on God and His servants. This can be a long-term challenge since the ex-Satanist will almost certainly play both sides of the fence for a while. Most remain cult-active. If a church community is afraid of being betrayed, it will not endure the struggle that is about to occur.

We despise the Pharisee who got up to thank God he was not like other men, and we admire the publican who prayed, "Lord, be merciful to me, a sinner." By the next church service, however, we expect the publican to be able to thank God that he is not like other men. Intense struggles keep reminding ex-Satanists that they are just like other men or women. These are the struggles we have chosen to share.

There is a danger here as well. Some cult survivors find a nice niche going from group to group with their stories but bolting when genuine change is called for by the community. Some appear to have invented their stories; others seem to be "plants" to disrupt church life. We can easily be deceived. Compassionate people are easy to dupe.

Some believers conclude mistakenly that God's nudge to befriend or love someone is an indication of that person's genuine faith, thus forgetting that we are nudged to love our enemies as well. Perhaps if we understood this better, we would not get so upset when we find out we have been taken in by an impostor. It should be noted that Satanists have lost more than one person they planted in a church to the power of love. Don't let their mission make you forget our Great Commission.

Helping ex-Satanists become part of our family requires the following caution: Do not unite ex-Satanists in a mutual self-help group like Alcoholics Anonymous. Not only is that an ideal way for a "plant" to reach all defectors with threats, but the conflagration of evil spirits in such a setting will cause the bravest person to shake. Further, you will not like what these people teach each other on occasion from their own theologies.

It does work well to surround each ex-Satanist with about fifty "normal" Christians willing to be involved. Seek people ready to have their families grow, particularly those suffering from an empty nest. These mature lay leaders can become spiritual parents.

Keep this work away from church leaders. Pastors should be informed, but others must form the major bonds. Pastors should avoid extensive involvement with ex-Satanists like the plague, because pastors can rarely make the commitment necessary to succeed, and young pastors lack the maturity to be elders.

10. Seek Healing

Be sure your community support includes some people experienced and gifted in the area of healing. If you know little about healing, then learn from watching, not from hurting someone. The first person I ever undertook to help told me I had done more to hurt her than anyone she had ever met. I was working alone and without experience. I still have her letter as a reminder to watch what I do out of good intentions.

The other side of this is that ex-cult members or victims can use all the support they can get. Don't stand back and watch others passively. Learn and participate. Let others know you are teachable and want to share in the healing, not just in bearing up with the suffering. That is part of your reward.

Even those who would rather bite a hymnal than be involved in healing know they are helping restore the image of God in minds and hearts. Those who believe that if ex-Satanists think correctly all will be well are in for a big disappointment. Clear, sound thinking helps because truth, when obeyed, leads to freedom, but freedom is not the whole of restoration. Following Jesus, as we saw in chapter 2, requires truth, power and relationship. God transforms identities through the bonds we form.

Having said that, let me hurry to add that traumas of the past maintain their power in the present only when the trauma is connected to some lie that is still active. Some prayer counselor training, such as that provided by Dr. Ed Smith, centers the healing process around identifying and allowing Jesus to correct the lies connected to trauma. Seeing the truth about our lives is one evidence of redemption. Dr. Smith's method probably exposes the counselor to less evil than most other prayer counseling methods.[7]

Here is a note to professional counselors that might help in the healing process: You would be well advised to teach a woodland chickadee to eat from your hand, and then cleanse the cuts in a wounded panther, as preparation for this work. Be part of a strong training and support structure. Do not mistake your training and license for maturity. Take responsibility to ensure that recovery plans are in place before starting the work.

11. Learn and Practice Discernment

One night my wife was awakened twice by a choking sensation unlike anything she had felt before. Kitty's immediate impression was that someone was trying to get rid of her. What was it actually? After a week of thought and prayer, Kitty concluded that it had been a spiritual assault permitted by a lapse in her normal prayer support.

It is a question of discernment, as older saints would say. Younger saints would say we need to know what is going on. Such knowledge comes through our spiritual eyes—known in Scripture as the heart.

The Holy Spirit speaks to our hearts and we learn to discern. This is mostly a function of spiritual gifts and practice. To put it another way, some people have gotten good at it.

Discernment is found among wise people, not necessarily among smart or old people. Beware of those who claim discernment but always discern the same thing. We know which people to ask if we want stock answers. Some will always say problems are caused by spirits; others always say they are caused by the person. Working with an ex-Satanist raises lots of questions about what is causing each problem to happen. Most of these questions will not be answered in Sunday school or even in seminary.

Nowhere is this task more complex than when helping someone with physical injuries, drug dependence, dissociative identity disorder, post-traumatic stress, problems with the law, emotional explosions and a fear-based identity that is also demonized. This grouping of problems is not unusual for someone reared in a cult. It can also be found, however, in long-time church members with responsible jobs. Life is not always predictable.

We cannot estimate the size of the job based on external factors alone. We need discernment. When we find someone with discernment, we can participate and learn what that person does. Discernment is a gift but it is also learned. We receive benefits from the wise.

12. Pursue Personal Integrity

Satan deserves his reputation as a tempter and tester. When we willingly expose ourselves to his lies and works, we are in for a tough time. Ex-Satanists have experienced a wide range of secret pleasures or powers that make evil look good. If we have never had to deal with the dragon's finest lures, we are in for a new tempta-tion experience.

Bonding with ex-Satanists exposes our every weakness. If we have problems with anger or vengeance, this work has plenty to tempt us. If we struggle with lust, we face intense sexual feelings. If we suffer fear, terror will rock us. If we need to make things fair, we are in for a crisis of faith. If we need to be sure about every-thing, we are in for confusion. If we are prone to escape into work, this job will consume us. If we need to be rewarded with a little something bad in return for hard work or suffering, opportunities will abound. If we want a fight, this one can be almost endless. If we cannot return to joy from anger, fear, shame, disgust or hope-less despair, we will be down for the count.

In all these weaknesses, Satan and our own *sark* (propensity to do evil and call it good) will reliably provide their own escapes, elixirs, potions and quick pressure releases. Consider the case of the drowning boy in the river. If you had been on the riverbank and known of a spell that would make you strong or let you move objects at a distance (like Luke Skywalker in *Star Wars*), would you have used it? Not even to save a life? Suppose you had cried out to God and the boy had still died. Would you have a crisis in faith?

To be a teacher, integrity and knowledge are needed. When the classroom is real life, we must know what we can do and what we cannot. Integrity keeps us within our limits even as we stretch them and grow. Integrity keeps us honest.

13. Prayerfully Seek Truth

We must be prepared to find the truth. The new Christian we are helping has been greatly deceived. Neither we nor he can trust what he has perceived, remembered or denied to be accurate. We cannot tell which of the dragon's threats or activities are real and which are illusions. We must seek the truth. We must also seek the truth about the ex-cult member and his or her identity. When deal-ing with self-deceived people, who have practiced deception and been deceived by others, solid ground is hard to find.

We must be prepared to hear the truth. One survivor said, "I could tell things that were literally true and no one would believe me. I could tell the sisters that I had crucified Jesus, and they would pat me on the head and say, 'We all have, sweetie.'" Can you hear what the little girl was trying to tell the nuns at her church? As a youngster this woman had participated in a ritual in which the child they were crucifying was named Jesus. How was she to know there was more than one Jesus? And what do you think it did to her mind to know that everyone had done the same thing?

We must be prepared to tell the truth. Ex-cult members have no reason to think we will act differently than their past mentors. If Christians distort or hide the truth, how will ex-cultists tell the players for God and Satan apart?

Under normal conditions little lies seem to have few effects, but as matters become more important, lying becomes more of a problem. I once set back the course of counseling with a survivor by making up what seemed to be a harmless and protective lie about where my parents lived. Fortunately she called me to accountability, or things might have never worked out. I should have told the truth and said I did not want to tell her where my parents lived.

Telling the truth can be a major disadvantage, however, at any given moment. As a boy I discovered that telling the truth would get people angry with me if it seemed I had done something wrong, which was often. This had a simple solution. "Creative portrayals of reality" (lies) helped me avoid unwanted attention. When I wanted to be somebody, on the other hand, the reverse (again, lies) worked.

The followers of the left-hand path are encouraged to make things up. This can be a great advantage for them. It is easier to make anything seem attractive if we need not limit ourselves to the truth. Anton LaVey wrote in *The Compleat Witch or What to Do When Virtue Fails*: "Most people need lies. This is one of the most important reasons why you, as a witch, must learn to lie when it is expected of you. . . . Lie and give pleasure. Lie and soothe consciences. . . . Lie and become a hero, for whatever lies are popular will always win votes."[8] In addition, as we have already seen, it is easier to make someone else look bad if we are not bound by the truth. Human beings are commanded not to bear false witness, but the father of lies has his children, and we can count on the opposition to tell lies about us.

If we have been scrupulous with the truth, however, it will be harder for them to convince our families that we are untrustworthy. Be truthful.

14. The Fruit of the Spirit Builds Love Bonds

Power can mistakenly become the main goal for the Christian as it can for the pagan. Believers sometimes get involved with power-seeking when they want the gifts of the Spirit. Consequently people drawn to power are often interested in the gifts of the Spirit. (Witness Simon the magician in Samaria; see Acts 8:9–24.) Much teaching about the gifts of the Spirit is focused on power, and the motives of Christians seeking power are hard to distinguish from those of spiritists seeking power. This is even more the case when we find people seeking power to avoid suffering.

While such power-seeking appeals to the ex-Satanist and doubtless meets a need, what separates the two spiritual powers for fear-bonded people is not their power so much as their fruit. The fruit of the Spirit characterize the way things are done by the heavenly Father. The means and methods are as important as the ends. In Satanism the ends justify the means.

The Satanist scoffs at the very existence (not just the power) of love, joy, peace, patience, kindness, goodness, faithfulness, gentleness and self-control. If this stuff were really strong, what person would sign up for Satanism? Satanists claim there is power in fear and hate. Victims understand fear power. A teenage incest victim will pick power over gentleness. Gentleness is not attractive if fear is all he knows. Power gets things done.

With fear as a power source, the world can be divided into weak and strong, masters and slaves, perpetrators and victims, lions and lambs. The fruit of the Spirit does not depend on which side of that dividing line describes our present state. Our actions do not change whether we are weak or strong.

The ways the weak and strong behave are different when fear is at work. Think what happens when an inmate gets hold of a gun and changes the fear balance in prison. But the fruit of the Spirit is not based on that sort of power. Slave and master are both to display the same fruit. The powerful are willing to suffer along with the weak. The rich serve the poor. It is this consistency, regardless of power, that often makes the difference for ex-Satanists. These, then, are the fruits we need.

The gifts of the Holy Spirit in people attuned more to power than to the Spirit's fruit can bring grief. Occasionally people full of faith-that-expects-power try to follow a power=speed formula for healing prayer. While I strongly support prayer ministry for all members of our spiritual family, disasters have come about in the name of spiritual power. I have seen prayer teams deal with their own feelings of helplessness by probing deeper, seeking words of knowledge and expecting powerful deliverances. They work intensely, extending sessions far into the night, fatiguing everyone, thus forming intensity-based fear (trauma) bonds in the prayer sessions. Even though the length of sessions is governed by group anxiety (fear), this fear is labeled as a spiritual attack or battle, and after these marathons the groups often fail to return to joy.

After forming fear bonds with the weak brother or sister, the prayer teams withdraw, breaking the bonds in the name of faith in God's power to heal. This cycle may be repeated many times, until the exhausted prayer teams break all bonds by saying that the person is depending on them instead of on God's power. The next step is often a psychiatric hospitalization with a very upset, suicidal person. He or she is out of control, convinced that bonds with Christians will not hold and that God's power is too weak. Some conclude that they are too bad for God or Christians to help.

This is the result of genuine gifts of the Spirit operating without the bonds of love. No wonder Paul the apostle began 1 Corinthians 13 by describing the Spirit gifts used without love. His conclusion: Without love I am nothing (verse 2).

15. Rest

Rest is a major theme in Scripture but not in Satanism. As a result it rarely occurs to ex-Satanists that rest is important. Oh, sure, they would like to rest, but it is not allowed when important things need to be done.

Since ex-Satanists' recovery is such an important thing, both they and their new families will soon be exhausted if the "babies" are allowed to set the pace. Satanists are up quite a bit at night. If you need a conversation starter, ask them how many times they have felt tired.

Rest in Scripture is closely connected to the Sabbath, blessing and faith. Rest is how we maintain our connection to God. Resting shows our faith because when we have done our work, we trust in God to perfect it. When we rest, God works and fights for us. It is better that way.

Resting involves a certain measure of giving up control. Since control is the purpose for most magic and occult activity, rest is, in Satanists' calculation, of little value. We rest because having our God as a Father is of great value to us.

16. Find an Anchor

Accountability is a big word these days, and well it should be. Too many leaders have run aground for us to want to hear of any more losing their moorings.

To anchor yourself, start with prayer support. While battling paganism, have at least ten people praying for you. Include at least three people who can listen to your worst fears and most perverse reactions. Stay close to at least one person who is not afraid to ask tough questions.

Rich has the gift of a prophet. He tends to rankle people at times because he is bigger on truth than on tact. He is a good teacher for the same reason. He loves God and understands His ways. Sometimes Rich's bedside manner can be like General Patton's. People like him make excellent anchor lines for compassionate helpers. As you might guess, it is his wife, Priscilla, gifted in mercy, who ministers best to the ex-Satanists. Rich can be an anchor to several people at once by keeping them honest. Get yourself a Rich.

17. Let the Ex-Satanist Minister to You

Most of the tragic situations I have encountered around the country involve people who are burned out from the nonstop demands of helping cult abuse survivors. In each case I ask, "How is the survivor ministering to your needs and hurts?" In each case so far, the helping person has been surprised at the thought.

But let's have a look. Ex-Satanists have many advantages that we do not have. They have already lived through the traumatic events that are shocking us to hear about now. They are weak, but God likes to use the weak. They need experience in ministering God's love to themselves and others. They are probably more sensitive to the spirit world than the average Christian. During the counseling session they have received healing for the very situations that have just shocked us. They are right there when we need them; we do not even need to explain what we have witnessed before they pray.

In a similar vein it has been interesting to notice how often missionaries come back from their field of work burned out for lack of fellowship. In many of these cases the missionaries have held themselves aloof from the people they were converting. As a result they are lonely, isolated and discouraged. The lack of people to ease the burden leaves leaders in a precarious spot.

Note how different Saint Paul, the missionary, is in his approach. He talks in his letters about how he misses people. He wants to hear of their affection for him as proof of their faith in God. At times he is unable to bear being apart from them any longer. The people of whom he speaks are coming right out of paganism. Their pagan worship resembles our Satanism in many ways. Yet these ex-pagans minister love and care to the apostle. They are his children, parents and family.

Jesus told Simon of the woman washing His feet that those who have been forgiven much will love much, while those who have been forgiven little will love little (see Luke 7:47). In time spiritual children are bound to love very much. Our children practice love by loving us. We need it. They benefit from our correcting their expressions of love and ministry. They imitate us. This makes good feedback and quality control. We both grow into increasingly godly forms of service.

18. Redeem Every Bit of History

The Bible and subsequent Church history are records of God's deeds. They are also records of human actions. We understand the meaning of both when we see how they fit together. To be really simple about it, God takes what man does and makes something good out of it. This is redemption.

I used to love to visit my Aunt Evangeline. She collected weeds and sticks and seeds. Out of old, dry pinecones and wire came beautiful wreaths. People would pay lots of money to take home her creations. It hardly seemed possible that they could be the result of all that trash.

My brother and I liked Mom's chocolate cake. Like many children, we preferred the frosting to the cake and loved to lick the spoons. Cookie dough was good, too. I noticed that the ingredient Mom used most in both was a white powder that she measured by the cupful and sifted out of a large metal can. *That must be good,* I thought. So one afternoon when I had the kitchen to myself, I opened the can and stole a mouthful. Puffing small, white clouds and feeling a pasty buildup form in my mouth, I ran to the sink. Boy, that wasn't good at all!

After scraping out most of the paste, I finally realized the truth: It was the chocolate that tasted good. *That* was the key. I headed for the tin of powdered cocoa to get the essence of cake and cookie joy. I should have stayed with the flour!

I can only say in retrospect that it is a good thing my nose put me off trying the lard.

Whether we think of history as stemming from individuals, events or stories, God is like my aunt and my mother, making beauty and pleasure out of unappealing ingredients. He is bringing redemption out of doubtful bits of human history.

Sometimes it is our own contributions that He is improving. We tend to object to the whipping, blending and baking. Often, as the recipe progresses, we dislike the people with whom we are being combined because they are too bitter and pasty or dry and prickly. Yet we need to know God can and will redeem it all.

The events in an ex-Satanist's past, and those in our own, receive the same treatment: redemption. This is always a miracle! Those events are often ugly and evil in the extreme. I am unable to understand or predict how it will be done, but God is not through with our history until it all becomes the story of how He saved us and made us like His Son.

Perhaps an example will help illustrate the point. As I stood by the riverbank downstream from the dam with its three whirlpools, I felt terrible. I realized my Red Cross book did not make my semi-paralyzed twelve-year-old body a match for a river with currents and whirlpools. Because of my interest in underwater swimming and in seeing how long I could hold my breath, I was aware that I had drawn three breaths since the fellow went under. Each breath filled me with greater dread; he must now be dead. My legs got weak and I dropped to the ground. Just then, near the opposite shore, an arm broke the surface. Immediately a coughing, sputtering young man bobbed up. One of his friends dragged him out of the current before he could be spun back into the river.

What keeps this from being simply another upsetting moment in a boy's life is not the happy ending. My upset feelings, once yielded to God, have been redeemed to teach me what it is like to feel powerless, afraid, ashamed, humiliated and hopeless. I would not have guessed this when I was sitting by the river that day. Now, however, it will serve to remind you and me to hold onto God and our brothers and sisters when we feel powerless in the days ahead. When I yielded the shame of my inadequacy to God, He cleaned that old wound of pain. I now see God using it for good.

You may be angry with me for not telling you sooner that the young man in the river survived. But there is a point to this. Most ex-Satanists, like him, are flailing under the water and do not know if they will survive. We do not know either. We cannot predict the outcome of these encounters, although we know who wins the victory at the end. Battle conditions are like that. It is to these difficult circumstances that we bring hope.

Hold onto that hope. Do not hold onto your pain. Turn it in for redemption the first chance you get, and teach others to do the same. Remember, if we try to discount the pain, ugliness and evil, we will reduce the redemption value as well. Worse yet, our healing will, to the degree that we minimize the evil involved, be incomplete. We can return to joy only from the misery we confess.

On the other hand, remember that God is the Master of time. He is eternal. He knew about each ex-Satanist for years before we did. He is rarely in a hurry. Moses was in the wilderness for forty years, David for twenty years and Jesus for forty days, but that does not mean our visits will be forty minutes! Some problems take a long time to solve because that is how God wants it. Feel free to tell Him to hurry up, if you like, and then rest—but rest with the flock.

19. Handle Hazardous Waste Carefully

I started the introduction to this book by saying it was uncharitable to tell you how ugly evil can get. Now that we have reviewed how God redeems ugly realities, there is still no incentive for those of us who have witnessed evil to tell everyone about the depths of corruption. We know people are healed and returned to joy by talking to others about their burdens, but here we reach an impasse of sorts.

If I hear an ugly story from an ex-Satanist about being used to breed a child for Satan, for example, it will hurt and upset me. If I pass that story on when I seek some healing for myself, it will affect someone else. Do we just keep handing pain down the line? If we respond instead, "No, I must turn this burden over to God," then why not have the ex-Satanist do that directly? Indeed, some people teach that he or she should do exactly this.

It is a nice idea that does not work because fear bonds can never return us to joy. Remember, joy means that someone is glad to be with me. Joy is always relational. Ex-Satanists cannot turn to God because they are terrified of Him, so God sends us to love them in their pain and thus demonstrate His love.

If our joyful identity (discussed in chapter 3) is not strong enough to bear all the grief, at least we who are spiritually mature know we are not alone. We know love. We have love bonds. We have a group with whom we share a joyful identity. Our group identity can bear more pain than we can alone, and the love of God spreads everywhere through our hearts. Our family will help us find joy.

But we must still be careful with the hazardous waste of evil. Trauma teams are left with a waste management problem. How should we dispose of the toxic remnants of evil? This is a major problem for every person who encourages an ex-Satanist, and it can cause helpers to become a burden to their friends and begin to show depression and post-trauma symptoms. This is equally true for professional, pastoral and lay counselors and family members. It happens when we face traumas bigger than our joyful identities can carry alone.

Here are six solutions that experience has proven helpful. You may need to adapt them to local conditions or you may need to change your local conditions.

Let the Ex-Satanist Minister Back

First, seek healing quickly from the people who will be most grateful to help—the ex-Satanists. As we have already pointed out, they will have the best understanding and the most faith, for they were just healed of their exposure to this same evil. Whenever possible, this immediate containment and clean-up is most effective and keeps counselors from carrying hazardous waste out of the room. It also restores the two-way flow of life in a broken situation.

Avoid Retelling the Actual Story

Second, when you have faced a new horror, tell support people how it has affected you without telling the actual story. This will help contain the toxic part but still let you share the burden of your feelings. For this you need people who believe you when you say you hurt.

216

You could say, for example, "I need your support and prayer right now. You know I am helping a hurt person to grow. Well, today I heard something terrible—worse than anything I've heard before. I'm really upset. Will you comfort me?"

To which your support people should be trained to say, "I know how bad the things you've listened to in the past have been. This must be awful! Let's take this pain to God together."

Your friends' faith in your words will bring comfort. Prayer will offer the pain to God for healing and redemption.

CONSIDER REFERRING DECONTAMINATION TO OTHERS

Third, unless you have been especially *called, gifted* and *appointed* to handle toxic waste, don't do it. We would not cut out someone's appendix just because the person needed it. We would not know what we were doing and, in any case, most of us could not stand the blood. Frankly, an appendectomy would be much easier to handle than this hazardous waste.

That does not mean we cannot adopt or guide an ex-Satanist. It means that trauma team work is not for everyone. It is enough to be family and to share our lives with another, if that is our place. Be wise. Refer actual decontamination work to someone with the joy to deal with it.

This probably means that many family members will need to say, "What you're talking about is too hard for me. Let's pray for God to contain that pain until you get to see your counselor. Lord, start right now to bring healing to this situation, and close this wound until help is available."

Sometimes we have to apply a little pressure to keep people from bleeding all over the place.

AVOID TOXIC BUILDUP

Fourth, flush your system regularly by praying and singing the psalms. They help us return to joy.

We also need to meditate on the law of God. I am serious! Deuteronomy is especially good. We need this meditation to develop the awareness of the difference between good and evil. Yes, the law is our schoolmaster, as Galatians says, to bring us to faith, and most of us have much to learn. When we encounter this kind of evil, we cannot understand forgiveness without first understanding the law.

Ezekiel is a very helpful book when we recognize that ritual abuse was occurring among the priests of the Temple and God was out to stop them. Nehemiah is the best model I know for nurturing ex-Satanists from the Church's perspective. Ruth exemplifies spiritual family relationships with ex-pagans.

Remember to Play

In church we are usually trying to get people to be serious. With an ex-Satanist, however, we are helping someone who already knows how to be deadly serious about his or her beliefs. So, fifth, we need to play together and enjoy the bounty of God's provision and love. We need times to be less controlling of everything and explore a bit. Something will usually go wrong when we try to play, but that must not stop us from trying again. Playing helps burn up hazardous waste and helps us be glad to be together again. Play builds our joyful identities.

Watch for Traumatic Bonding

Sixth, keep an eye out for the development of traumatic bonding. Traumatic or intensity bonds are fear bonds between family members and the ex-Satanist. Traumatic bonding is a clear indicator of toxic waste residue. Unhealthy traumatic bonding occurs when someone becomes emotionally attached to something or someone who is hurting them. The helper wants to stay very close to the source of the pain because he or she feels anxious. Often the helper is afraid the person will explode or get hurt or go out of control if the helper is not close enough to prevent the problem.

When anxiety is producing this attention and concern, making it difficult to leave the other person alone, then a traumatic fear bond has formed. These are the same sorts of bonds that frequently connect ex-Satanists to their abusers. If we as helpers stay connected to that chain of fear, we will soon start to be controlled ourselves.

Perhaps an illustration of a traumatic bond will help show its power. One woman I treated hated men. Holly spent most of her life controlling her rage at experiences she had suffered.

One day she said to me, "Don't you ever come near me when I get into a rage, or I'll kill you!" She glared at me to tell me she meant every word.

I kept out of range.

218

About a year later she was crying and in pain, so I moved close to hold her hand. We had done this often. About a minute later she flew into a rage.

As she struck out around her, I was caught by glancing blows. My training said to stay calm and comforting, but my insides said, *Run quickly before she kills you! Go! Go!*

I stayed.

The rest of the day I could not keep from worrying about Holly. Was she all right? I felt compelled to call and find out but restrained myself with great effort. My concentration was gone. My stomach and digestion were busy on the meals I did not eat. It was all I could do to get my mind off Holly. Something was wrong; I was far from joy.

When I stopped to examine my experience, it became clear that feeling I might get killed or badly hurt had been traumatic for me. I was stuck in terror. Focusing my attention on helping Holly had kept me from noticing how badly frightened I was.

After accepting the fact that I was afraid to be near her again, and that I was afraid to abandon her as well, I asked God to heal the trauma. Next I had to study seriously the issue of my personal safety. Fears should neither control us nor be dismissed.

Trying to prevent a recurrence of the upsetting event often covers a trauma bond. This is particularly likely when the helper is driven to stay involved and cannot pass the problem on to others who will help. If no one else will help, of course, then such trauma is guaranteed.

Often these traumas are caused by witnessing reactions that are scary or painful. Sometimes they are caused by manipulative threats yielding the same result. They are also caused by exposure to the extreme intensity of emotion that hurt people can express. Helpers and family members often overlook just how hard it is to watch these things, and they become traumatized without knowing it happened.

Breaking a trauma bond requires us to call the trauma terrible and evil. Fear bonds are broken by identifying them and then healing the injury. Helpers and family members are in constant need of healing, and often require brief counseling to help them recover. By sharing a painful event with someone, we return to joy, and the power of the trauma is broken. Then it is time for rest and fun.

RETURN TO JOY

The ability of an individual to recover from the right hemispheric memories related to a trauma (see chapter 1) is limited by two factors: the strength of his or her joyful identity in the right prefrontal cortex (chapter 3) and his learned capacity to regulate the negative emotions and return to joy. Several key emotions to be regulated are terror, rage, shame, disgust, humiliation and hopeless despair.[9]

An individual is unable to tolerate a higher level of those negative emotions than the capacity he has grown to experience the positive emotion of joy. Thus his emotional capacity to contain a traumatic event in memory is only as big as the joy he has grown in his prefrontal cortex. This makes his joyful identity, as well as his capacity to return to joy from negative feelings, the limiters of trauma recovery.

The strength of the joyful identity of the trauma recovery team also defines the capacity of the team. The group identity is able to return to joy from much more pain than one person alone could ever carry. Working together also increases the joyful identity and capacity to return to joy of each team member. Joy means we are glad to be together. Teams must remember that joy is more important than memories, understanding, ministry or getting finished.

Joy is the natural state of our hearts. We must return to joy as individuals, families and communities-of-the-self. When we find ourselves outside of joy, we know we are away from home. When we see others without joy, we need to recognize their need. Someone must be glad to be with them, join them where they are and share their burden. That someone must see them through the heart Jesus gives and bring the orphan and stranger home to joy. Don't stop until we are all back in Camp Joy.

Beyond the Trauma Team

Restoration begins with the Holy Spirit at work building bridges where there were none. The trauma team steps in for the cleanup, but restoration is only beginning. The greatest growth comes from the spiritual family. When we receive an ex-Satanist, we are spiritually adopting an abused child. No matter how this person got into Satanism or at what age it happened, we receive a hurt and frightened child. It is reasonable to think of adopting an abused child as a fifteen-year commitment—maybe more in some cases. God has promised to bless His followers with children. How much blessing do you want?

God surprised Kitty and me with our first child at a time when it was most inconvenient, and I was not sure we were ready. My first ex-Satanist came the same way. I guess if we are married and enjoying each other, we should not be surprised by babies. If we are the bride of Christ and enjoying fellowship with Him, we should also expect children. Let's remember this when they keep us up nights. So long as we do not try to be single parents, we will be rewarded with joy—but not before we change in ways we never thought we could.

Keep close to our family and we can all catch a nap.

Gifts of Maturity

Growth, Repair
and Transformation

For nine months Mommy's tummy grew bigger. Priscilla was a slight woman whose progress was easily noticed. She had never grown out like this before and everyone was excited. All her friends were excited, neighbors were excited, the smallish church on Casa Grande Street that Kitty and I attended during seminary was excited, her husband was excited, some even thought their parrot, Erica, was excited. The major transformation was just weeks away when the whole young adult community went for a camping weekend.

As we enjoyed the wild desert around Owl Canyon, Priscilla began to swell up. Her fingers, toes, face and arms stayed dented when we pressed them. She kept getting worse until Rich took her home. By the time we got back, tragedy was confirmed. The next day Nathan's body was born without him. He had taken his last transformation before his first.

Much of the community that would have given Nathan his identity, and helped him grow, met in the smallish church to say goodbye. His parents, pastor, playmates, babysitters, teachers, reprimanders, encouragers and family came, grieved that we could not give him life. We grieved that he had not been able to repair himself or make the first of what we all hoped would be many transformations in our midst. We grieved not seeing him grow tall or smart or naughty or even make bad puns like his father.

Nathan had gone ahead into a community whose existence formed the very purpose of the church on Casa Grande. His family changed from the natural to the spiritual, leaving all his would-be life givers peering after him through puffy eyes. We wanted to see him grow up, because helping him grow and transform was our natural function.

Parents, brothers and sisters, relatives, close friends, teachers, babysitters, neighbors, pastors, pediatricians, godparents, television characters, pets and spirit beings all shape a child's identity. While family is the core of this group, many unwelcome intruders, from burglars to drunk drivers, can change a child's identity in seconds. We call this group, as we saw in chapter 3, the community-of-the-self. We are ready to look at this community in far greater depth and see how extensively and intricately we are connected. This community is the emotional equivalent of an ecosystem for identities. The community-of-the-self is made primarily from the two groupings we call family and community, with the family at the center. Because words like *tribe, village, neighborhood* and *culture* each miss the point, I will use the awkward term *community-of-the-self* for the extended system of loved as well as unwanted beings that determine our identities and bonds. I say *beings* because this group includes humans, animals and spirits. Arranged in its own unique structure, this community greatly influences the development of each self.

This community-of-the-self is a complex group identity. In setting up His people, God arranged us in marriages—families that included several generations, towns, clans, tribes, nations, families of nations, cultures, languages, even larger communities extending into the past and future—and then into the spiritual worlds of God, humans, angels and fallen angels. God intended for all these structures to be intact and functional so in them we could grow our true identities as individuals and groups. Most of us do not have even a small fraction of these structures intact.

The structures were also to be connected by bonds of love. Instead there are two networks of bonds—one of love bonds leading to God, and a second of fear bonds leading to the fallen angels. All people currently living on earth are caught in both.

When we first discussed the community-of-the-self in chapter 3, we discovered that it builds children's identities by creating bonds, stories and symbols. Then we studied identity disintegration in chapters 3 and 4; love, fear, weak and intense bonds in chapter 5; the relationship between symbols, stories, bonds and identity in chapter 6; raising strong, joyful children in chapter 7; and replacing fear and intensity bonds with love bonds in chapter 8. Now we are ready to find answers for a damaged community-of-the-self.

The Split Community-of-the-Self

Each community-of-the-self is tainted, distorted, contaminated, divided and indispensable. We fight it and cling to it. All selves in the community-of-the-self are contaminated to some degree by evil fear bonds. We will call this partially contaminated community the *natural community*. Every self in the natural community is responding in some way to the lifelong process of decontamination. The final, decontaminated community-of-the-self will be structured differently because of these responses. This decontaminated community of pure love bonds we will call the *spiritual community*. Nathan shocked us by skipping almost all of the natural community and entering directly into the spiritual one we cannot yet see.

Because both the natural and spiritual communities exist at the same time during decontamination, there is a split sense of community and identity in each self. We see our natural community with our physical eyes and the spiritual one with our hearts (provided this organ is working). During decontamination we could accurately refer to two communities-of-the-self operating simultaneously with different structures and different rules. Through spiritual processes our natural community-of-the-self is being transformed. We live in the natural and are moving toward the spiritual.

We could have drawn Nathan's family tree according to his natural family. His parents would be Rich and Priscilla, and then there would be four grandparents, aunts, uncles and cousins, with other relatives going back for generations. These genealogies are often recorded carefully and sometimes include famous people. But Nathan has a second genealogy going back through Jesus and Abraham into the family of faith. We might find the same parents and grandparents in both genealogies, but before long differences would appear.

These two genealogies represent a small part of the natural and spiritual communities-of-the-self awaiting any child. The spiritual community is greater than the natural one. Spiritual community is not some kind of supplement but rather a natural community *plus* some very life-giving bonds. The main difference between the spiritual and natural communities is this: The spiritual community has only one exclusionary division while the natural community has many. The spiritual community-of-the-self includes those being decontaminated and excludes those who refuse decontamination. The spiritual community forms according to the love bonds of the Father of lights. Those who refuse adoption stay with the father of lies—the old red dragon.

The natural community-of-the-self is often divided according to biological or blood ties, wealth, status, race, ethnicity, education, sex, nationality, criminality, attractiveness and ability. We do not consider as family those who fall "below" us on these standards.

The spiritual family accepts no such distinctions. Nor do the structures of the spiritual community-of-the-self line up with even the central core of our natural community—the family. That is to say, our spiritual family structure will never match our biological family structure. Furthermore, the natural family structure is less "real," for it is a symbol pointing the way to the spiritual community structure.

For the spiritual community, decontamination is called *redemption*. Redemption is entirely God's work. On earth the community that chooses decontamination can be called a *redemptive community*. It is a split community, both natural and spiritual at once. The same human community would not be redemptive if it rejected purification, no matter how nice its members or perfect its structure. A redemptive community-of-the-self heals the split between our spiritual communities-of-the-self and our natural communities-of-the-self by allowing, tolerating and abetting decontamination.

225

In doing so the redemptive community finds both its structure (bonds and members) and its identity changed.

The redemptive community is one in which symbols, stories, bonds and identities are being brought constantly into harmony with the spiritual structures. There people learn who they are and how to act like themselves. Redemption itself cannot be structured and has a constantly disruptive effect on natural structures because it seeks to change them. This change is more than mere restoration or repair of the existing structure by eliminating the bad elements; it brings about something altogether new, along with the death of the old.

The redemptive community is a natural community responding positively to redemption while continuing its natural work: growing people. The natural direction of this growth is always toward maturity. Both natural and spiritual maturity come through growth, repair and transformation of the self, followed by growth, repair and more transformation. In the redemptive community, natural and spiritual transformations all bring us closer to our true identities.

The Washing Machine, Vacuum Cleaner and Garbage Disposal

The redemptive community is like a washing machine, washing people and their histories. Inside the washer we place dirty clothes until they have become clean and sweet-smelling. If the agitator is broken or if we forget to add the detergent, the machine will tear the clothes or simply not clean them. This chapter will cover the design and maintenance of good washing machines and the next chapter will cover how to wash dirty clothes. Obtaining a usable washing machine, of course, precedes the discussion of washing clothes.

We select an efficient washing machine precisely so we can put dirty clothes into it. We build desirable individuals, families and communities so we can add the undesired. The washing machine accepts dirty clothes and works them steadily until it has separated dirt from fabric. The dirt is then sent down the drain and away from the washing machine and clothes. The washer welcomes dirty clothes—in fact, its exclusive interest is in dirty clothes—but it does not seek the dirt and will not keep dirt for long.

The vacuum cleaner, on the other hand, looks for dirt, pulling dirt into its very middle and keeping it there. Satanic cults are like vacuum cleaners sucking in filth. The vacuum cleaner does not separate good from bad, nor does it enhance anything that it sucks inside itself. Nothing comes back out smelling nice, looking beautiful or even better for the experience. The vacuum seeks out dirt more aggressively than the washing machine, but it likes the dirt, not the cleaning. If you feel worthless as dirt, a waiting vacuum cleaner may seem more welcoming than a closed washing machine.

It may be the garbage disposal that helps the vacuum cleaner's cause most. The garbage disposal, like the washing machine, is connected to the drain. Like the washing machine, it exists to clean things up. Unlike the washer, the disposal takes waste, grinds it up and sends it away.

The graceless church community is like the garbage disposal. This kind of church separates out bad people and, after chewing them up, sends them away. The *sark*-driven church purifies itself and its community by ridding itself of all the evil it fears.

When dirty-feeling people see the garbage disposal at work, they decide to hide their own garbage so they will not get shredded and sent down the drain. In garbage disposal communities-of-the-self, people keep bad things secret. They do not know evil is meant to be redeemed. I think the red dragon prefers the garbage disposal to the vacuum cleaner.

Some washing machines wash the same load over and over; others run full loads for one sock. This chapter is about what makes a good washing machine. We want a machine that will not chew up delicates, leave dirt in jeans, run only hot or cold water for all loads and get stuck on spin-dry for months at a time. On these subjects we will find common agreement among Christians and non-Christians. Everyone wants a clean, efficient machine. Everyone wants a good self, good family and good community. Everyone, that is, except for the red dragon and his vacuum.

In the next chapter we will look at redemption in more depth. We will examine how we may become redemptive agents, when redemption changes the structure of the natural community we call family. First we must review how the natural community-of-the-self builds maturity. Without understanding this, we cannot speak meaningfully about what happens during the transformation of redemption. Worse yet, we may confuse redemption with the transformation that occurs naturally during maturation.

Growing a Mature Self

Maturation is a combination of *growth* and *repair* followed by *transformation*. The natural community-of-the-self is responsible to provide all that is needed for these three processes.

We do not leave prenatal nutrition to chance; we provide treatment for injuries; and we take great precautions when a child is born. Maturity will be cut short if any of these three aspects is neglected by the natural community. Each individual must also work to achieve these three parts of the maturing process. Embryos must keep growing bigger and repair what goes wrong, or they will develop severe birth defects or die. If Nathan could have repaired what was going wrong with his body, he would have lived to see birth—his first transformation.

Maturity requires growth, repair and transformation at their proper times. A man might grow to three hundred pounds, while fifteen pounds for a fetus is pushing the limit. Rather than continue to become a larger and larger fetus suspended in water, babies are born to become air-breathing, mouth-feeding beings. Transformation is required before more growth can begin. Kitty's second pregnancy went ten months. The tenth month did not produce increased maturity; in fact, the baby lost weight that month. Complete growth requires timely transformations.

Birth is the first transformation in the maturity process and death is the last (at least, as far as we can observe). The Bible seems to permit a view of maturity in stages: unborn, infant, child, adult, parent and elder. Each stage has its own growth requirements for the individual as well as for the community-of-the-self. Between each stage a transformation allows the old identity to die and a new growth stage to start.

The main objectives of the six stages of maturity are these:

Prenatal: growing a working body
Infant: growing a working, joyful identity

Child: learning to take care of oneself
Adult: learning to take care of two or more at once
Parent: growing children by giving life sacrificially
Elder: growing a community

Each stage builds on the previous ones. When we have finished learning how to receive care and to express our needs as children, for instance, we continue to do so as adults but add the ability to include others' needs and expressions as equal to ours. When we become parents, we add the ability to give without receiving in return. Parents can and must still receive at times, and exchange equally with others at times. Nothing is lost from stage to stage but new strengths are added.

Maturity development is blocked by the two types of trauma. We can heal from some of the bad things that happen (the type-B traumas) like cuts and contempt. But the type-A traumas block growth for as long as the necessary good things are still missing. The absence of a loving relationship can block the development of a joyful identity for a lifetime if love is never found. Repairs cannot be made until the traumas stop.

The ideal ages for each stage are:

Infant: birth to age three
Child: four to twelve
Adult: thirteen to birth of first child
Parent: first child until the youngest child is an adult
Elder: youngest child reaches thirteen until death

These ideal ages are rarely achieved. Development can lag far behind or never be achieved at all. This blockage is common when either A- or B-type traumas are not redeemed. The opposite is also true: These stages and their tasks cannot be achieved ahead of schedule. Stages cannot be skipped without severe damage to both the individual and the community.

Essential tasks for the community-of-the-self and the individual are part of each stage and transformation. The *LIFE* Model lists these in detail.[1] Each stage has many tasks. Here are just a few:

Stage	Community-of-the-Self	Personal Tasks
Infant	Delights in the infant's unique existence.	Organizes self into a person through relationships.
Child	Teaches and allows the child to articulate needs.	Asks for what is needed.
	Gives time, encouragement and direction to do what the child does not feel like doing.	Learns what brings satisfaction.
Adult	Provides the time, place and activities to bond with peers.	Cares for self and others simultaneously in mutually satisfying relationships.
	Gives important tasks.	Contributes to the community.
Parent	Provides spiritual parents and siblings for children.	Protects, serves and enjoys one's family.
Elder	Recognizes elders.	Gives life to those without families.

Without completing these (and all other) requirements, our identities will not mature, grow, repair or be transformed free from deformities. We will stay immature.

Less obvious, perhaps, is that some people continue repairing identities they long outgrew instead of undergoing transformation. Some stay self-centered children long after they should have become men and women. When they wear spandex, we cringe. Maturity requires the timely application of growth when growth is needed, repairs when repairs are needed and transformations when transformations are needed.

Repairing the Self

All earthly structures are flawed and incomplete. Constant maintenance is necessary to keep us from falling apart. From our houses to our identities, nothing is perfect or stays perfect. Businesses, churches, families, relationships and identities all need repair. Death alone ends the repair efforts. The self requires its own repairs and is only as good as its maintenance record.

While maintaining a strong self is not the only goal of life and faith, it is more important than physical health.

Normal Repairs to the Self

When we disintegrate, we temporarily stop functioning because what we believe about ourselves and the world is not working when we need it to work. We feel overwhelmed, anxious, out of control or paralyzed because we know that something about our identities is wrong but we do not know what.

Disintegration, which we studied in chapters 3 and 4, along with its concomitant anxiety, are the signs of a self in need of repair. We are not granted the luxury of skipping repairs. During times of stress and distress, we need more repair. Each of us needs connections to someone who can tell us who we are when we begin disintegrating. We are at the mercy of our families, community and the spirits that surround us, as we discussed in chapter 3.

Proper identity repair belongs to God's loving relationships. These occur in the split community-of-the-self, which is both spiritual and natural. The job of repairing identities has not been entrusted to experts but to the heart. It is accomplished every day in almost every person's life by the people around him and by the voices in his mind.

Who lets *you* know who you are? Your spouse, parents, friends, boss and dog all have a part. Each of us is surrounded by our own group. Within our ecosystem we also repair the identities of others. How well we do depends on the quality of our bonds, for we will be treated differently by those who love us, those who fear us and those who are indifferent to us.

All of us possess incorrectly assembled identities, even when our parents were great. Judy's folks wanted to be the best parents ever. Her father figured that being a good accountant and providing a comfortable living were his greatest contributions to the baby's first few years. Not that he would have shirked a responsibility, but weren't mothers the ones in charge of babies?

Judy's mom took to reading books and asking pediatricians how to raise a child. They recommended that children be fed at regular intervals and allowed to cry in between. "Children will do that because they need to cry," she was told. Bedtime was the same way. Mom checked the clock, tucked Judy into bed with a kiss and then let her cry.

Judy was a bright, sensitive, perceptive child who began to learn who she was earlier than most. What she learned was this: *Clocks are more important than I am; how I feel makes no difference to others; I should not bother important people; they will not be there for me* [God was an important person in this child's mind]; *it is better to be passive and inexpressive than try to meet my own needs because activity makes me bad; if I wait long enough, relief will arrive, so I do matter some.*

Most of these beliefs were developed by seeing how she was treated by her natural community. Her experience helped define her identity. The odd part is, her parents would have been appalled by several of her conclusions. Some were actually contradictory; none was taught by words. Judy put these "facts" together out of her experience.

As an adult Judy looks for "don't-bother-me" messages from important people to maintain her faulty identity. When an important person says, "Come by and see me," she becomes so anxious that she starts to fall apart and runs the other way. She is carefully repairing an identity that does not fit her. Judy needs a community to help her see herself. She needs to heal the hurts of having good parents who did the "right thing."

Most people, I believe, are capable of knowing when those to whom they are close are starting to fall apart inside. Blessing others on a regular basis, especially when they are under stress, helps to repair their identities by telling them the truth about themselves. Paradoxically those who have been taught incorrectly who they are will react with anger and anxiety to the truth. "Oh, shut up!" and "You don't mean that!" and "Are you trying to make fun of me?" and "Just go away!" are common responses. Occasionally I get hit for my troubles, although usually not very hard.

We resist having our identities transformed, even when we do not like them. Letting an old identity die is frightening, and people with fear bonds avoid frightening things. At the same time we are being drawn constantly to the truth. This tension continues so long as we have incorrectly formed identities.

There are times and activities that create their own momentary and partial disintegrations of identity. Falling asleep, orgasm, hypnosis and trance states, meditation, panic and intense pain are a few. Some of these disintegrations occur regularly in our lives. As a result people are careful about the potential effects on their identities at each vulnerable moment.

People have their bedtime rituals and sexual habits. This is why Christie, whom we met in chapter 3, told her sexual partners to "talk mean" to her. She was afraid her identity as a worthless person would fall apart and then she would have no identity at all. By timing the right messages with a momentary disintegration caused by sex, she could rebuild her identity and continue to be worthless a bit longer. Repair prevented transformation because her fear centers (amygdala) oriented her life. She could see the things she feared but not the joy set before her. Her community-of-the-self included some men who were far too eager to perpetuate her old identity. Good men did the "right" thing and stayed away from her because they, too, feared getting close to a woman. There were no elders around.

As adults we can choose who will define who we are. When we are falling apart we naturally seek out people who repair us in the ways we are accustomed to be reassembled. "Do you have any drugs?" says one. "Hit me," says another. "Get mad at me," says a third. "Screw me." "Go away." "Pray for me." "Hold me." "Cry with me."

"Tell me who I am! I am stupid, lazy, ugly, sexy, a hard worker, a child, loved, hated, invisible, unimportant, an outcast, disgusting, dirty, precious, good, bad, good for hitting. I don't belong to anyone. I am falling apart and need to be put together."

Some seek reassembly through food, work, someone who will do anything for them, more faith, comfort, safety, danger, cutting themselves, being raped, cleaning the house, finding someone to blame, friends, addictions or a good, swift kick. Fear-bonded people will seek the approval, help and opinions of the people they fear. They will make scary people join their communities-of-the-self. All these fear-based repairs are momentary.

If at this point you are beginning to think you have been programmed in all the wrong ways, then good news is here. Please take courage. God means to heal the identities of all of us. If there is a problem, we come for healing. There is no need to despair or fear, even though at times He must blow our identities beyond repair so that we might find transformation. Simultaneously we seek to build the best communities-of-the-self that we can because we dare not welcome everyone's opinions about our identities.

Because of the truth it brings, there is more power in seeing others through the eyes of heaven than in commanding all the abuses of hell. We cannot repair ourselves; it happens in our communities-of-the-self. When our communities are based on love bonds, we remember what our symbols say about us and what our stories tell. In a good community-of-the-self, we can be reassembled more accurately each time. We let the community act redemptively. When we recognize the needs of others and respond with love and correction, we will soon be blessed by maturity in both our own lives and in those nearby.

Identity Repairs between Husband and Wife

Once we grow up and leave our parents, the single-largest contributor to our communities-of-the-self, unless we do not marry, is our spouses. Husbands and wives have a special role in identity repair with each other because of their sexual relationship. A brief examination of sex and identity change will help us understand why so much sin is related to sex and why married couples sometimes avoid sex when it is available to them.

The sexual experience, and in particular the orgasm, as we have noted, is a disintegrating of the self. It is a moment when the self is open to change and to being redefined. Whatever is true of our experience at that moment goes deeply into our identities. If we are thinking and feeling worse than usual about ourselves, we will avoid sex. We are not inclined to make those temporary bad feelings a permanent part of our identities by opening up to a sexual experience.

Also, as I pointed out, people are reluctant to disintegrate themselves. Some people so fear falling apart that they never have orgasms. If it were not for the pleasure involved, perhaps few people ever would.

People with sexual abuse histories, whose internal identities are in such turmoil that they are in constant danger of falling apart, can be just the opposite. Sex means they are wanted. They are glad someone can stand being with them. Some believe they need lots of sex. They use sexual activity to maintain their crumbling identities.

The conscientious lover should be aware that he or she is establishing the identity of the partner with each encounter. What we say during those times, when the ability to consciously correct or resist messages is greatly diminished, is important. The lover should take every opportunity to say, "You are special, enjoyable, valuable, worth having and protecting, attractive, fun, memorable, beautiful and uniquely suited to be married to me. I trust you to be the one who holds me when I disintegrate and to reestablish me again."

Nonverbal messages count very heavily at these times as well. On the negative side, any disrespect, indifference or disregard plants messages that the other person has little or no value. People who have married sexual abuse victims are well aware that such messages come to the surface at these times. On the positive side, nonverbal attention to our partners' needs before, during and after disintegration leaves them knowing they are valued and that their needs really do matter.

These nonverbal messages are also forced into our identities by self-produced sexual experiences. How we treat ourselves, what we say or think and the context we establish all become locked into our identities. As Christians seeking growth, we should seek to establish the most accurate view of ourselves that we possibly can. If you cannot think of yourself as a deeply loved child of God during such experiences, then look for healing to help you change.

Identity Repair and Redemption

Redemption adds something to identity repair that the natural community-of-the-self cannot. Redemption decontaminates from fear bonds and pulls each identity toward the spiritual community-of-the-self. Thanks be to God, maturity builds on a sanctified base. The power to forgive bad secrets lies at the very foundation of Christianity. It is this power that protects us from evil. If there are no bad secrets to be kept, evil has no leverage. Evil spirits have nothing to thrive on where there is truth.

Increasing numbers of people are committed to helping Christians and their churches break the silence on addictions, shame, abuse and other secrets.[2] More important, they are addressing the needs behind the silence. These churches are the antithesis of Satanism. It is not surprising, then, that several of these ministry-oriented churches report opposition from Satanist groups. The dragon hates a good washing machine.

Wherever there are pockets of openness, you can be sure that people with secrets will be attracted. There is relief in being able to know and tell the awful truth about our secrets. When old Simeon blessed the Baby Jesus in the Temple, he said, "This child is destined to be a sign which men reject; . . . and thus the secret thoughts of many [hearts] will be laid bare" (Luke 2:34–35).

This creates an interesting dynamic in church life as people begin to reveal increasingly worse secrets. Heightening truthfulness creates the impression that things are getting worse. If this truth-telling is met with fear and rejection, it will not be long until people are keeping secrets again. Telling ourselves the truth is limited by our ability to love each other, as we will see in chapter 11.

There is ongoing tension between secrets and forgiveness. Where love and forgiveness lead, increasingly worse secrets come into the open, requiring us to grow in love to match the demand. This is new wine, and those who try to contain it in old wineskins will have a mess. Those who try to hide the mess start a new series of secrets, and love dwindles. Those who take their new mess to God find forgiveness and grow in love once again.

What our churches need most is not truth but life—not that these oppose one another, but because truth is not complete without life. Life comes directly from the love of God within us, and that love comes from being forgiven. This is what Jesus told Simon about the woman washing His feet: Her great love showed that her many sins were forgiven (see Luke 7:47).

Anti-Identity Theology Blocks Maturity

Some Christians directly oppose teaching about the self, condemning it as evil. Likewise many Christians deny that we have any real needs except for spiritual ones. Self and needs are rejected as the accouterments of secular self psychology. Intelligent, influential Christians hold modified versions of this position.

Without a self, maturity is not possible. But garbage disposal theology has made many of us afraid of the self. Like money or sex, the self can be worshiped and can dominate our lives. Repairing an outgrown self can keep God from transforming us by reconstructing our minds. Consequently some say we should get rid of the self because it is an agent for the flesh and the devil. This thinking is fear at work.

Paul tells us in Romans 7:13 that even God's own holy law is used by sin to kill us. Indeed, nothing plagued and threatened the New Testament Church as much as the supporters of God's law. Does that mean the law is bad? "God forbid," Paul says. This is the very law on which the psalmist said we are to meditate day and night. The law is not to be abolished but fulfilled.

Similarly the self is not to be abolished but nurtured, transformed, redeemed, sanctified and matured. "For we are God's handiwork," writes Paul, "created in Christ Jesus to devote ourselves to the good deeds for which God has designed us" (Ephesians 2:10).

But fear and anti-identity theology block many Christians from developing a strong self so that they never mature. To a lesser degree fear blocks the growth of the community-of-the-self as well.

These fears are founded in misunderstanding and confusion about maturity and redemption in at least three areas.

1. Developmental Stages Leading to Maturity

Confusion about developmental stages leading to maturity is the most regrettable lack of wisdom in the debate about identity. Some oppose investing in the self because in order to build a self, they say, the child's needs and feelings must be more important than the parent's needs. Indeed they believe that children should begin early to put their "selves" on the altar. But believing that children should be taught to put self on the altar before they even have one leads to deforming the self. Children do not belong on altars. Jesus did not ask any children to sacrifice themselves, leave their parents or go to Gethsemane. He wrapped them in His arms and told the disciples not to bother them.

If we try to teach children that as children they should die to self, we have it all wrong. Then we have foolishly asked them to be adults. This will not work. We can teach children not to worship their identities but to allow redemption to transform them. When they reach the adult stage of maturity and have solid selves, these precious but twisted selves will need to die. Because of the pervasive contamination of sin, we cannot hope to raise them carefully enough to avoid such spiritual transformations. In much the same way, we do not teach children to drive cars, but we do teach them that by the time they are sixteen, they should be able to learn the art. There is a big difference.

Biblical teachings for adults, parents and elders do not apply to children. Children cannot lay down their lives for God and should not be taught to try. There is no wisdom in this. It takes away the parent's chance to learn sacrificial giving and the child's chance to learn unmerited favor.

2. Human Evil

The second area of confusion among Christians over identity relates directly to human evil.

Confusion about our two natures is not a new problem. "What?" said Jesus to Nicodemus. "Are you a teacher in Israel and you do not understand these things?" (see John 3:10). How can we construct a positive self-image out of being dead in trespasses and sins? In addition, most of us have the distinct impression that not everything in us is so estimable, and that the condition has been with us a long time.

All children are born dead, as Jesus told Nicodemus. Yet in that state they are still to be esteemed by their parents, just as God esteems them. Children are to be taught that this value is truly part of them. All children should learn of their great value, which does not come from their own actions. We possess this value even when we are dead, for "while we were yet sinners, Christ died for us" (Romans 5:8, KJV). Another way to say this is that our value never comes from our own goodness.

There are two things wrong with the self. The first is the presence of the *sark*—that is, we are plagued by the impression that we can tell good from evil on our own. Such a simple judgment as calling someone "selfish" may be the *sark*. It is this very capacity to decide what is evil that anti-identity theology has harnessed. With it *sark*-guided people go about trying to rid themselves and others of their bad identities. These are the authoritarian and religious enemies of the self, operating in fear. Instead of removing evil, they become destroyers while quoting Scripture to justify themselves.

The second thing wrong with the self is its size. Each self is too small, but this evil cannot be corrected by anything we do. We cannot raise a child with a good enough self, even by following scriptural principles. When godly parents follow the best principles and raise their children faithfully to have the best selves possible, it is still not good enough. Left that way, children are both dead and deadly. We fool ourselves when we think we can rear or train our children in such a way as to eliminate or even reduce this problem. The problem with the self is not so much something bad that must be eliminated—after all, our old nature *(sark)* will stay with us until we die—but rather something good that is missing from it. What is missing is the life we cannot give. This new life comes through the new heart Jesus gives us.

There is, nonetheless, a part of life we can and must give.

3. Self-Worship Cults

Self-worship cults like humanistic psychology also scare Christians away from self-esteem. Such cults—and some of Satanism is a self-worship cult—deny that children are born dead and need to be made alive. Some self-worshipers in humanistic psychology believe the self is alive and good and should be esteemed for that reason alone. This is why their children are at risk for cults as much as ours are. We must come to terms with both the good and the bad within us.

Denying the evil in us makes us deny our value. We need identities that include both parts. Yes, we are loved and we are evil, both together. Satan does not love us because we are evil. God does not love us because He has been fooled into thinking some of us are good. The God who loves us sees the evil in us and is prepared to transform death into life.

It is clear to me that failing to build strong identities in children leaves them open to anyone who wants to tell them who they are. Christians who run away from building identities in their children will find themselves doing the devil's work for him.

Growing a Community-of-the-Self

The self continues to develop after childhood as people become adults, parents and elders. At these later stages the self has an increasing number of ways to give life in the community-of-the-self. From adulthood on, each individual begins to have responsibility for the other selves in the community. The maintenance of others' identities plays an increasingly important part in each stage of growth. Growing a self becomes increasingly tied to growing a group identity. We must grow strong families, churches and communities.

Growing strong identities in children is a high priority for families and communities. All who gather around and shape a child's self-concept become the community-of-the-self. This community-of-the-self is mediated by the family. The family bonds connect inward to the child and outward to the community. We want the community-of-the-self to be as close to perfect as possible. Many "selves" make up the community-of-the-self for each individual. These family and community groups each have their own identities, stories and miniature subcultures.

The structure of the community-of-the-self is critical to its function. The giving of life must flow from elders toward children, through parents or adults, and never the other way around. The responsibility for life-giving always lies with the persons at the top. The more you are given, the more is required, and adults have more than children, parents more than adults and elders more than parents. All of them have more than infants and the unborn. Thus children are in a receiving position in relation to everyone except other children and infants.

Just to avoid misunderstanding, I do not mean that children do not give. I am speaking of the *responsibility to give life*, which is never the child's place. We must never make children responsible for rearing other children. We should not force or allow them to take adult responsibilities. Nor should parents, incidentally, try to be elders. The responsibility for life-giving lies with the ones at the top. This is the structure of the healthy natural community-of-the-self and the spiritual community-of-the-self. It is this structure that must be maintained, or all kinds of trouble is on the way.

The top-down structure for life-giving lets us make sense of the fact that all people of faith become children of Abraham, the father of faith. Adam, therefore, sold the farm for all of us; Levi tithed to Melchizedek (see Hebrews 7:9–10); and through Isaac we have all been traded for a ram (see Hebrews 11:17–19). The structure of the spiritual community-of-the-self transcends time and surrounds us like a great cloud.

Growing a natural community-of-the-self involves our human institutions (structures) like marriage, family, community and even government. Because all these institutions are contaminated, nothing they do is free from the required decontamination process of redemption. Still, we are constrained to produce the best selves we can—the best friendships, marriages, families, communities, schools and governments—even though none of these structures can give contamination-free life. Ours is the choice between giving contaminated life or giving death. We give contaminated life because we trust in redemption.

Redemption is not structured by our natural or spiritual communities and cannot be. Anyone may become a redemptive agent at any time. Samuel may speak to Eli—a child to an elder. Miriam spoke to Pharaoh's daughter; an ass spoke to Balaam; Abigail spoke to David. There are countless examples of redemptive actions that go against the flow of natural structures. It may well be that children are redemptive agents far more often than elders.

Redemptive community structure is still very important, not for redemption but for growth toward maturity. The group identity needs to grow in ways that are life-giving. Much of the book of Numbers is devoted to arranging the structure of the natural community-of-the-self to resemble the spiritual structure.

Repairing the Community-of-the-Self

Repairs to our group identity usually involve getting our structures (members and bonds), stories and symbols back in order. Repairs are continual. We must accept that all our best repair and maintenance efforts are defective to some degree. We will never get it right and keep it right. Selves, families and communities will always be defective. As the wisdom literature says, "That which is crooked cannot be made straight" (Ecclesiastes 1:15, KJV), yet it is our burden to continue trying.[3]

Our good news is that these firstfruits of community portend a harvest beyond death. We wash clothes because clean robes will one day be the standard. Although we will not be totally free of fear bonds before death, we begin the cleanup now in tearful, joyful anticipation of total decontamination.

Repairing Structures

From the bad shepherds in Ezekiel's day to the pastors who have disgraced churches today, the community-of-the-self has needed to correct the false elders who take and consume life rather than give it away. The community has needed to correct death-giving parents and adults and remove children from places of authority. These repairs correct the structure of the community-of-the-self

241

The reason to grow a strong self is so that it can die properly. The reason to work with all our might to produce the best natural group identity is so that it can die. Everything in this book so far, as we will see in the next chapter, is a preparation for how to die. With fear bonds this makes no sense. With love bonds it makes all the sense in the world (see 1 Corinthians 15:44).

In the love story, death is the normal completion of our contaminated lives. We know the basic significance of death from the short history of the world we reviewed in chapter 6. God established death as a visible sign of His determination to destroy evil. Each death shows us that only good is eternal and that everything contaminated by evil will come to an end. Whenever we see death, we know that the cleanup of the universe is underway. Only God can decontaminate others because only God is pure. For us becoming pure is a process. Death tells us that no one and nothing will escape the cleanup.

Adam was told this right away. The soul that gets contaminated will not go on forever; it will die. Carrying toxic waste subjects us to cleanup procedures, because God will not allow toxic waste forever. This is great news, even if we are contaminated. The sicker we are, the better we like the news that this illness will not continue forever.

What happens, then, if a kitten or child is murdered in a black mass? God's unavoidable symbol informs everyone present that all things touched by evil will come to an end. This first death, which is more like sleep, points to a second death, which is final. Death is a visible sign, then, that evil is not eternal. Evil loses. Decontamination orders are inescapable.

Because of this we do three things. First, we do not fear the evil still within us, but we wash regularly. We freely admit that we are both clean and dirty. Second, we boldly reclaim and clean up our world, symbols, stories and lives. We surrender nothing to the dragon. And third, we accept that we can decontaminate no one, not even ourselves. Consequently we lead everyone eagerly to Jesus, the one Source of cleansing.

Point three is the dividing line between Christians and others. Not that we want to divide, but to relinquish this point is to cease being Christian, and to accept this point is to become Christian. The hideous truth is that Christians believe decontamination came only through a voluntary death. This one-time event makes us all killers and God the only life-giver. What life we can give is given first to us, and then only when we confess our deadly state. The price of admission to the Christian faith is the confession that the best we can do will ultimately kill our selves, families, communities, governments, planet and even God—if we could get our hands on Him.

To be a Christian is to admit being a killer who has let himself be killed in order to receive life and become a life-giver. We carry as our symbol a killing device called a cross. We join the church by the symbol of death in baptism, and we symbolize the new life we receive in the sacraments. We anticipate the end of time when the second death will permanently remove the need for this symbol, which has become our enemy (see 1 Corinthians 15:26). Our families and communities differ from all others because we both accept that we are killers and we repent of it, that we might receive and give life.

Because of this life, Christians should provide exemplary models of families, companies, churches, schools, courts, hospitals and other community structures. We pray, "Thy will be done on earth as it is in heaven." The Kingdom of God is like leaven, you see; it grows and permeates everything. Evil must try to avoid us. Light spreads everywhere.

"Tell your God to leave me alone!" one Satanist told me.

"He doesn't take orders from me," I said. "Besides, leaving you alone is against His nature. He goes everywhere."

We are to be growth-oriented. Passivity and avoidance do not go with the Spirit we have been given. We need not fear people or the world around us. We should be wise but remember that, as the cleanup crew, we were not sent here to fear dirt. Our growth is always in the context of a battle with evil.

Faulty Repairs

Transformation of our natural group identity produces an increasing similarity to the spiritual community. Many so-called repairs, however, do not serve this purpose. Like the garbage disposal, they try to decontaminate by subtraction. These faulty repairs remove what we fear by destroying or rejecting the sources of our concern rather than by removing our fear. Redemption does not work that way. Faulty repairs actually increase our fear base by causing us to fear evil. One of our symbolic stories, one we looked at earlier, says, "I will fear no evil, for thou art with me."

Frankly I have grown tired of Christians reacting in fear to Satanism, New Age, spiritual warfare, secular humanism, cults and other forms of evil. We have given up too much of our birthright to the persistent advances of occult contamination. Some believers run from ugly things or try to ignore them. Many are simply afraid to know about evil. As a result of this fear, our hampers are full of dirty clothes while our washing machines stand idle. We have no need to fear people who have become contaminated or filled with evil. We do not need to isolate ourselves.

I can understand not wanting to know about the disgusting, loathsome nature of evil. But the fear of evil deserves no long-term place in the Church. Those afraid of being overcome by evil should be on their way toward freedom from that distorted reaction. The fear of evil can be expected in children who have no sense of history. And it can be worked with in adults while they become part of redemptive history. We can even expect the fear of evil to crop up occasionally in parents. But it should be absent in elders. Parents and elders are expected to know that God is the Redeemer of His people and His world. They are to teach others not to fear, as we saw in chapter 8.

We need not fear the world around us. Nor do we need to reject everything that was not created by Christians. Then we would need to refuse to use metal or even musical instruments, for example, because of their origins, which are clearly spelled out by the Bible as pagan. This would be nonsense, however, and I know of no serious believer who would endorse such a position. Even the Old Testament allowed both metal and music in the Temple. Modern churches that exclude musical instruments do so not because of their origins but because instruments are not mentioned in the New Testament worship texts.

If the point is that we as Christians should not do what God has strictly forbidden, then this becomes a discussion of God's laws. That topic is far beyond the scope of this book and the object of much ignorance by the Church at large. Still, some reference must be made, in any discussion of evil, to God's law.

Saint Paul makes it clear that even God's holy law becomes deadly in the hands of Satan (see Romans 7:10–13). We can be sure everything else will become deadly in his hands as well. The solution, according to Paul, is grace, which far exceeds the power of sin's contamination.

We will fail to come to the truth about any symbol or activity, therefore, by seeing how or if Satanists, occultists or pagans use it. We will find out even less by trying to discover if they originated the idea. The worst they can do is to take signposts that originally pointed to God and point them somewhere else. Our job is to get the signs pointing in the right direction once again.

Evil will try to contaminate everything good. For this reason we are constantly having to say, "Hey, give that back! It belongs to us." Then we have to clean it up before we can use it again. Cleanup amounts to clarifying the use of every symbol, activity and structure in proper relationship to God. Thus we can pray even though Satanists pray—but our prayers are to God. The relationship bond is crucial. As Paul points out, even the greatest abilities used without love (a proper relationship) are of no value.

Motivated by the fear of contamination, some people place themselves in just the position they wish to avoid. Instead of growing a strong self so that it can die, they attack the self. If self-worship is bad, they become self-destroyers. In trying to avoid evil, they become contrary and reactionary, doing the opposite of whatever they think is bad.

What Redemption Does to Maturity

The natural community-of-the-self grows mature, strong people. Yet we need more. We form identities and communities that are always too small and will kill or cripple us without timely redemption. Redemption forces us out of the tiny worlds of our control. We cannot do this for ourselves.

I am not saying there are two selves—a good one and a bad one, one to kill and one to save. The *sark (sarx)*, sometimes called our old nature, is not us. "Clearly it is no longer I who am the agent, but sin that has its lodging in me," the apostle Paul tells us (Romans 7:20). That hallucinatory form of spiritual vision misleads us to believe that we can discern good and evil, but the *sark* is not us. The transformations of normal maturity do not rid us of it. The transformations of spiritual maturity do not rid us of it either. Only the physical deaths of our bodies will rid us of this evil.

Our one and only, hand-crafted, repeatedly transformed, carefully nurtured identities must not only die the deaths of going from stage to stage in order to grow, repair, transform. They must die the deaths of going from the natural to the spiritual communities-of-the-self. This latter process we call spiritual maturity.

Because not everyone chooses decontamination, there will never be a complete match between the natural and spiritual communities-of-the-self. Redemption will always disrupt the natural community, causing anger, misunderstanding, hate and pain. Redemption is not popular with fearful people and it cannot be tamed.

Redemption and magick are opposite processes. Redemption brings spiritual order to our natural structures, while magick applies our natural community dynamics to nature and spirits (as we saw in chapter 5).

Redemption is not the only force to change the natural group identity. Politics, from Communism to tribalism, as well as various religions, seek to change the natural community. The largest competitor for Westerners is education. We believe that education and its byproducts, like science, medicine, economics, ecology and psychotherapy, should change the natural community into a more enlightened one. Consequently we grant divorces, take children from their homes, place them in foster care and require them to spend more time with teachers than they ever will with their parents. This process, like redemption, also causes anger, misunderstanding, hate and pain.

More Westerners, however, believe in education than in redemption. Consequently every book I have read on Satanism stresses the importance of education to combat teenage Satanism and prevent it from growing. But education is not redemption. Neither is therapy or government.

The first sign of spiritual maturity, caused by redemption at work, is a change in the meaning of pain.[4] But our big, gorgeous, almost-healthy selves must die to find out. If we can give life on our own or decontaminate ourselves, this would be a stupid move. But we are powerless. Not only are we unable to do what needs to be done, but we are unable to remove what we do not need. If we destroy ourselves trying to be purified, that only makes us destroyers.

Well-intentioned Christians have thought to help God along by destroying their personal identities and those of their children. Satanists do this, too. It is wrong. We cannot leave the subject of normal development until we address how we are to teach our children without becoming self-destroyers.

At the beginning of chapter 8 I recounted part of my conversation with "Mr. Choice." He saddled me with the task of explaining the difference between a Satanist killing his children and the actions of Abraham and Isaac. It is time we took a look at Abraham, the father of the faith.

Abraham and Child Sacrifice

However upsetting this comparison may be, there is actually little difference between the actions of Abraham and those of a Satanist conducting a human sacrifice. Yet because the small difference is significant, all followers of Abraham must follow his example with their children.

The first point is that when this test of faith took place, Isaac was not a young boy. When he was weaned, Abraham held a feast and introduced him to his community. Everyone celebrated the boy's ability to feed himself. His capacity to care for himself grew until he was able to travel away from Mother for a week and climb a mountain carrying a bundle of wood. The indications from Scripture that a long time had passed after weaning (see Genesis 21:34–22:1) would make Isaac at least a teenager, and perhaps as old as thirty, when the would-be sacrifice took place.[5] Isaac was neither an infant nor a child. This means Isaac had a well-developed sense of self with which to understand and interact with his father.

This is also true in the story of Ishmael, who was sixteen or eighteen when he was sent away—about the same age as Mary at the birth of Christ. An important point, I believe, because Isaac, Ishmael and Mary were not children when they were tested. These young adults had already formed selves. From this I conclude that tests of faith are not for children.

When Abraham and Isaac went up the mountain, God demonstrated three things—not the central point of the Genesis narrative, but crucial to child-rearing all the same.

First, God revealed Abraham's character to Isaac. Abraham was a killer; otherwise he would not have gone along with the plan.

Abraham climbed the mountain carrying a knife and fire—symbols of death and destruction. Abraham showed his son the knife in his hand. Even though he was the father of faith and promise and many nations, Abraham was by nature a killer. Faith does not make us less deadly. True people of faith must eventually show their children the knife. We must admit we can kill but cannot give life.

Second, God demonstrated to Isaac that he was not a suitable sacrifice, even though he was the child of promise. As special and miraculous as his birth had been, Isaac did not make the grade. A better sacrifice was needed to make any difference at all. Isaac's father was a killer by nature, and Isaac himself was disqualified as a source of redemption. There are no uncontaminated sources of life here. Through Abraham and Isaac, all children of faith are also ruled killers and unfit sacrifices.

Third, God became the One who provided. Abraham killed the ram with the knife, destroyed it with the fire they built together, and he and Isaac came back down the mountain. God alone was able to give life and find a suitable sacrifice. No human, not even the father of faith, could give life. No human, not even Abraham's son, was accepted for sacrifice. It was a double failure for the natural community-of-the-self.

My point is that Abraham was not the destroyer of Isaac's identity while his son was growing a self. He did not rear Isaac with a knife hung over his cradle, warning him each day, "Someday Dad will kill you." He did not withhold the feast because the boy might get a swelled head about his importance. Abraham raised his son to be strong, mature, thoughtful—and only then did they go to the mountain. Only when they gave their best could it be proven insufficient.

The sacrificial lamb described later by Moses had to be perfect. In normal Christian life we raise our children, improve our families and grow our churches to try to make them perfect. We help our children grow big, healthy selves, excellent bonds, fine relationships, bright minds, strong wills, so they will become their very best. Then, when we are called for the trip up the mountain, we can say with Abraham to our young men and women, "My very best will kill and destroy you. God will give life because He can and does." We can say with Isaac, "I cannot decontaminate you from your killing nature, or even save myself. Only God can save us now." Our best goes onto the altar, and the sanctifying process of redemption begins a transformation from natural to spiritual that will shake our identities and the whole structure of our communities.

Are mainline churches dead in Europe and dying in America? It is because we have built strong, safe, healthy communities-of-the-self and not shown our children the knife in our hand. We have become garbage disposals, cleaning out heretical or antiquated beliefs until we retain only the truth. We have become such clean washing machines that we never put in a load of dirty clothes. I am not against denominations; we need our own clan—not to keep others out but to provide a structure that redemption can disrupt to bring them in. But we have made our denominations into the Way and the Truth.

In both denominations and independent churches, we have chased our children around with knives and fire almost from birth. Our fundamentalist and Pentecostal Sunday schools and Vacation Bible Schools often become preschool altars. Justifying ours as the "right" way or even "God's way" to rear children, we have prohibited infants and children from needing, asking, feeling, wanting and sometimes even thinking about themselves. Students from some Christian schools and boarding schools lack strong enough selves to make decisions, let alone do hard things against pressure. These children grow up deformed.

As a result, revival meetings become places to pick up girls for one night of intensity bonding, as Paul Simon recalls in his song "Lincoln Duncan." Our communities stay full of pain, turmoil and compliance. We push our garbage down the disposal as quickly as possible or else we load dirty clothes into washing machines that do not work. One machine constantly agitates, one spin-dries unbalanced loads, another leaks, and many have burned-out motors or slipping belts. We refuse to fix ourselves and we call it faith. The result: lots of agitating but few clean clothes.

Growing a Self, Then Letting It Die

Here the road forks again. Non-Christians could not follow when we spoke of transformation through the only sacrifice that decontaminates. Those who do not live by faith left when we narrowed admission to killers who would show their knives and confess. Now Christians take two different roads. Those who have no working washing machines can stay in this chapter to build strong communities-of-the-self. Those who have strong family and community structures can go on to chapter 10 and see how they must let redemption mess them up.

In our normal, healthy, happy, tiny communities-of-the-self, growing, repairing and transforming must yield to something we cannot do. We admitted to the knives and fire in our hands. Now we are ready for redemption to go deeper—to destroy all we have worked to build. Only in this way will our best efforts not kill us or others. Those who have built strong individual and group identities are invited to let them die. Only admitted killers and failures are allowed beyond this point.

The Gifts of Christ

Merry Christmas, Red Dragon!

The good news of Christmas that "unto us a child is born" upset a great guy named Joseph. He first heard the news as, "Your fiancée is expecting someone else's child." This was not the way Joseph planned to start his godly little family. It was not his dream come true. And Joseph, a righteous man, knew this was not God's plan or structure for a family. His hopes died and his family plans were changed beyond repair. Merry Christmas, you say?

Redemption had begun. Long trips for taxes, babies born in cattle pens, death squads for children under two and refugee flights into Egypt all heralded the catastrophic advent of redemption. Relational structures of human community were mangled; marriage, parenthood, family, home, community, country and the world were rearranged. It was a terrible stress on Joseph, his family and community. Redemption was at work. Merry Christmas?

If individual rights, the preservation of the family or maintaining the community were the most important values, then the course

253

of redemption would have gone quite differently. We are structure-builders; that is our job. But redemption cannot be structured. What began by disrupting the life of one godly man soon devastated the structures and bonds we all treasure most.

If Joseph had only been a secular American, we could have warned him. This process was not *his* idea, it was not *his* plan, it was not in *his* best interests. Probably we would have recommended an abortion to help *his* career plans and preserve *his* hopes for starting *his* family when *he* was ready and things were more stable (no pun intended.) Redemption gives no such priority, however, to individual will or choice. Joseph's plans died.

If Mary and Joseph had been American Christians, we would have recognized at once that the highest priority in God's mind was the preservation of the family structure. We would help Joseph and Mary understand that they must not let this child come between them or interfere with their sex life. Their most important commitment must be to their marriage and each other. We would make it clear to those young people that this way of having children is *not* God's will for marriage or family.

Neither marriage nor family structure, however, had the highest priority during redemption. No parents, husbands or wives were asked before families were disrupted. The families' hopes and plans died.

If Mary's family or Joseph's family or their community had come from almost any tribe or village around the world, the most upsetting part of the story would have been the violation of community process and structure. No elder, priest or shaman was consulted. Community traditions were violated. Redemption did not follow community guidelines. Preservation of the community structure is clearly not top priority for redemption. The community's plans died.

National, religious and political leaders and structures fared no better. This Baby of Mary's brought ruin to the towns around Bethlehem. He brought ruin to kings. If Mary and Joseph had given priority to their government, community, family or themselves, death squads would not have been raiding towns and killing Jewish babies. Redemption stands, then, as a direct challenge to all who uphold the priority of the individual, marriage, family, community or nation. Almost every culture in the world has trouble here. Merry Christmas, indeed!

In chapter 9 we learned to grow strong individuals, families and communities. These strong group identities are necessary so we can let *us* die and be transformed. Dad cries as his daughter walks down the aisle. The family he grew will end today. It is a time of death. Yet because he can predict a new and larger family, he will sit down, brush away the tears and smile.

Redemption leads us to an even greater change. From here on we will study its effects. After we see how redemption requires spiritual adoption, we will observe its effects on established community relationships as well as on strangers who are weak and wounded. The last part of the chapter examines how our structures are transformed by including weak and wounded people, like cult survivors. People suffering the effects of anti-identity theology will see this chapter through fear bonds and think it means that growing a strong individual or group identity is bad. These people are not ready to die. Other, more mature people must die daily for them first.

Redemption Is God's Plan and Responsibility

God plans to set things right again. This broad definition of redemption does not stop with regeneration but extends to sanctification, justification, restoration, spiritual adoption, healing, deliverance, spiritual gifts and all other restorative activities on God's part. These activities take place among the people of God and among those who are drawn to the light.

The People of God and the Stranger

The redemptive community-of-the-self has long been called *the people of God.* You may have heard of them. The people of God provide the structure, framework, matrix for God's loving community in the world. From the beginning God's people have been commissioned with the care of the *stranger*—the one without a supportive community. The care of the stranger has always been a here-and-now concern for the people of God.

Christians refer to the people of God as the *Church,* although many prefer the term *Kingdom* because what is locally seen as the Church is often a cluttered, lifeless structure. The New Testament provides many metaphors for this structure. We will examine two: the *body* and the *family of God.*

THE BODY

If we consider the church as a body, we recognize within it organs with special functions that exist for the care and maintenance of the whole body. These are the body ministries. Elders maintain these organs so their services can be used by the body at large. These temporary functions are provided through the ministry gifts of the Spirit.

Body ministries include prayer ministry teams for healing, deliverance, intercession, prayer altar and counseling, to name a few. Ministry groups help victims and abusers in the areas of drugs, sex, domestic violence and religious abuse. Ministry to specific problem areas, such as personal debt, chronic or terminal illness disabilities, deafness, hospital visitation and care for the poor, develop in response to specific needs. These ministries, provided by competent, trained and gifted people, lead toward wholeness.

THE FAMILY

If we consider the church as a family, it is the network of all supportive, enduring, eternal relationships. Elders are parents for the orphans in this family and maintain the identity of the community. They also have charge of the well-being of the "ecosystem"—the functioning of the community-of-the-self. This family is where we belong forever and the group on which we depend for our very lives and identities.

Unlike the gifts of the Spirit, which do not require a human bond, the fruit of the Spirit flourishes in the enduring relationships of the family of God. Joyful life among the parents, children, brothers and sisters of faith is made possible by the fruit of the Spirit evident in every believer. All believers participate, whether they have found their gifts yet or not.

The spiritual family is needed to protect, serve and enjoy each member. With this care everyone can grow, mature and transform. This is how God gives us life and where we can give it to others. We are continuously discovering new relationships and bonds in which we can share life.

The Stranger

The Scripture makes more than one hundred references to the *stranger*. The stranger is one who lacks the necessary supportive relationships and can, therefore, be easily ignored or used by others. Strangers are mentioned in the company of widows and orphans, who suffer the same problems. The treatment of these groups becomes the test of true religion for Old Testament prophets and, according to Christ, the test between sheep and goats at His throne (see Matthew 25:31–46).

After taking my state licensing exam, I can say that Matthew 25 is not the test for qualified mental health professionals. Supporting the unsupported is the Church's business.

Spiritual families must include those who would not otherwise have a family. We must remember the widows, orphans and strangers in our midst. Who are these widows, orphans and strangers? Divorced people are usually widows. Children of abusive or divorced homes are often orphans in some area of their lives. And many new arrivals, cult survivors and members of minority groups are strangers, lacking the necessary sustaining relationships.

Many individuals lack a natural community-of-the-self because:

- Divorce causes family disruption, breaking the extended family and reducing community support for the family itself.
- Communities are often fragmented socially and economically and divided by age group.
- Multicultural communities do not share the same family patterns, leading to a misunderstanding of the needs of other styles of families.
- Mobility makes moving easier than working things out.
- American individualism militates against asking for help or support.
- Our culture believes that the only ways to obtain more family (not just children) legitimately are sex, marriage or adoption of minors, thus isolating singles and seniors.
- Cult claims to be "families" have increased conservative reluctance to embrace such concepts.
- Zero population growth and wealth conservation have convinced us that having children is a liability. As a result God's

257

promise to add children to the righteous is seen at an emotional level as more of a curse. Few parents want to see their *personal* spiritual families grow. Since this desire is a significant part of the growth of the Christian community, its absence will produce little growth. The desire for spiritual family is often limited to those who have no one but themselves to offer.

- We fear problems as though the spiritual family had no strength. It is strange when spiritual family members back away from hurts, bitterness, anger, depression and fears. We need to greet injured souls with the expectation that they are due for healing. We should congratulate those with the faith, courage and humility to bring all the devil's footprints to their spiritual families for removal. Jesus came to undo all the enemy's works.

- Some people expect that prayer and admonition should change problems instantly. As a result badly hurt, truly upset and therefore unhappy people do not find a spiritual family in some churches.

- We lack elders. Elders do not fear the death that transforms individuals, groups or family structures. Elders allow redemption to disrupt lives while continuing to remind groups of their greater identity.

Elders and Redemption

In our culture we do not expect people to be elders. Seldom do we respect maturity or expect elders to parent the stranger, widow and orphan. Old age means the end of any important contribution to the elderly person's community. Once parents are through raising their children, they are free to get Winnebagos and travel. Others wait for grandchildren to spoil. Our cultural vision for seniors is too limited, and older people as a group have few visions for themselves. Elder men do not often encourage or establish younger men; the same is generally true for women. Many face an empty nest or retirement wondering what difference they will make now.

Because of our failure to follow God's instructions about resting, many people reach the age of eldership all tired out. Elders need to know how to rest, or they will fall prey to codependency and other evils. Tired people should be put out to pasture for a while to learn again how to play and pray. After all, Ezekiel tells us that evil shepherds, not God, drive the strong sheep with ruthless severity.

Being an elder is more demanding than being a parent. The Scripture is clear about this. No one should be an elder, Paul tells us, without first mastering parenthood. With their maturity elders are ideally suited for adoptive relationships because of their life experience and because they do not find control as appealing. Eldership requires sacrificial giving, however, at the very point when our culture says it is time to enjoy our own agendas for a change.

To do anything effective about evil requires elders to become involved at the community level. Here the experience they have gained by guiding their own children through the growth-repair-transform cycle lets them encourage mature families and communities to let redemption disrupt their lives and structures. By long practice looking through their hearts, they can sense what God is doing and help others through the death and transformation of redemption.

According to W. T. Purkiser, redemption always involves three things:

1. Removal from a state in which a person cannot get out on his or her own but needs the help of another.
2. A cost to the redeemer.
3. A new attachment.[1]

Redemption is not possible without spiritual adoption. But removal, new attachments and costs are not isolated events. Redemption is disruptive.

Removal from a Place We Cannot Leave on Our Own

Christians are accustomed to thinking that redemption removes us from a state of sin, but we often forget that sin is a failure to act like the selves God intends us to be. Redemption removes from us the inability to act like ourselves—and this is not a one-step process (recall Ephesians 2:10). In this chapter we will see that redemption removes the weak and wounded, as well as the strong and mature, from the fear bonds they cannot break alone. By putting us together, God frees us all from a web of fear bonds and connects us to a family of love bonds.

God removes cult members from a place they cannot escape on their own and puts them into established communities. The weak must leave and the mature must receive. The host community might think, *It's time to make them like us now*, but that is not true. God has just begun removing the strong community from a place it cannot escape on its own. Strong people must leave their homes and let their family identities die. This is what strong families fear most.

For the established community it is a time to die. For the weak and wounded stranger it is a time to live.

COST TO THE REDEEMER

Both removing and attaching people involves the disruption of whole social structures. Thus the cost is never paid by one person alone. It is also an expensive process. Joseph, Mary and the mothers around Bethlehem all paid a high price for redemption. The response of the redemptive community is to accept death and give life. They must let family structures change to accommodate the new attachment.

Both removing someone from a state in which he or she needs the help of another and forming new attachments have costs. If I took all my money and paid for a family to escape genocide in Rwanda and to relocate in the United States, there would be a steep financial cost and risk to both rescuers and pilots. The removal process from Rwanda might even cost lives. While I might be considered a humanitarian by many, this action would cost me options. Some would question why I did not spend the money on crime in Los Angeles. My children might ask why they had no money for college, weddings or medical expenses.

Forming new attachments also carries shared costs. The neighbors might protest the use of tax dollars on services for foreigners unable to work because they have no Western-style skills. The neighbors might not like the way these strangers live or hunt for food in our neighborhoods.

A NEW ATTACHMENT: A THEOLOGY OF SPIRITUAL ADOPTION

As Kitty says, we can tell who "family" is by seeing who we turn to in times of disaster. I say "family" is where you know you belong on Christmas Day. Christmas is the story of a family during a time of disaster. The families we join by adoption are families for good times and for the hardest times.

Christ's birth was a difficult time for His family, which should warn us. Unfortunately we have romanticized the Christmas story. As much as I like to sing about the friendly beasts who stood around Jesus, it is sobering to remember that Saint John the elder tells the Christmas story this way:

Next appeared a great portent in heaven, a woman robed with the sun, beneath her feet the moon, and on her head a crown of twelve stars. She was pregnant, and in the anguish of her labour she cried out to be delivered. Then a second portent appeared in heaven: a great red dragon with seven heads and ten horns; on his heads were seven diadems, and with his tail he swept down a third of the stars in the sky and flung them to the earth. The dragon stood in front of the woman who was about to give birth, so that when her child was born he might devour it. She gave birth to a male child, who was destined to rule all nations with an iron rod. But her child was snatched up to God and his throne; and the woman herself fled into the wilds, where she had a place prepared for her by God. . . .

Revelation 12:1–6

John tells how God took care of the woman this way:

Meanwhile near the cross where Jesus hung stood his mother, with her sister, Mary wife of Clopas, and Mary of Magdala. Jesus saw his mother, with the disciple whom he loved standing beside her. He said to her, 'Mother, there is your son'; and to the disciple, 'There is your mother'; and from that moment the disciple took her into his home.

John 19:25–27

We find the disciple John already standing next to the mother while the dragon is attacking. As the Child is snatched up to God and His throne, the disciple takes Mother home. The brief adoption ceremony was presided over by Jesus Himself. Merry Christmas, red dragon!

The fact that John and Mary were both adults did not reduce their need for adoption. Both had lost Someone very dear to them. John, who in time became an elder, understood that love is at the center of the family of God. Little wonder he tells a Christmas story different from how we usually hear it! It sounds like Christmas stories told to people I know and love. These family members know the cost of Christmas.

261

Does God still prepare a place in the wilds for women whose children the dragon kills but cannot devour? I believe so. This story serves as a model for us in dealing with those whose children have been snatched up to God from a dragon attack. Through them we can know the blessing of Christmas as well—a blessing found only through involvement.

John knew where to stand to receive a blessing—close at hand offering his support to Mary. As a result of his involvement, he was blessed with new family. While most of us would like to have Mother Mary in our homes, we avoid the spot at the foot of the cross where adoptions are performed.

Redemption for Established Communities: A Time to Die

The grow-repair-transform cycle lets us die to our identities as a fetus, infant and child by the time we are adults. As young adults we begin growing a group identity in earnest, as we saw in chapter 2. The need for a group identity is exploited by gangs and cults but often ignored by churches, which protect their organizational structures from the disruptive energy of young adults. After working hard to get things "right," good people are reluctant to see their work undone. They maintain and repair their existing group identity structures until they decompose.

God, in the process of redemption, seeks to disrupt strong family and church identities by adding immature, weak and wounded strangers right in the middle of our best bonds and group identity structures. In so doing He changes the structures of the natural family and community to conform with the structure of the spiritual family and community. In response to redemption, the group can either repair itself and reject the new member (like a failed organ transplant) or else die and be transformed.

Let's return to the washing machine analogy from the last chapter. God does the wash by attaching the weak and wounded to the group identities of the strong and mature. We grow a mature community-of-the-self so that God can help it die. The greater the distortions of sin in the natural community, the more severe the adjustment produced by redemption. To conform with the spiritual community, our natural attachments must be broken and remade elsewhere. Decontamination disrupts the natural structures we have built.

Redemption changes individual, family and community identities, whether we resist or cooperate. Our consent is neither required nor requested. But our response is crucial. Redemption is never something we can do for ourselves; it occurs only when others pay the cost for us or we for them. Our choice lies in the response we make to redemption. We may choose to receive redemption and pay the price for others to receive it also, or we can protect our structures and wither.

As a redemptive community we should not think we are redeeming souls, although, like Isaac, we are the children of God's promise. The price we pay is not the atonement for sin. Mary's Boy Child did that. Merry Christmas! He is God's gift alone, paid in full. Staying on the altar, then, as though we were a suitable sacrifice for sin, is an abomination. The cost of redemption we pay covers only the earthly lives of our new family members. We pay for their redemption with some of the life we have been given. We are paying so others will have a better life here on earth, yet we are paying with life we did not earn but was a gift to us in the first place.

Transforming the Redemptive Community

The redemptive community is a huge matrix, connected on one side with fear bonds to the pyramid of fallen angels, and on the other side with love bonds to the eternal spiritual family that lives in the center of the Trinity. God adds new members to this matrix and disrupts its structure in order to complete it. These new members are transformed—but so are the existing members.

Almost any compassionate person can see why immature, weak and wounded strangers need a loving community. What is not so clear to most of us is how much a strong community needs the presence of the weak and wounded. Here are a few reasons:

1. *Revealing hearts.* The weak and seemingly insignificant are God's light to reveal the secret thoughts of our hearts. It is not how we treat the rich and famous that shows our character but how we treat those who can do nothing about it—children; the poor; the weak and wounded stranger. These will be called Jesus Himself at the judgment. Our hearts are revealed, as Simeon told Mary and Joseph, by whom we reject.
2. *Breaking fear bonds.* Redemption often means that the very people we have tried to avoid, we must now welcome. Ana-

nias of Damascus must adopt Saul of Tarsus. Redemption makes avoiding the people we fear impossible because the dirtiest clothes get dumped right in our midst for washing.

Job said, "The worst of my fears has come true; what I dreaded most has happened" (Job 3:25, Message). The three Hebrews at the fiery furnace; Esther before King Ahasuerus; Daniel amid the lions—all found redemption bringing about their worst fears. The weak and wounded Satanist cult member will also cause us to face our relational fears. When our fears come true, they lose the power to bully us.

When we build relationships, we try to eliminate the problems we fear. Our friends do not push us too far or expose our shortcomings, and we return the favor. Wounded strangers are not so graceful. They expose our fears and limitations, sometimes with contempt or anger. They cry out, "I thought you were a Christian!" We must confess how little we love, care or will suffer, and we will be redeemed ourselves—far more than we ever wanted to be.

3. *Purification.* The wounded are almost allergic to evil. Small amounts cause them great pain. They also look us over with exceptional discernment—when it comes to our flaws. The weak and wounded make it necessary for us to confess and be redeemed of our harmless-looking pet sins.

4. *Growth.* Each transformation that produces a death of an old group identity brings us a larger identity in which to grow more loving and less fearful.

5. *Receiving grace.* It takes tremendous grace for the immature, weak and wounded person to put up with resistance, fear, self-deception, ignorance of evil, suspicion, pride, rejection, judgment and self-centeredness in established communities. It is a tribute to God's grace that they stay at all.

6. *Witnessing God's mighty works.* A front-row seat in the lives of those who are just escaping the red dragon allows us a truly awesome view of God's power in action. As His witnesses we must see what He is doing.

7. *Giving life.* Providing new attachments for others transforms our own identities. When we become the suppliers of life to others, our identities must expand to include *life-giver* among our attributes. Only those who have received life can give life because we are dependent creatures.

A redemptive community must submit to God's adoptions, in order to produce a transformation, in at least two ways. First, it must be willing to change its structure to accommodate new attachments. This change is rarely easy and often not welcome. A community-of-the-self protects itself. It keeps loved ones far from distress or bad influences. But redemption means Joseph must raise the Baby.

Second, the community around the newly adopted members must form strong love bonds with them. This is done by meeting them in their pain and returning them to joy. This active process requires the strong to seek out the weak and wounded in their pain and to share it with them. Sharing the memories of painful life experiences, along with the daily ups and downs of healing, adds pain to all members of the group. This pain is part of the cost of redemption and develops both character and love in the community. Through paying this cost we give life.

Kelly Crane sells real estate. When Rose, a survivor from a satanic cult, was looking for a new home, I suggested that she work with Kelly to find one. Rose trusted no men. All the men she knew had been perverted with her. With my encouragement she went with Kelly and found he was different. Mr. Crane treated her with respect as they drove around in his car, and he changed the course of her feelings toward Christian men. All the time he just thought they were looking for a house.

Kelly won her trust without knowing he needed to. When Kelly showed her houses without making a pass, he did far more than help solve Rose's housing problem. He showed her a new, more truthful view of her identity. She was someone different than she had ever thought possible. She was a sister, a woman with value. Her identity changed. When he invited her to church with him and his wife, she found new attachments.

While Kelly Crane practiced his gift of helping, other members of the community made their contributions; they provided furniture, employment, camping trips, car repairs, people to go to lunch with, friends to go shopping with. Some helped pay for the extensive therapy that victimized people can require. In these different and simple ways, many people became a source of life to Rose.

The average cost of recovery for a cult survivor around 1990 was two million dollars. Much of that expense came from hospital costs needed to provide victims with a "therapeutic community." For

Rose, having a supportive community meant that most of her community needs were met by the donated time and activities outlined in the previous paragraph. That cut cash costs considerably. Rose, who talked to me along with many other counselors in the course of her recovery, could never have raised two million in goods and services needed for her restoration. Only her redemptive community knew that it existed in part to pay the redemption costs for the earthly life of a stranger.

These relationships were difficult at first for the community but transforming to those who persevered. It was not just Rose who, after a while, saw herself differently. Many began seeing themselves differently through Rose's glasses. Their isolation and self-sufficiency looked uglier and their life-giving looked lovelier. Mutual effort helped numerous brothers and sisters overcome their isolation.

Transforming the Family

The part of the community-of-the-self we call family is what we protect most from outside forces, including redemption. There is little doubt that hurting people and cult survivors bring distress with them. Consequently we do not want them attached to us or to our families. We know they need attachments but the cost is too high. We want to believe that some other church or family is better equipped. We are overloaded as it is. The inn is full. Merry Christmas!

While Christians have not made an idol of natural identities, we have raised the natural family to sacred levels. People need strong bonds to real family, but which family is real, the natural or the spiritual? The answer is, Both. When redemption transforms the natural family, it becomes like the spiritual one. When natural communities resist redemption by keeping their natural shapes, they destroy themselves. If we give top priority to our natural or blood ties, redemption will pass us by and we will die pointless deaths. Salvation is not just an individual matter for individual change; it is for us and for the whole house.

It is not simply that every individual in the family must be saved; the entity we consider "family" must also be saved—that is, transformed and given life. Our efforts to protect ourselves and our children will kill us because we always build communities-of-the-self that are too small. We allow few people into our homes without an appointment. We build small so that we can be in control. Our control kills us and our children. Our family structures will not save us, and our identities will kill others unless we are transformed.

We also try to protect our families by hiding from evil. In so doing we must hide our own evil and deny the knives in our hands. At our best we, like Abraham, are killers granted faith. We dare not deny the knives in our hands. Only redemption can disrupt the deadly results of our best efforts to form a family. Only God can save us and our children.

Redemption arrives when mature families include the weak and wounded. These spiritual adoptions ferret out fear bonds in families. In any fear-based family a change of structure brings up specters of abandonment, replacement, betrayal and rejection. These spawn the green-eyed monster of jealousy with its friends— hate, criticism, backbiting, strife, gossip and pride. Family members feel threatened by the presence of someone new, and from the richness of their hearts, their mouths speak. Others keep their mouths shut but close the doors to their hearts as well.

The very presence of this fear, jealousy and rejection proves how desperately our families need redemption. Confronted by adoption, our hearts are revealed. Faced with the cost of attachment, we can no longer hide our greed and fear in the corner, where we have taught our families to leave them alone.

Providing a new attachment for the weak and wounded transforms mature families. This change in family structure is not in our power to produce, since these are divinely appointed relationships. We have our hands full with the care and nurture of our biological families, and we do poorly enough at that. God must build this new family in His own time and way. What we are asked to do is allow this change. We are not to fight God and seek our own comfort.

What are the effects of redemptive adoptions on natural family members? The greatest deterrent to my sons becoming interested in cults has been their involvement in creating a spiritual family. As young adults they began being brothers to those who, through no fault of their own, needed a family. Jamie and Rami looked forward to such involvement and rate it as the best experiences of their lives.

Working together sometimes meant their going with me to put a shelf on Rose's wall or to move furniture. The boys learned that simple acts of kindness really did matter. We included new people at Thanksgiving dinner. This proved easy with the help of another Christian family who shared the same vision. Playing board games for an evening with a cult survivor or giving birthday parties were simple activities through which my children could include others.

In a spiritual family brothers and sisters often play a central role. These are the relationships with give and take, and the times that teach fair play and conflict resolution. These are the places to learn sharing and including others. Brother and sister relationships help us meet our immediate needs, and those of others, by including everyone. When codependent people participate in brother or sister relationships, it develops maturity and even brings great relief.

In ministering brotherly love to ex-Satanists, there is no doubt that what my sons do is important. As young adults they are a source of life to others. I might add that they are greatly loved in return. Because of this, each member of our spiritual family is drawn toward relationships with others. As you may recall, hopelessness about finding love or relationships greatly contributes to the attractiveness of Satanism.

All the weak and wounded are not coming out of cults. One day Jamie came to me with a new concern. A school friend had cut her wrists but acted as though it were humorous. He wanted to know what he should do. He already recognized that he was to be a source of life to his friends and knew enough not to be a brother by himself. This wisdom came from helping create a loving spiritual family. How much better to help him solve these problems than to try to find ways to keep him away from drugs and other activities that young men without a vision can create!

God uses many kinds of weakness to change our natural families into spiritual ones. For some people adopting orphans becomes a way of life. Other mature families may be called to receive neglected people whose type-A traumas require their love. Some respond most when bad things happen. They provide comfort in a crisis.

Rami went to Mexico for a weekend with a Sunday school class and built a house for a mother of eight children with another on the way. Her husband had abandoned her and the kids. They were living on a single mattress with a twelve-inch board over their heads for a roof. One end of the plank was propped on the ground; the other was supported by a barrel. That was home for a family of nine. For two days the Sunday school class worked in the rain and mud, leaving behind a house for the family. Rami came home a changed young adult. He had seen his spiritual family at work. Now he has brothers in Mexico.

Developing a loving spiritual family takes all the knowledge and power that a young man can obtain and use. My sons found ample use for their spiritual gifts and knowledge. It was good for them because they needed a group identity built on truth and power in relationships.

Combating the effects or presence of evil is a great deterrent to joining the other side. When one has worked to get rid of graffiti, it is no longer as tempting to deface property. When one supports a counseling program for sexually abused children, it is not nearly so tempting to buy pornography. Being part of overcoming evil and its effects is the best way to keep ourselves, families, churches and communities safe. Our group identities change by combating evil together. We become family and community to each other.

Staying in the battle is the best way to avoid becoming a casualty. Having seen damaged lives—the worst results of fear and pain—redeemed by God's love shows children that love is superior to fear. In addition, when young people watch elders share the pain of others, and then share some pain themselves, they do not desire to produce pain. Not that they do not try it occasionally, but they quickly discover how dissatisfying it is. Everyone is being changed.

Redemption for Weak and Wounded Strangers: A Time to Live

A tremendous change of identity occurs when passing from death to life. This new identity is transformed continually by redemptive adoption by God and by His family. Healing, growth and sanctification transform actions, attitudes, thought patterns and many other bits of self. Redemptive family bonds change the identities of immature believers. These changes in newly adopted members are usually welcome—until they start ministering truth to our pet sins.

Redemption removes everyone from their old attachments. While Christian families struggle to keep spiritual and biological families together, believers coming out of multigenerational

Satanism struggle to let go of their cult families. These Christians really need the Church to provide what their pagan families will not give. Spiritual families must provide more than hugs at church when the pastor tells us to hug the people next to us. We must also furnish birthday celebrations and Friday night suppers, like a family. This way we begin to see the faint outline of the spiritual community and our real families.

Those whose biological families are intact rarely recognize the gap between spiritual and natural family. Many people are being left—through migration, death, crime, illness and even old age— with no natural family. With neither natural nor spiritual family, it is soon obvious that adults have little hope of gaining any family except through marriage or a cult.

We do not want to duplicate the spiritual family lives of cults. Cults use a perverted form of spiritual family to their advantage. Many attempt to destroy the natural family ties of their members. Satanism often replaces natural ties with unnatural ones, while many other cults attempt to destroy ties altogether. Spiritual families and adoptions are seen in most cults as the only desirable or real relationships. This is done to ensure that only the cult has permission to tell members who they really are, and so increase members' dependency on the group. It increases the distance between *us* and *them* in a way that benefits the cult.

Someone whose entire family is in a destructive cult will need a complete change in natural community, therefore, when he or she comes alive. The families of the redemptive community must also change to receive new members. New Christians left in the care of cult families have little hope of nurture, and a chance of being abused or even killed for defecting. It is not hard to see why they need spiritual adoption. It is a bit harder to know how to participate.

In Bangladesh, I am told, a person who accepts Christ is immediately ostracized from his or her natural and biological and social family. The Christian Church provides a family that adopts the new convert as her own. Family growth is viewed as a good thing. As the psalmist David pointed out, the line of the ungodly is cut off (loses its children) while the line of the righteous endures (continues gaining children.)

Redemption of pagan individuals, then, requires removal from their pagan communities-of-the-self in which they are unable to help themselves. It also requires a new attachment with the redemptive community. Costs include sharing in their struggle, facing opposition and disrupting our well-built and smoothly running lives—perhaps for a lifetime. This redemptive activity transforms not only the individual but also the structure and identity of the redemptive community.

Community-Based Care

Hope for the weak, wounded and immature members of our family springs from community-based care. The community we speak of is the redemptive community. The care of this community is provided through:

1. Prayer ministry
2. Trauma teams
3. Spiritual adoption into the family structure
4. Including the weak and wounded in the church
5. Deliverance teams
6. Community life

Community-based care is more than psychotherapy, recovery programs, pastoral care ministry, prayer ministry or discipleship training, although it relates to all of these. Community-based care is giving life to those who need a spiritual family. Care is provided by teaching others through example to live.

Community-based care is *not* about the healthy helping the sick. Ever since the medical model of mental illness brought compassion for the mentally ill, Christians have been struggling to decide who is sick within the Church and who is healthy. Disconnected members of the spiritual family roll around like so many loose rocks and pile up on any church that is compassionate enough to offer help. These churches often become predominantly "sick" because the "healthy" people head for the hills to avoid becoming overwhelmed. Some big churches decide to hire professional help to start programs for those who can afford to pay for services.

The professional counseling industry has grown enormously but has been unable to provide service to the same population that received help previously from churches. As a result an enormous pool has grown of needy and economically stressed individuals who need counseling of some kind. Most cult survivors fit into this group. These individuals are marked not only by their emotional needs but also by their economic problems and the lack of significant social support from their communities.

Because professional counselors are encouraged to maintain complete detachment from the lives and communities of those they counsel, they often leave all supportive functions to others. In addition, because of detachment and confidentiality, they have neither the time nor the ability to assist in building family.

It is my contention that just as well-fed English sailors developed scurvy because they were missing a key vitamin, even so professional counseling has left a hole—not so much because of the cost but because there is a key need that, Christian or not, it cannot fill by the very nature of its being "professional." Christian counselors in clinics, private practice and even churches are not able to address the need for a supportive community adequately. Without support from family and community, many of the changes produced by counseling are either not possible or else they will not endure. Support groups have proliferated for this very reason. The psychological version of support groups is to gather isolated individuals for mutual support. It certainly beats isolation but in no way resembles a family; it is a grouping of strangers. Support groups are a poor replacement for the care of spiritual family with its diversity.

Some churches resemble a support group instead of a family. These churches are stratified by age and resources so that even within churches, strangers must group with strangers. These bonds between strangers are easily broken if a struggle for resources ensues. This is a non-bonded family, perhaps more interested in preservation of resources than in having children.

Community-based care, by contrast, starts with spiritual adoption as its basis for giving life and changing identities. If we look at the reclaiming of identities as a war, then prayer teams are the invasion forces. They drop in across enemy lines where no contact is possible by human means.

PRAYER MINISTRY

In prayer ministry God often reveals the unknown and jumps across enormous barriers. He opens contact to parts of our souls that were inaccessible and unknown. The gifts of the Spirit do not depend on knowledge or relationship skills we have formed. The Holy Spirit makes the first contact where an attachment can start to grow a bond of love. People need support and attachments, but prayer and trauma team members are often not gifted in this area. Family members must surround prayer teams.

During these early hours of the battle, prayer ministry can be focused or general. By bathing every aspect of life in prayer, new territory can be soaked with God's grace. Groups of Christians can minister this soaking in prayer and soften years of hardness in every aspect of life. See "Guidelines for Prayer Teams" on page 318 in the appendix for details.

Community-based care requires the availability of prayer ministry teams. All ministry should include teaching. We teach ministry by example in the hope that those who receive ministry will also grow and minister. It is not for the purpose of training others that we minister; such a purpose would insult both God and the recipient. We do not care for our children simply so that they will grow up to have children. But even these first encounters teach life-giving ministry. Every aspect of our lives should enhance the recipients' desire and ability to live as we live.

Prayer teams work to open up new territory where there are no existing bonds. Trauma teams can subdue the territory and make it habitable by building the first love bonds. The community then gives life and vitality to the territory by building eternal family bonds.

TRAUMA TEAMS

While prayer teams are great at opening up new territory, trauma teams are needed to build bridges into these new regions. We discussed the work of the trauma team extensively in chapter 8. This work requires time and care. Healing is done through the fruit of the Spirit exhibited in bonded relationships. As these roads are opened, there may be continued battles and deliverance, but loving bonds develop rapidly during this phase.

Trauma recovery cannot safely be separated from community life. Every stranger, widow and orphan who requires healing of emotional wounds and deprivation needs adoption before he or she can recover. This means that no one should be sent for counseling who is not accompanied by a support person. Community-based care is coordinated by elders in the community and addresses both healing and maturity needs in each person adopted into the family.

Healing is the work of God through the Holy Spirit in our lives. Through healing, both pain and the continued working of evil are stopped. Healing does not always restore complete wholeness. Scars and gaps often remain. If a leg is cut off, healing may close the wound and remove the pain but it does not replace the leg.

Restoration is usually a long, slow process that depends largely on relationships and hard work. It does not always restore the original condition but it works toward the original function. A missing leg may be replaced by a prosthesis, or new skills for locomotion can be learned and strengthened.

SPIRITUAL ADOPTION INTO THE FAMILY STRUCTURE

As the land is conquered and the war is being won, people must come to live in the land. Families must form and grow. Bonds grow into adoptions, or adoptions grow into bonds, as we discover how God is arranging our spiritual communities-of-the-self. The community must occupy the land or it will revert to wild beasts, chaos and ruin. To conquer a land but not to build houses, plant little gardens, grow trees and flowers, then sit down to eat with young and old is a great loss.

Support from the family of God should begin with elders and pastors and work its way down to the pillars and officers of the church, and from there to the members, and finally to the weak. Ensuring that such support exists and is being utilized is the first task of community-based care.

INCLUDING THE WEAK AND WOUNDED IN THE CHURCH

Wounded people—cult survivors in particular—need to be taught how to pray, worship and know God. These personal aspects of community life are learned through intensive teaching, prayer and praise. Various churches have implemented programs of this type. Specific guidelines are found in "Steps for Including the Weak and Wounded" on page 316 in the appendix.

DELIVERANCE TEAMS

In order to be effective, we must see our communities through the eyes of heaven. Our enemies are not people but the spirits that deceive them. Anyone seeking seriously to see through God's eyes will encounter the interference of other powers soon enough. Resisting these powers is also a community effort. Many times I have been saved by someone saying, "Look out behind you," or by being able to say, "I'm tired. You take over for a while." Spiritual warfare is a central part of helping our communities. Dr. Neil Anderson, Dr. Ed Murphy, Tom White, Dr. Charles Kraft and Dr. James Friesen have all written extensively on this topic; check the bibliography.

COMMUNITY LIFE

Elders represent the center of any family, community or support structure. If they abdicate their roles, the whole structure will be shaky. Elders have the maturity gained by raising their own children to adulthood and are able to raise a community into its true identity. Community-based care is the work of elders building the community-of-the-self around each individual. They direct the redemptive steps of the natural community toward realizing the bonds and structure of the spiritual community or family.

Spiritual family life is not feasible without the direct teaching and involvement of pastors. These shepherds help everyone discover the desirability and absolute importance of having their own personal spiritual families grow.

Although elders and pastors build structures, redemption (as we said at the beginning of this chapter) cannot be structured. Healing ministries flow among all believers bringing comfort and love. Those who minister are greatly loved by their families once the bonds have formed.

Community life centers around worship—that is to say, the proper appreciation of the Source of all life. Praise and the stories and symbols of reconciliation become part of individual and community identities. Meditation, singing, prayer, rest, play and spiritual disciplines guide members toward the sources of real life. Bonds of love slowly replace fear of pain and loss as the best ways to find life. The natural community becomes more like the spiritual one.

Redemption for All: Spiritual Adoption Is a Three-Way Bond

Having seen that redemption is God's activity through which He brings strangers to the people of God, we have begun to appreciate His methods. We have discovered that without weak, wounded and immature strangers, God's community would not be transformed. Through this dying process, strong, mature community members are purified of their remaining fear bonds to the dragon. We have also discovered that strangers cannot find life or maturity until they became family with the people of God. Because redemption disrupts our family structures, both strangers and the people of God resist participation out of fear. Often we do not give in until our need is desperate. For most the cost is too high and they go back home to wither and die. For the strong who are willing to die, and for the wounded who are willing to live, spiritual adoption brings transformation inside and out.

Our spiritual family grows when we are connected to God and to each other. A three-way bond is formed among the individual, God and the people of God. Everything works in harmony when we love God with all our hearts, souls and minds. Growth occurs by reclaiming the children of the evil one. We are committed to retrieving as many of the people he has stolen as we can. We are all retrieved from this same condition, so all of us carry wounds and fears. We all need God and His family.

Spiritual adoption is the process by which *everyone* enters the spiritual family. How wonderful when our natural family has preceded us, but it is adoption and not natural ties that brings us into the Kingdom of God. The spiritual family grows only and always through adoption.

Adoption is not an isolated act. When people become members of the household of faith, they naturally seek their places of attachment. They are aware that the structure of the family has now changed irreversibly; at issue is how long it will take for the natural community-of-the-self to catch up. To find a place in a family requires the family to make a place for you.

Through spiritual adoption, family structures in the natural and spiritual communities are changed. Adoption is a redemptive process, which means that:

1. Adoption removes people from a state from which they cannot remove themselves.
2. Adoption involves a cost paid by the ones doing the redeeming.
3. Adoption means new attachments.

hide in our hearts we keep hidden for good reason. Envy, fear, jealousy, strife, criticism, hate, greed and pride are exposed. Whatever we have hidden from redemption appears and waits for confession so that we may also experience redemption. Adoption cleans house as it builds a new one.

Those who think God is showing them a parent or child through spiritual adoption should consult the "Guidelines for Spiritual Adoptions" in the appendix of this book. All spiritual family members should examine "Guidelines for Redemptive Bonding" in the same source. And because adoption produces identity change, elders, parents, pastors and counselors may wish to consult "Guidelines for Identity Change."

The results of spiritual parenting on healing can be truly remarkable. One cannot recover from the absence of necessary good things until the lack is supplied. It is certain that many people will never recover without receiving a new family and parents. Perhaps that is true for all of us, for without our spiritual families we will not reach the fullness of Christ.

To the degree we believe we can be independent and take care of ourselves, we will disregard our need for adoption and demand that others "grow up," too. Rebellion toward our dependent state is deeply set by sin, as Larry Crabb showed us in *Finding God.*[8] The certainty that parent-child bonds produce dependency also raises the most common mental health objection to spiritual adoption in America: But won't it foster dependence?

Maturity, Dependency and Spiritual Adoption

We often measure maturity in terms of independence. Perhaps this comes from learning to button our own shirts and tie our own shoes. We think that the more independent we are, the more we have matured—but this is false. We are and always will be dependent creatures. No amount of physical, emotional or spiritual maturity will remove or reduce our dependence. Because we are dependent, we will always have needs—physical, emotional and spiritual. Maturity becomes, then, the natural and authentic expression of our dependent nature, for God alone is independent.

There are Christians who claim we have no needs except to love God, but this is not true. We are dependent creatures who rely on our Creator for each breath. Dependency is our natural state. At the Great White Throne, Jesus does not say to the sheep, "I was hungry, thirsty, naked and in prison, and you prayed for Me to love God." No, the sheep met needs.

One may not substitute one need for another. Increasing spiritual maturity does not eliminate physical or emotional needs. Nor does emotional maturity eliminate spiritual or physical needs—as older folks in nursing homes will tell you. We are naturally dependent in every aspect of our lives, and it will stay that way. Maturity is learning to live fearlessly with this dependency.

We are dependent on God in our bodies, our ecosystems, our two communities-of-the-self, our nations and our planet. We cannot mature our way out of dependency during our life span. Redemption will not help us opt out of dependency but teaches us to appreciate it fully. As we mature we become increasingly aware of the vast extent of the communities we depend on for our identities and existence.

We depend on our natural families. Although the degree of immediate dependency varies throughout life, we always remain dependent on our communities-of-the-self. If we define family so narrowly as to include only parents and children, then this is not true at times, for we may exist for a period without either. At both ends of the life span, however, it becomes clearly true that without family we suffer and die. In case of misfortune at any time, the same becomes immediately evident. Only when our family connections are strong are we free to act *as if* we do not need them.

This dependency is real, it is by design, it is irrevocable, it is not optional or escapable. We need the very people who carry knives and fire. Dependency is the source of our terror when redemption strikes the structures on which we depend for existence, and it promises to change it. Decontamination alters the structure of the natural family profoundly.

We depend on our spiritual families. Paul instructs the spiritual family to "admonish the careless, encourage the faint-hearted, support the weak, and . . . be very patient with them all" (1 Thessalonians 5:14). We support the weak because they cannot function independently. They need help from their families.

It is the spiritual family that ministers redemption to us when our natural families would kill us. We tend to think of *spiritual* as "not real," so let me be clear. The spiritual family is the real structure of our life-receiving and life-giving bonds. It lasts beyond all legal, biological and natural bonds because it is *alive*. In the end only the spiritual family is real; everything else will have killed itself.

DEPENDENCY IN THE WEAK AND WOUNDED

People with no experience in loving relationships must pass from the realm of no relationships (the first phase) into the next closest thing—emotionally dependent relationships (the second phase). It will take them years before they arrive at mature relationships (the third phase). Fear bonds must be replaced by love bonds that are stronger than their fears. They must develop bonds with their spiritual parents that resemble the relationship every newborn child needs with Mother. Mother must guess what her baby needs without much help from the infant, and be available when those needs arise. This dependency is quite demanding.

The intermediate dependency phase in spiritual adoptions will likely last from two to five years. In the interim a basic, loving relationship has time to grow. The people who could not previously relate learn to ask God and the parent for the care they need. It is not clear whether they learn to love God because they are loved by one of God's children or whether it is the other way around. But in time they learn that they, too, can love and give, which begins to bring them out of emotional infancy and the need to depend on another person in order to feel loved.

The ability to resolve this dependency phase rests, in great part, on the emotional development of the parent. Mature people set others free while keeping the relationship intact. Childish people become frightened at the thought of allowing others to act on their own. If the parent is childish, then a painful severing of the relationship is the most likely outcome.

Only people not prone to codependency should sustain adoptive relationships with dependent people, or else the third stage of mature relationships will never be reached. Those attracted to dependency from others should take up making quilts, preparing meals, fixing cars and painting houses for those who can use short-term help from brothers and sisters. These ministries are of great value and will provide joy rather than hurt.

Here is the catch, however: The people who can best do the jobs are those who are most reluctant. An act of the will is needed to accept the Holy Spirit's offer to become a spiritual parent. Starting a relationship that will be painful requires vision seen only by the heart that Jesus gives.

Hopeless people heading in or out of Satanism, severe abuse or destructive cults usually lack the maturity, experience or hope necessary to form relationships. In other words, they are hard to get along with. This strengthens their belief that they have been cursed and doomed to a life without love. Many of those most attracted to Satanism are greatly impaired in their ability to sustain a relationship at all. Some teenagers can relate to others only through sharing drugs or fantasy role play.

In chapter 1 I talked about Greg, the boy who received a love spell from the Satanists at his high school. He needed love because his Christian parents were full of violence they could not stop. Good advice and godly counsel rarely worked with them longer than fifteen minutes. Although they were learning slowly, they usually functioned at an infant's level of maturity. The family disintegrated before they grew enough. Had a mature person—an elder—lived with this family for a year, much change would have been possible.

Ted and Joyce Cooper, whom we also met in chapter 1, are parents of three preschool children. Both parents came from multigenerational Satanism. Imagine the difficulty these two had figuring out how to rear their children after what their lifelong experiences had taught them! A six-month search to find someone to stay with that family produced almost no results. It was a potentially dangerous job and four churches declined involvement.

The Coopers did receive an offer of help from some feminist witches. That Wicca group was opposed to men and male violence. On behalf of the goddess they were ready to take a stand against the violence in Satanism. These witches wanted to teach the Cooper family a different way of life from what the parents had experienced through Satanism. Whatever our Christian repugnance for witches, the offer from this Wicca group was a real step up for the Coopers.

The parents declined the offer because they wanted to be Christians more than they wanted to be safe. But before we clap our hands in holy glee, we must ask, Where were the elders from the Christian Church?

Dependency versus Codependency

Emotional immaturity is a hallmark of our society. Codependency is an unhealthy emotional dependence between people who maintain childish relationships. While all parties are afraid to lose the emotionally immature relationship, the codependent party tries to control the other by adjusting his or her personal identity (boundaries). This fear-based bond aims to control whatever they both fear. Control and fear together stop growth.[9]

The movement to correct codependency has led some to view the Church once again as family and to correct dysfunction in the relationship patterns within congregations. Churches often take advantage of immature people. Those whose natural development is immature make great church workers; they cannot say no. Addressing codependency in churches is neither redemption nor sanctification, however, but developing natural maturity that also has its place in church.

Hurt people often take their need for spiritual family very seriously. In my experience the first people who volunteer to help others are often emotionally immature themselves. They recognize distress in others—but they may also be responding to God's voice within their hearts. This may be the gift of mercy spotting needs in others with sensitivity born out of their own weakness. Because they are weak, they recognize what our individualistic society denies: that needs and weaknesses are real. We really are dependent. We always stay dependent. Recognizing this point, the weak have become wiser than the strong.

Codependent brothers and sisters, in pain themselves, cannot stand to see their spiritual siblings ignored in their need. They try, therefore, to be spiritual parents. The results of having emotionally immature people acting as parents are often disastrous, because children usually understand rescuing far better than healing. It is impossible (as we have seen) to rescue people from the pain they carry; they can only be healed from it. Desperate, hurting people demand rescuing rather than healing, and only wisdom knows when each is needed.

Dependency, Pain and Spiritual Maturity

Having just examined the interaction between maturity and dependency, we will look at the single-largest reason we do not mature: pain.

It is easy to cause pain to dependent creatures by depriving them of something they need. Our weakness is real, and when our communities-of-the-self do not provide what we need, we hurt. When we fear hurting, we stop maturing, until redemption appears to get us through.

For children pain always means they have no value. If they were important, someone would care enough to protect them. The spiritual community-of-the-self sees pain differently, and must teach us all that pain reflects our value in the face of evil. Paul told the church at Philippi that his suffering was their glory. He meant they were so valuable that it was worth going through all he had suffered just for them. If he had not told them that his suffering meant they had great value, they might have thought it meant Satan was stronger than God.

Paul told the church at Colossae that it was his joy to suffer for them. He did not mean he enjoyed pain, the way Satanists would have it. Paul's joy was to be like his Lord, who preferred to endure hardship so that others might see who they really are. God gave His only begotten Son to die for our sins, it is true; but God has sent many more sons and daughters to suffer and die so others could know they are loved. Paul knew he was a son given as a gift as well. Merry Christmas!

Is joy more powerful than pain? We may judge in our own lives. To find out, we must bring our pain to God and see what it means. Just as mothers return their infants to joy, God and His people meet us in our suffering and bring us back to joy. Those who hide their pain will never know what heaven sees and be healed. Loving relationships are necessary for that trip to heaven. We know that those who love us do not want us in pain. The power of love comes from its ability to suffer pain it does not deserve—this is the cost of redemption.

When we suffer, we are the source of good things. This is the truth of who God's people really are. This is what we see with the eyes of heaven. We are good to be around because love flows from us. Our bonds grow strong as we return to joy.

Christians should respond with joy, then, to detecting pain and damage in our lives because we know we are due for healing and will be shown a mystery. Elders are to know this and teach it to parents, who then teach it to children. We are given God's eyes to be His witnesses. We see, in part, the wonders He does and teach others His mysteries. This is the nature of spiritual maturity.

Redemption Returns Us to Building Maturity

Redemption ultimately helps us all act like our true selves. As we are redeemed, we return to our natural function: building maturity. Each time we submit to correction, we emerge more fearless and loving. We can act more like ourselves, hurt more like ourselves and belong better among our people. This purification is evidence of God's sanctification in our lives. With it we can build a community-of-the-self that is even closer to the spiritual one. Now the natural maturity we build will be closer to our real identities.

The combined efforts of maturity and sanctification bring spiritual maturity. With it we no longer see ourselves and others through the eyes of our senses but through the eyes of our hearts. We recognize who others are to us, and we live into that spiritually created reality. Through living out spiritual relationships here on earth, we overcome the type-A traumas in the lives of all of us. For some this means their need to receive life will be met, while others will meet their need to give away the life they have received. Together we build our families once again, certain that redemption will rearrange them soon enough!

Redemptive decontamination changes the natural community by transforming individuals, their family and community structures and identities, breaking fear bonds and deadly attachments, and replacing them with attachments to the spiritual family. This is done in the midst of much pain and real weakness. Through redemption we learn how to live as dependent beings while changing our bonds and attachments. It is a process in which there is no informed consent, no uninvolved observers, no non-participation, and without which we will all surely kill ourselves, our families and communities.

We are the gifts of Christ to each other. He will use us to disrupt one another's lives enough for His redemption to reach places we did not know redemption was needed. Come and see what He did to mine.

REDEMPTION COMES TO MY HOUSE

MAKING ELDERS BY FIRE

YOU ARE a hard man to be married to," Kitty said to me. "I love you and I'm glad to have a godly husband, but I can't take any more of this ministry of yours."

The lentil soup started to get cold in my bowl as my appetite drained away.

Here we go again, I thought.

"You and the boys are first," I told her again that night. "There's no doubt about it. Still, we have spiritual children, brothers, sisters, mothers and fathers to consider."

My face portrayed more confidence than I felt. At times emergencies careened along at such speed that I despaired of balance or rest.

I handled those hard times better than some simple times. When my wife and sons talked, laughed, took bike rides or went camping, it made me sad. These simple, loving experiences were missing from survivors' lives. When we enjoyed a simple meal without a cross word, my family was unaware of the contrast it pointed up in my mind between our life and the barren existence of some survivors. I lived in affluence, it seemed, while my spiri-

288

tual children lived in poverty. I was painfully jammed between two worlds.

"Why do you have to go and have other children?" Kitty asked, sometimes plaintively but at other times with an accusatory note to her voice. "Sometimes I wish there were no such thing as ministry!"

At times a spiritual family could seem more like a burden than a blessing. Perhaps she was the only minister's wife to think so, but I doubt it.

We married young and had spent many years by now creating the best family we could. Our vision for our family had changed gradually. At first we thought of adopting unwanted children instead of having our own, but we received a surprise instead. We were blessed with a son just as I was about to start graduate school. Kitty and I attended Lamaze, La Leche and all the prenatal doctor visits together.

Jamie did not make graduate school any easier, but we enjoyed him so much that we decided to have a second child. Not only could they play together, but Kitty liked the birth process and was eager to repeat it. Rami was born at home with the help of a visiting doctor and his assistants. We did this to provide a warm family atmosphere for the birth. With the assistance of another home birth mother, we included Jamie in a way that would weave our growing family together.

Kitty carried both boys on her back, the way she had learned as a missionary kid in Africa, to help them bond. She stayed home with the children until they were in school. We joined a food co-op to buy good, low-priced health food. We stopped cooking in aluminum pans, planted a garden, childproofed the house, limited television, drank bottled water and hugged freely.

During graduate school we went to therapy to prevent marriage problems because we had heard that more than half of the married students in the program were divorced by graduation. Kitty and I practiced honesty and openness. We went to marriage seminars, attended church together, camped as a family and I worked at home as much as possible. My coffee mug said, "Please interrupt me, I'm trying to study." We spent time together building a marriage and family.

For our companions we selected families with parents who could be our friends and whose children were good for our own. Young marrieds support groups and Bible studies expanded into group camping, sharing skills and working together. We were building the best marriage, family and community-of-the-self possible for our children. When people commented that they had never seen a long-term happy marriage, I would point to Kitty and me and our friends to show that it was possible. We were happy, well-liked and respected at work, home and church.

I worked 45 minutes from home in a different community to ensure that my children were not exposed to any of the people I was counseling. Everything was neat and clean. My first book was published telling how I helped my sons become men. I began receiving directorship offers from counseling centers. When I was named to the who's who of fathering advocates in America, the only credibility problem I had was that no one believed our family was that good. But it was.

Just then redemption came to my house.

The Need

The same year that our son Rami was born, I began working at a Christian agency that did counseling and research while training churches how to minister to the weak and wounded. When I finished seminary and was ordained, my denomination assigned me to this counseling ministry as part of its outreach to "strangers, widows and orphans," particularly those who had suffered abuse. Because our agency had connections to more than two hundred churches, we saw more people in our two busiest years than the Los Angeles County facility in our area.

By tracking the progress of cult survivors in counseling, I soon realized that those with a community-of-the-self got better, while those with no currently functioning community-of-the-self, or with one based on fear bonds, did not improve with counseling. Those with redemptive communities improved the fastest even when their damage was worse. The same was true for those with trauma-based identities. Identity change requires a community.

I worked with a large team of counselors whose caseloads evidenced similar results. Traveling around the country consulting with professional and lay counselors revealed the same patterns. Reading all the books I could find brought me to the same conclusion: Really big problems do not heal for isolated people. As a result, my first goal became finding communities-of-the-self for survivors.

The reports I gathered suggested that the best choice of community was always some part of the family of origin—provided that fear and trauma bonds could be replaced with love bonds. Parents were often more interested, however, in continuing their destructive patterns of control, intrusion and intimidation and would not change. Sometimes siblings, aunts, uncles, grandparents or other relatives would help, but most often it was a marriage partner who provided the necessary community. Because many marriages were based partially on fear bonds, these survivor marriages needed quite a bit of restoration. Typically both marriage partners were isolated individuals with no one but themselves to offer. Still, it was easier for married people to add to their communities than it was for singles.

Trying to enlist some part of the family of origin resulted in many failures, but I, like most of the lay and professional counselors I consulted, kept any vestiges of family that could be saved. Even family members who refused all redemption might someday change, so no door was permanently closed except by death. But, as Proverbs 13:12 says, "Hope deferred maketh the heart sick" (KJV), and people grew sicker waiting for their families.

People with some community-of-the-self often had mixed bonds. They could not think straight if the intense fear and trauma interactions with their families continued overwhelming them. For them temporary separation from confusing relationships allowed them to grow. Their progress was slow, but by joining support groups with other survivors, they were able to learn about love bonds. Then they were able to grow strong, loving relationships with people they knew slightly through church and family. The most common connections came about when they became friends with the parents of the children who played with their own.

I thought of Rose, a widow and grandmother whose relationships with her children were suffering because she had no community for herself. Rearing children to adulthood had taught her something about bonding. Group therapy and prayer teams had shown her new patterns. But now she needed people to see who she could really become.

Those with no community-of-the-self or whose few contacts were based on fear and emotional intensity might bond with their counselors, but bonding did not spread from there. Counselors had to take the person out into a community and teach them how to bond with others. But here came the challenge. To find a community-of-the-self requires someone to want you as family and to love you when you do not know how to bond that way.

Once I had found communities for everyone I could, there were a few people left over. I talked in chapter 5, for example, about Wendy, the petite blonde poet who wanted someone to pray with her each morning. Survivors like Wendy bonded to me through anxious, fearful attachments but would not bond with anyone else. They had no viable communities-of-the-self. Left this way their identities did not change after years of the same kind of counseling that produced recovery in those who had community. My colleagues said, "Low prognosis." "Impossible case!" "Borderline." "Poor protoplasm."

The only choice left was one I hated to think about.

Most professional counselors protected and isolated their personal communities, just as I did. But occasionally they ventured out of their offices and into their communities. They deconditioned some agorophobics by taking them into their communities and desensitized responses until the patients could go out on their own. Community treatment was practiced in AIDS hospices, homes for behavior-disturbed children and other groups labeled "low-functioning." Professionals tended to prefer consulting roles, however, and left the bonding to assistants and "houseparents."

Across the country, however, certain untrained lay counselors were finding success bringing isolated people into the counselors' own communities. By sharing their communities-of-the-self, these counselors were building bridges and bonds until isolation was overcome. Not only did abandoned people need bonds that were stronger than the abuse, fear and abandonment they knew, but they needed a nest full of bonds.

I had only one nest. There was not enough time in the day for me to participate in two different communities deeply enough to call both family, keeping one for myself and one for survivors. I would have to introduce these abandoned people around the community I knew as my own.

In several ways using my own community was as bad an idea as I could generate. First, I worked in isolation from my community and had spent years building the highest walls I could between it and my work. Second, I got nervous in free-flowing situations with more than one person involved. Third, most of the time I worked alone so that community time was in addition to work time. Fourth, the idea went against conventional wisdom, which asserts that the best counseling happens in offices and total privacy.

Could a consistent bond be maintained in many contexts? These untrained lay counselors around the country were doing so successfully. Although they worked in multiple roles, contexts and activities, they maintained a single, consistent relationship bond— a parent-child bond that gave and received life. Through it they came to share a community-of-the-self. And several books documented that, in spite of the difficulties involved, trained counselors could accomplish this as well.

A Good Idea

I asked Kitty what she thought of the idea. She read the books and decided she liked it. She agreed that, since helping our sons prepare to become men as they turned thirteen, they were growing rapidly into their own activities and away from her. She was tired of being kept out of my world. If anyone was going to show people how to be family, she thought, it should be strong families. All the same, she read a dozen books to help her think things through. Finally she felt it was time.

As we carefully considered all the ramifications, however, I missed one. Little did I know that redemption of my house was underway.

Our sons were agreeable and ready for action. But they were not motivated enough to read a book and were not grasping the immensity of our effort. Our friends were similarly agreeable. We were surrounded by the best and strongest families we knew and we enlisted their help easily. They, too, seemed unaware of the effort required. I prepared my sons, friends and church with lessons that eventually covered spiritual warfare, Satanism, dissociation and community life.

I hoped this would not take long and that loving bonds would soon grow among brothers and sisters, aunts and uncles, parents and children in the spiritual family. By careful modeling and guidance, I hoped, love bonds would grow, forming a strong spiritual community-of-the-self around the people who were failing to thrive.

We began with a night of prayer on Halloween. An all-night prayer vigil for cult survivors and friends was a way for survivors and church community to meet and mingle in God's presence. It was during that night that Wendy met the family she tried to bond with for a year. Initially it looked like a great success and it took me only ten hours' work. For a time she had a woman to call for prayer in the mornings.

It was on that Halloween night that redemption first showed up in my family. Kitty met Rose on her way to the restroom and recognized the grandmother as a survivor. Rose said hello to Kitty, and my wife froze. She was so unnerved that she left and went home early.

Kitty had little idea why Rose had triggered such a strong reaction in her, but decided to overcome it. Soon Kitty's eagerness returned and she begged for another chance to reenter my world. I was more reluctant. She seemed too eager. I reviewed the costs, and she repeated her earnest intentions to minister near her husband. Both women and men were needed, Kitty pointed out, in every community and family. She was as right as she was determined.

So she and Rose slowly began to form a relationship. Attending church, Sunday school and special seminars together expanded the relationship base for both of them. By participating on prayer and worship teams, Rose began to find connections with many people in the community.

Meanwhile Kitty and I were trying to grow in the area of hospitality and joint ministry, so we opened our home to our spiritual family. We both noted that hospitality was on the apostle Paul's list of characteristics of elders. Since isolation described us better than hospitality, we arranged, supported by the Birkey family, to host a dinner.

We invited those who had no family to join us on Thanksgiving Day. Some had cult or criminal families. Some lived far from home. Others had no living relatives. A few had families in such violent turmoil that they could not go home at the moment. No matter the cause, all would be alone on Thanksgiving. Rose and Wendy were part of the group of fourteen around our table.

Halfway through the day, I felt an icy chill coming my way from Kitty. That night she exploded. She was upset and jealous of the time I had spent with others. Over the turkey she had seen people turn to me with their feelings. She felt left out and unimportant. The apparent bond between me and the women particularly bothered her.

I responded as I do whenever action is called for and I withdrew—first to silence, then to angry defensiveness, then to the other room. Hey! Wasn't this what she wanted? Hadn't Kitty wanted to be part of my world?

We fought for the next three years.

Few subjects have produced such discussions between my wife and me as the family nature of church relationships. Kitty would argue that kinship ties were the dependable ones in times of trouble. The church, she insisted, used family as a metaphor only. There was little real substance to it when something went wrong.

As Kitty and I began seeking assistance from our church friends, it appeared increasingly that she was right. Once Kitty panicked, everyone we knew bailed out on us.

Children are a gift from the Lord, and spiritual children are the reward for faithful ministry from the same Lord. A spiritual family is God's provision for our edification and joy. Yet in Kitty's experience as a child of missionaries, ministry by her parents seemed to provide more losses for her than gains. Spiritual children usually represented competition for available time and love rather than a blessing. Still, at crucial times when I lacked courage regarding some spiritual son or daughter, it was Kitty who said, "He needs you to go after him. You'd better go quickly. It's what a good father would do." Her face registered both determination and the wish that it were different.

"Community begins at home," my friend Mike Coppess says. So does family. God must think so, too, because He left me no way to ignore the distress this ministry caused in our home. Redemption was showing us the defective nature of our marriage bond and our self-satisfied identities. Simultaneously God left Kitty with no way out of the pain.

We began to be redefined, refined and relinked. Slowly and almost endlessly our hurts emerged for prayer and healing. Sometimes it was Kitty who hurt; other times it was my turn. When we were both down for the count, despair would creep in to visit us. Months dragged into years. We grew very tired.

Learning the Truth about Ourselves

Often the rights or obligations of spiritual and biological family members toward one another became a pointed discussion. Kitty and I were grateful that our immediate family was part of our spiritual family. We did not need to choose one or the other. Yet a strain remained. We tried to maintain both.

It is a trap to spiritualize the family and deny the importance of our kinship ties. In some ways each family is more important than the other. Raising one kind of family to exclusive importance always ends in folly. How, then, does one keep a good natural family and yet become a spiritual family to others? I attempted to succeed by trying harder. Redemption made rubble of my hard work.

Kitty started keeping track of how much time I spent with each person. Her tally sheet was an attempt to help her gain control of the situation. She took it to friends and family, alternately asking for support and expressing her grievances. The very fact that she was so upset was enough to convince all our friends to back off. Their withdrawal confirmed what Kitty had always believed about the church—that they are not there when trouble comes. Since the church did not function the way I said it should, she concluded, then my own motives must also be suspect. It could not be my faith that motivated me but something more sinister. I wanted to replace her with another woman. She started keeping more careful records of my activity to find out who that woman was.

My work was very demanding. Doubts plagued my mind about almost everything I did. Never having faced anything so unpredictable, complex and evil as Satanism, I was constantly stumbling, failing and mired in uncertainty as to my next move. It was a time of feeling incompetent and overwhelmed. My colleagues were all reporting the same reaction, so we comforted one another by checking to see who felt the most incompetent each week.

My home life was often more consuming than my time at work. Keeping my internal commitment to spend twice as many hours each week with Kitty as I spent with anyone else took all my determination. Needing to find reassurance and comfort for my own pain and insecurity gave me less tolerance for questions I could not answer satisfactorily. So I became defensive.

Subtly the enemy sneaked in, robbing the joy from my blessings. It took the wisdom of Solomon to remind me:

> Here is an evil under the sun which I have seen, and it weighs heavy upon men. Consider the man to whom God grants wealth, riches, and substance, and who lacks nothing that he has set his heart on: if God has not given him the power to enjoy these things, but a stranger enjoys them instead, that is emptiness and a grave disorder.

> Ecclesiastes 6:1–2

Kitty worked hard maintaining her marriage. One day she bought a new white dress with a slightly daring cut. She knew I liked white. She bought some peach-colored candles and cooked a roast with vegetables. The boys had left for their activities by the time she put on the music, took a bath and dimmed the lights.

Coming home from hearing yet another grisly murder and rape story, only to find the table set for a romantic meal, was too abrupt a change for me. I tried to be happy, but the distant look in my eyes brought Kitty to tears. There was no point explaining. The evening was ruined and we were both brokenhearted.

Kitty got angry. She did not like my spiritual children and began rejecting them. What she wanted was something exclusive, so any activity I shared with someone else she refused to share with me. If I hugged someone, she refused hugs. If I shared a meal, she would refuse the food. If I used a certain tone of voice and then she heard what she considered the same tone used toward her, she would leave the room.

It got worse. Kitty bird-dogged me to find the other woman in my life, and alerted the community to do the same. She talked to my colleagues at work, pleaded with my friends, wrote to our families and questioned everything I did. There *were* other women in my life, I said; they were daughters. Kitty said she hated fathers and daughters. Why would a man want a daughter unless he was perverted?

It was Kitty who had first persuaded me to accept Wendy as a daughter, but that was back in the days when Kitty and I had a nearly perfect marriage and family. We had invited her in to take a look at our home and become part of us. When everything blew apart,

297

Wendy needed reassurance that she would not be abandoned, so she turned to me. Every time Wendy felt something was upsetting Kitty, she called me to check, and Kitty made a note in her log.

Meanwhile, after meeting Kitty at Halloween, Rose was particularly eager to see a good family and marriage, and she put ours under a microscope. Never having known a man who was not sexually driven, she went, naturally, to Kitty for reassurance that I was not on the prowl. Her questions did not reassure Kitty at all.

Remember, when Kitty and I started this, we both thought it was a nice idea. That was before redemption began to show us what was hidden in our apparently ideal lives. We stayed with it because there was no way out with integrity. I had given my word and would not abandon either my biological or spiritual family. But I also harbored some secret fears. I feared betraying, hurting or abandoning those I loved or even making them angry. Kitty stuck it out, refusing to let her personal comfort become our family god, no matter how upsetting life became. She also feared that people might find out she was not a perfect wife or mother.

Simultaneously my wife was not at all sure that any of this was redemption at all, so she asked several of our friends, who were prominent Christian leaders, to intervene. They asked her if God had called her to this work, and she said no. They asked if she felt her place as a wife was secure, and she said no. It seemed to her that I was trying to replace her with Rose. They asked if she had doubts about my motives, and she said yes. They asked if she felt she could handle what was happening, and she said no, adding that no woman she knew could either. So they told me, "God will not call you to something and then not equip your wife. God is not in your plans."

With that, my invitations to speak around the country dried up. Kitty became really frightened and despairing. The best Christians she knew were of the opinion that I was out of God's will and self-deceived. She soon concluded that either God or I hated her and loved making her suffer. She was at the mercy of a madman husband.

I was having serious self-doubts. Nothing was going as planned, every situation was getting worse and my wife had turned on me. She could not leave me alone and her angry attacks were escalating, as she demanded control of every aspect of my life.

About then my parents sent me a set of tapes about spiritual warfare based on the life of Moses. When Moses showed up in Egypt, saying, "Let my people go," he made things worse. Then the Israelites were made to gather the straw themselves and still turn out their same quota of bricks. It was not until the fifth plague that the people started breaking even. Clearly not everything goes smoothly and succeeds from the start just because God commands it to be done. I decided to persevere.

Christmas

As Christmas approached my family had seen little of me. There had been a series of crises at work that consumed most of my time. On top of that Kitty had been ill for several weeks. Hemorrhaging had led to tests for cancer. We were waiting to see if there would be surgery. The medication she was taking produced depression. What my family needed was a good vacation and a happy father. What they had was a father giving them insufficient time, trying to keep other people alive and feeling quite overwhelmed. It seemed to be too much. This was definitely more than I could handle.

How I longed for rest! Perhaps I could find a bit of time away from the struggle. Perhaps there was someone who could take over for me for a day or a week. Perhaps we would win the war and everything would be wonderful. Tired or not, I kept asking, "What does it mean to be part of the family of God just now?" Others, however, were saying about me, "He takes his work too seriously."

Kitty was not the only one undergoing medical tests. Wendy received confirmation from her doctor of her abuse. Until then she could never believe that certain things really had happened. Her memories linked her abuse, moreover, to Christmas time. Now, during the holiday that is especially difficult for those who want loving families but lack them, she had no family to comfort her, no home to visit and no one she trusted to share her pain. She had very little reason to live. She was angry, withdrawn and hurt.

At Christmas good families want private time with those in the inner circle of love. For most people this means their nuclear families. In times of great loss and grief, too, we need to be surrounded by loving family. Yet if one's family created the tragedy, it is better to be alone. But if we really are alone with our losses, there is very little connecting us to life.

Wendy had few of the community resources that had helped the Cooper family years before. You remember the Christmas Eve I described in chapter 1, when the call arrived from the Cooper family saying they had been contacted by the Satanist cult. You might recall how they escaped with the help of their spiritual family. By being surrounded for the holiday, the family found they were safe and loved. True, it disrupted everyone's Christmas plans, but the burden was shared by many.

Wendy felt she lacked the personal resources to cope with her devastating tragedy. Christmas seemed like a good day to join the dead. Feeling hopeless and despondent made all celebrations abhorrent. She could not go to church and act pleasant or have a happy Christmas Day alone with her agonizing memories.

So Christmas Eve I baked cranberry bread and took some down to the cold, bare apartment where she lived. Kitty sat crying as I left with that bit of home-baked care. "You don't love me anymore" hung in the crisp night air behind me. Sometime while I was gone, Kitty shifted the focus of her fears from Rose to Wendy.

Driving in inner city Los Angeles at night was unnerving, but sitting in the tiny, unheated kitchen while Wendy searched for a second coffee cup was worse.

"Why didn't Kitty come?" she asked.

"She didn't feel up to it tonight," proved to be enough of an answer.

Wendy found the butter and we each had a slice of cranberry bread. I took in the bleak surroundings and could not believe my daughter was living in such a place, or that I would leave her there.

Not wanting to hurt Kitty any more than I already had, I left as soon as possible.

"Can I call you on Christmas?" she asked as I left.

"If you need to," I answered. "Merry Christmas."

She was crying as I drove away.

The next evening Kitty, my sons, various friends and I went to a party at Rose's house. There we were each given an ornamental box and slip of paper on which to write our birthday gift to Christ. One at a time we hung them on the Christmas tree. Our meal was a retelling of the Advent. Every item of food symbolized some part of the Christmas story. Quiet meditation and songs reminded us all of the One whose birthday made us family. Kitty and Rose got along quite well.

Redemption Reaches the Community

The next spring was tumultuous. Kitty could not find her place in the spiritual family. She found that she could not trust God's intentions toward her. Some days she would insist that I was better off alone and plan to leave; some days she insisted on being mother to everyone and on being obeyed. Once she threw down her wedding and engagement rings and left for a day. Kitty insisted on being included in everything and then got overwhelmed and ran away. The only good news was, she did not have cancer.

We sought counsel from an endless stream of people, with mixed results. The only pattern I noticed was that Kitty inevitably talked about my actions and her upset, while omitting mention of her own words and actions. She would conclude by saying, "Jim doesn't spend any time with me and doesn't care how much I hurt." Any of my statements to the contrary brought anger and the charge that I was trying to make her look bad to everyone.

Our plight became public knowledge. Invitations to teach at church dwindled to nothing. Finally we turned to the man I trusted most with spiritual discernment. Over dinner at his home, Kitty told him her story and he pulled my plug. God had not equipped Kitty for this work, he concluded, so I must have made some mistake.

This was the last straw. With anyone else I could have argued, but I trusted Tom more than anyone to speak for God. This meant I had hurt Kitty for nothing, betrayed Rose's trust and would have to abandon Wendy. I was through.

Unable to trust my own thoughts, I went home, got into bed and waited to die. It was, of all things, Father's Day. I refused calls from Wendy and Rose.

The next day was worse. I canceled all my appointments and would not take any calls. Kitty began to panic and called my colleagues. She offered to go away and die if it would make me feel better. Wendy was desperate but Kitty sent her away, telling her she was not really family. I put my face to the wall. What could I say?

Everyone concluded that I had cracked under the stress of well-intentioned but misconceived plans. I was relieved of part of my

301

workload, including all writing or speaking. All my staff was assigned to other supervisors. Evaluations were made of whether I needed hospitalization for a nervous breakdown.

I wanted to die. How could I have missed so totally what God wanted? Kitty was hurt and angry. Rose felt betrayed, and soon told me angrily that she was not my daughter and that I was no father. Wendy felt terrified, furious and abandoned. This disaster represented all my worst fears come true.

There was no escape. Disaster had come from my most careful, thoughtful, prayerful actions. This authentic expression of the best, most loving part of me, based on my deepest knowledge of God, had failed. There I was, exposed for the whole world to see, with the knife and fire in my hand.

Even leaving the ministry now and becoming an electrician was not a viable option, because no matter where I went, I would still hear what I heard and believe what I believed. I could act or think no differently. Inevitably I would live out my beliefs, which was exactly how this mess had come about. There was nothing to stop me from doing it again. My deepest fears had come true.

On the third day Kitty came in quietly and we talked. In tears I told her that everything I knew pointed me in the way I was going. My alternative was to serve her. I could live to prevent her distress and guide my life by what kept her out of pain. But I could not trust myself to know what was right.

"I will not be your God," she said. "You must do what you believe is right, and I will get therapy to help me."

It was the first time she had agreed to look at herself.

"Jane has agreed to counsel me," Kitty continued. "Her colleague Marie will help Wendy. I can't handle this father business of yours anymore."

The next day I went back to work.

Change but No Relief

By late spring it seemed that everyone was fighting with each other. The staff where I worked was in turmoil and many quit. Our support people at church were fighting. One prayer team that had helped Kitty disintegrated, as did one of our supporting churches. The support network for Rose plunged into turmoil. Enmity sprang up between her and Wendy. Wendy's few developing support people disappeared amid strange circumstances.

As the problems spread, peculiarly, so did neck pain. Almost to a person, each one who succumbed to the conflict developed severe neck, shoulder or back pain. Even the counselors who came in contact with any of us became afflicted. A prophet, a prayer warrior and an itinerant spiritual warfare teacher each told us independently that this was the work of religious control spirits. Practicing spiritual warfare made both the pains and misunderstandings subside.

After Wendy watched a drive-by shooting on her street, Kitty and I helped her find an apartment near us. Our close community pitched in to help her move.

Meanwhile Kitty underwent one last drug treatment to head off surgery. The medication was making her depressed and irritable. Her moods were unpredictably erratic. Rage, tears, terror, jealousy and loneliness galloped out of control. By summer she was scheduled for a hysterectomy. Losing her ability to have natural children highlighted the intolerance and inability she felt toward spiritual children. She began to hate everything about daughters.

My support came from the three men who became my prayer partners, as well as the men's group at church. Each week they scrutinized my actions and motives, sharing my agony and helping me stand against my fears. Together they led me out of the identity disintegration of Father's Day into a new identity as a father. No longer was my fatherhood defined by my roles or governed by the fears and hurts of fatherless women. I did not need to fear the anger of women or the devoted love of daughters. Best of all, I did not need to fear uncertainty, because God knew my limitations and could build His family through them. I began learning to embrace Kitty even when she was really mad and accusing me falsely.

All the women I knew, except for one, concluded that I was a terrible husband. Rose watched me like a hawk for any sign that I was betraying Kitty. She presented me with any flaw she found. Wendy detected any lack of closeness and underlined it. Having spent her life in search of good intimacy, she did not want anything to be wrong with mine as either a husband or a father. This obliterated my long-term pattern of withdrawing. Not only was the reaction to my withdrawal immediate; it was intense and persistent from all three of them. No blink, glance or swallow was exempt.

No degree of exhaustion or confusion was an excuse; if anything, these intensified the testing.

Most of the women counselors at work likewise examined me. They questioned my theories, motives, techniques, beliefs and subconscious desires, interpreting my silences, patterns and family history. They compared information with one another, with Kitty, with people in the community and with clients. The women questioned me for hours. They generally assumed that while women can have intimate relationships with their mothers, children and other women, married men should have intimate relationships only with their wives.

Kitty would laugh occasionally and say, "Boy! God must not want to leave any flaws in your character!" Redemption was hard at work. The women at the office examined my relationships and the men challenged my passivity while my family demanded and scrutinized my most intimate involvements.

I had the fear burned out of the bonds I had formed within our spiritual family. When each of my fears came true, it lost its power. When I was rejected, the fear of rejection lost its hold. When I was misunderstood, the fear of being misunderstood lost its grip. When I could no longer prove I was right, the fear of disapproval turned to ashes.

Kitty and I could see the fire burning through our lives but could not make out whether it was our destructiveness or God's purification at work. Thinking it was our own doing, we kept trying to put the flames out. Onlookers were certain that our distress was caused by my failings. This was more certain as the fire laid bare more and more of my faults. People who did not believe redemption could disrupt a marriage brought their structure to our lives. Their formulas failed, but so did my discernment. Yet through my failure, redemption saved our house.

Neither Kitty nor I was particularly thrilled as our deepest flaws became community property. Kitty could no longer run away, hide or pretend she was fine. Perhaps the boys and I had let her do that, but redemption did not. Increasingly she sought healing rather than become angry at whoever exposed her.

Holiday Strain

Christmas Eve arrived again, and with it Kitty's parents. The yule log burned most of the night. The tree blinked to the music. The boys lost the annual wrestling match to their dad. It was a quiet, peaceful night. A careful observer might have noticed that Jamie and Rami were showing signs of the turmoil in their parents' lives. They were a bit detached. The time Kitty and I had spent fighting had left a big hole in family time.

Redemption has its cost. Showing hospitality or compassion sometimes leads to having things stolen. Adults lose possessions. But when children pay a price, it can be more costly yet. Some parents of young children have undertaken to help others, only to find that their children have been molested by those they were helping. This has been the case even when the families were giving hospitality to visiting ministers.

In our home the battle against evil had certainly been costly. The most excessive costs had come when we worked without the help of the rest of the Christian community. When we alone supplied spiritual family, it had taken a toll on our family's emotional health. When I had provided almost sole support to both survivors and to Kitty, it took time away from our sons. This should not be—but it happened.

Wendy had also paid a price by enduring suspicion, rejection, jealousy, uncertainty, anger and turmoil in return for membership in her spiritual family. She was terrified that the problems between Kitty and me were to be the end of her. She had not trusted Kitty, and God had not exactly protected her all her life. On this holiday our doors again locked her out, but this time she was not alone. Wendy spent part of Christmas Day with Marie and her family.

Later in the day Kitty and our sons went with me to Rose's house for the symbolic Christmas birthday meal. We were all a bit strained. No one else came this year. Spiritual family had left Rose more lonely than she had ever thought possible. The turmoil at church and at my office had cost her many of her friends, and she had been blamed for the trouble in my marriage. The absence of people in the room spoke almost more than we did.

On New Year's Day I took the kids cross-country skiing, an activity that was beyond Kitty's ability since her hysterectomy. I came home to find my wife gone. A fire blazed in our fireplace, but in Kitty's place and body sat a little girl. When I walked in, she looked up at me sadly and said, "I built the fire myself. I can do it myself because you never spend time with me."

She ran to the bedroom to hide from "those boys" who came in the door just then.

At bedtime the little girl asked where she should sleep because it was "naughty" to sleep with strange men. Eventually she went to sleep in our bed. She slept; I did not.

The next morning Kitty woke up disoriented and upset. She could not remember the day before or the little girl. She called her counselor and told me this was the end of the line. Ever since we had met with Tom, she had been praying and had heard nothing from God in all this time. While I claimed to have daughters, grown women were not little girls. Frankly, she was through. Either God was going to tell her something or she was walking out.

Together we decided to pray and fast until we heard an answer.

After a few days Kitty got sick and needed to start eating. I kept fasting. Although I am six feet three inches tall, my weight fell to 145 pounds, which spawned rumors that I had AIDS. God stayed silent.

First Light

Then Kitty heard from God. The message on my answering machine at work said, "Hurry home! God has spoken." In my spirit I knew this was it. I drank my first bit of fruit juice and headed for the car. It was early evening, February 6.

Kitty sat silently after handing me this note:

Dear Jim,
Praise God, He spoke to me. I finally heard what He is saying.

First of all I asked why it took so long. God told me certain things had to happen first and not to blame myself. God needed to give me a taste of severe pain to be able to draw me close enough to reach me.

What God told me then was that your being a spiritual father was what He had planned. I am to trust you and even reach out to our spiritual family, too. God will teach us together what that means, but some of the little things that upset me are not, in the overall plan, very important. I am to keep my eyes focused on Jesus.

He also told me that our spiritual family would continue to grow. You and I will be bound tightly together in rest and support, but not always will our hearts be in the same direction. God has planted a small seed of interest in my heart for sign language; it will be my focus.

God gave me a new heart some time ago, and the pain He has given me recently is a taste of the pain He suffers when we are distracted and He wants to spend time with us. I have looked to you for my strength and security, but God has broken us down and shown me a soft, tender man—the man he has made you. I need to get my strength and security from God—not drain you. I can also have an important role in God's Kingdom and service by passing some of the strength from Him to you. God is in the process of making me a sweet fragrance and a sparkling jewel. Remember how you used to talk about my sparkly eyes? They will return!

I am sorry for all the pain I have taken you through. Since we are united as one, it is hard for one to hurt and not affect the other.

My job now, God said, was to change the position with others from what it has been. I am to state boldly to all that I have heard from God and that He has declared you are a spiritual father—in stronger ways for some than others. He said to watch Him work. I will begin my work promptly as I am sent on God's service.

Loving you so dearly,
Kitty

I cried. Kitty cried. We went to bed early and slept better than we had in years.

A few days later there was a fire burning in the fireplace and the little girl was back.

"Who are you, mister? Why don't you like me? See, I built a fire. I can do it myself."

"I do like you, but I don't know you very well," I answered. "Have you ever met Jane?"

"I've seen her, but I've never talked to her," the little girl said.

"Let's call her and she can answer your questions about me."

She picked up the phone and a doll. I left them on the phone and went to the living room.

The mountains were barely silhouetted against the night sky. I turned off the light and felt the wooden dowels of the high-backed chair press along my spine. The oak-grained Formica tabletop felt cold on my elbows. The fire offered a faint warmth from across the room.

Slowly a picture came into focus. It shook me to my core. I saw a little blonde girl wandering the darkened halls with her dolly. No one came when she called. Whatever she did, she did alone. Now, after all these years, the little girl was back. She and her dolly were down my hall talking on my phone.

What chilled me to the bone was realizing that the red dragon had used Christian missions to produce the same personality damage that satanic cults produce. Good intentions plus fear had led to the same end as bad intentions. The road between us and them was not as long as I supposed.

As I stared at the lights from the transmitter towers on Mount Wilson, more of the story dawned. The pixie-haired girl had cried to empty arms but had not cried to empty skies. The glow of the fire carried into our lives by Rose, and fanned into bright flames by Wendy, had illuminated the darkest corners of our lives. Together they had helped find little Kitty, and Kitty in turn had helped me reach them. God was as determined to heal the results of the garbage disposal as He was the vacuum cleaner. Redemption had come to my house.

After a while Kitty wandered out into the living room.

"When did you get home?" she asked.

New Identities

That year was a great improvement from the last few. Father's Day came, and this time copies of my book on fathers and sons were passed out to every father in our church of three thousand. Offers to teach and write books reappeared, and I was asked to supervise again. Jamie dropped out of high school and went to college. Kitty also went to college and studied sign language.

All of us began to collect a spiritual family. Kitty found brothers and sisters as well as children. Jamie and Rami found spiritual parents and a brother at the Birkey house. Simon Birkey became Jamie's roommate at college. Rose also developed brothers, sisters and children. She was constantly in search of ways to share what she had experienced. Wendy found brothers and sisters among Christian teachers at the school where she was teaching, and poured her life into her students.

Kitty stayed volatile for a year and a half after hearing from God until she began taking a newly discovered medication for depression.[1] Prior to that she was easily overwhelmed and could not participate in spiritual family activities without becoming, angry, jealous, afraid or hurt. Within a month on the medication, she was able to do the things she purposed to do. Within six months she was consistently staying an adult. For the first time in more than three years, I had a wife and she had a life.

Kitty smiled and laughed. We started camping again and bringing Rose, Wendy and her students, our friends and even dogs along. Kitty worked with the deaf and blind. She took trips with Rose. With the help of her prayer partner Bonnie Jakeway, she even started to like Wendy a little. Actually, she liked Wendy more than she wanted to admit. For Kitty, the real pain came from seeing daughters who were loved and parents who came when they were called.

A few months before she started the medication, Kitty began reading in earnest about spiritual mothering. Not long after that, I introduced her to a young woman named Evelyne, who began almost immediately calling Kitty "Mom." What followed was a joyful, meaningful time for both of them as Kitty discovered that her mothering extended to daughters. Not long after, Rose also became a spiritual daughter for her. Both daughters responded with dramatic growth.

Evelyne soon became a spiritual child for both of us. Kitty and I enjoyed working together for the first time. This smooth start did not preclude severe storms to follow. We are told by St. Mark that when the disciples obeyed Jesus' order to take their boat across the lake, a furious squall came up and the boat nearly sank (see Mark 4:37). With Kitty and me at times, the Lord seemed to be as asleep as He had been in the disciples' boat—but that is another book.

While Kitty and I now bailed and sailed together, we needed more family than ourselves. Our sons had their own lives well underway, so we turned again to the spiritual community. Kathy Dillman, who rented a room from us, was a major part. When spiritual family was absent, we were slammed around. With community participation, tempests were livable. We expect it will always be this way.

Kitty was now doing the impossible without demanding control. "I tried to control you," she told me one day, "because you were easier to control than my emotions." We reflected for a time on how much pain and pathology was hidden in our lives before redemption came to our house. Were it not for our love for each other, we would not have gone through the pain. Neither would the others.

309

Redemption showed me that I could and did abandon my wife and children at crucial times. The fear of women's anger that led to my Father's Day meltdown had ruled my life. That pain made me a little boy who ran away and climbed a tree to hide. My love made no one better. Redemption revealed in me an identity that was all split up to match the context and differed depending on who was around me. Redemption's surprise was that God used me just that way.

Redemption also used Kitty in her distress. It is no surprise that through the weakness of others, redemption reached my house.

After the Fire

Christmas was again approaching. For the first time Kitty and I were planning for our whole family—biological and spiritual—to join together. Jamie would be home from college and was talking about an engagement. I was invited to a convocation on sexual abuse in Texas the week before Christmas. Even though it was our anniversary, Kitty thought I should go. She could care for the family while I was gone, she said. So I left without misgivings, prepared to speak on community-based treatment for survivors of severe abuse.

Flying both ways and rooming with Dr. Charles Kraft built the relationship behind the "Guidelines for Prayer Teams" in the appendix of this book. Barbara Moon, who wrote *A Bridge of Love*,[2] taught eloquently on living in community with survivors. David and Carol Brown made me feel warm just being in the same room with them. It was a good trip.

Chuck Kraft, who lives nearby, dropped me off on his way home from the airport. As I entered the house, everyone was in Rami's room. Kitty was grinning. There on Rami's bed, curled between him and Wendy, was a floppy-eared puppy.

Kitty's eyes fairly sparkled. "We got Wendy a puppy."

The story bubbled out among giggles and delight.

"Free!"

"Even better than on sale!"

"He's three-quarters golden retriever," announced Wendy, "and one-quarter Brittany spaniel. I want to call him Cacey—which means watchful."

Cacey it was.

Christmas Eve Rose went to stay with her children. Her biological family was being reunited with her spiritual one. At our house the tree flashed to the carols on the stereo. All our mattresses were arranged on the living room floor in preparation for a night by the fire with music and lights. Rami and I wrestled while Jamie watched. In the morning he would fly up with a ring to surprise Stacey, and perhaps he felt too mature for the fracas. I think he was afraid he would get pinned.

Kitty wrapped the last few presents while the yule log crackled. Friends dropped by with gifts and greetings. We had oranges with candy canes for straws. Kathy Dillman and her family joined us for Santa's arrival complete with jingle bells.

Eventually Kitty and I kissed everyone goodnight and climbed under the covers. She snuggled up next to me, waiting for the children to fall asleep so we could load the Christmas stockings. As usual I would watch the fire and add logs should it threaten to go out during the night. This year's yule log promised to be a good one. In fact, just getting it into the fireplace had taken quite some work.

The family lay in a row across the middle of the room. I wondered if Jamie would carry on the tradition when he got married. My gaze moved from him to Rami, whose six-foot swimmer's frame left arms and legs protruding everywhere while he slept. Next to him two yellow heads poked out together from under the covers. The golden-haired girl smiled and hugged her reddish-gold puppy. The cheery fire added flickering highlights to their hair. She reached across for my hand and fell asleep. Each time the fire needed tending, she and the puppy were there all tussled up together.

I smiled at Kitty. She wrapped her arms around me and whispered dreamily, "Merry Christmas."

EPILOGUE

We have not finished until we answer the question "Who is my family?"

At that a man stood up to test him saying, "Rabbi, who is my family?"
And he answered saying, "A child went down from Jerusalem to Jericho and fell. . . ."

APPENDIX OF GUIDELINES

Guidelines for Community Life

- Build joy.
- Practice grace with truth.
- Seek integrity for everyone.
- Recognize in each individual heart the characteristics of Jesus.
- Challenge cultural rules or assumptions about bonds and relationships with the requirements of Christ.
- Constantly explain the meaning of any departures from cultural norms. If you do something differently from what your church or community might expect or understand, try to explain why.
- Allow all members to receive and give life.
- Use affection as the major deterrent to sexual sin.
- Have a clear responsibility structure for nurture.
- Allow redemption to disrupt your structure.
- Leave room for transformation in your procedures and organizational structures.
- Encourage freedom for all members to come and go without breaking bonds.
- Always lend power to the weakest.
- Be aware that who is the weakest is constantly changing as you lend power.
- Let people feel upset.
- Return to joy ("We are glad to be together").
- Support others so they can bear their feelings and not be controlled or try to control others with them.
- Don't let the most anxious person take the lead or control.
- Operate with the understanding that all community members are dangerous.
- Prevent anyone from being a predator by watching those who do not admit or take responsibility for their own destructiveness. (Seduction is as destructive as rape, and withholding love as destructive as assault.)

- In a crisis remind others tirelessly of the objectives—that is, to establish our true identities.
- Watch for spiritually accelerated or intensified conflict and take spiritual steps to stop it.
- Don't expect survivors to know how to work through conflicts with each other for a *long* time.
- Admonish only those who have forgotten what they are able to put into practice. Weakness is real. Carry burdens for those who cannot. Constantly encourage the fainthearted.
- Be very patient with everyone.
- Intercede often.

Guidelines for Community-Based Counseling (from the LIFE Model)

E. James Wilder, Ph.D., and James G. Friesen, Ph.D.

Community-based care seeks to change the structure and identity of both the individual and the community in order that both may be redeemed.

1. Love is more important than recovery. Healing is more important than pain reduction. Pain reduction is more important than proving faith, hope or independence.
2. Carefully assess the severity of each problem.
   Catalogue the two types of trauma involved for each person:
   Type-A trauma: **A**bsence of necessary good things
   Type-B trauma: **B**ad (evil) done to him or her
   Record the age of onset for each trauma. (The younger the person when it occurred, the more severe it is.)
   Discover the positions of trust and number of perpetrators.
   Record the amount of isolation, distrust and loss.
   Examine the person's ability and methods for forming attachments (bonds).
   Rate his or her overall maturity level and plan your care accordingly.
   Prayerfully assess deliverance, healing and adoption needs.
   Note the degree of overlap between the person's biological and spiritual families.
3. Provide clear community structure in all matters of responsibility. Appoint one elder to oversee and coordinate the nurture of each deeply wounded person, including:
   Advances by prayer teams
   Trauma team decontamination efforts
   Bonding and family life
   Meeting of needs
   Work-rest-play recovery cycle balance

4. Undertake only the level of change for which you have available resources and Holy Spirit guidance. Evaluate resources by seeing which of the following are true:

   Individual

   Has good personal resources (see "Guidelines for Assessing Resources," p. 326).

   Desires to seek healing for wounded parts.

   Accepts the saving presence of God in his or her life.

   Regularly strengthens and utilizes healthy parts.

   Therapist

   Desires to have God in the center of his or her life.

   Does not base his or her identity on roles, thus artificially separating life in and out of therapy. (Prayer and worship belong in both places.)

   Considers dividedness a specialty area and seeks ongoing training.

   Is part of a team for consultation, education and support.

   Has a clearly defined relationship or bond with the client (as coach or supplemental, stand-in or replacement parent) and lives it out with awareness and integrity.

   Is involved regularly with key people in the client's life.

   Community

   Seeks redemption and develops maturity.

   Sends an elder or "therapy partner" to attend therapy/prayer sessions with client regularly.

   Includes the wounded on the giving end of the ongoing ministry of the local church, utilizing their gifts without putting them prematurely in leadership.

   Is familiar with and accepts dissociation, spiritual family and identity change at the highest levels of the local church.

   Emphasizes members' love for one another and commitment to meet one another's needs.

   Values and works toward freedom from fear, especially fear of pain.

   Living environment

   Is safe and non-triggering.

   Provides house partners who are understanding and involved in recovery but not rescuing or codependent.

   Has antidepressant medications available in case of prolonged stress.

5. Don't let anyone go through counseling alone, if possible. No "stranger, widow or orphan" is sent for counseling by himself or herself. Privacy is not the highest priority.

6. Seek identity change, not role change.

7. Allow, encourage and train *all* community members to minister redemption. The highest must be willing to receive from the lowest.

8. Let the restoration work be done by a group resembling the abuser team— that is, a woman to restore the damage done by a woman, a man for a man, and a group for a group.

9. Consider all options, including medication, anointing, secular programs, law enforcement, consultation, radical personal reorientation and perseverance.

10. Remember that our goal is to receive and give life, not to produce recovery. A person needs to have a life more than he or she needs therapy or ministry. Recovery is a side effect of life-giving, not its final goal.

Steps for Including the Weak and Wounded

E. James Wilder, Ph.D., and James G. Friesen, Ph.D.

Churches can provide enrichment programs for members who are developing redemptive relationships with weak, wounded and immature people, like cult survivors, who need more than individual counseling. Spiritual children need a program designed to help them receive and give life within the church family. When the program is designed only to give life to the weak and wounded, they do not benefit much and neither does the church.

1. Church leadership must be prepared.
   United support for the program must include the senior pastor. Support means inclusion in the church budget.
   There must be willingness on the part of leaders and mature members to invest the time needed to oversee the process.
2. Church membership must be prepared.
   Several members must understand the benefits of a Christian framework for trauma recovery.
   Volunteers must be found with the gifts to run the program.
   Necessary training must be provided for volunteers.
   Intercessory prayer teams must be in place and operating.
   The church must desire and practice spiritual adoption for all.
3. The wounded (cult survivors particularly) must be prepared.
   Badly traumatized people must have individually guided counseling beyond that provided by the community.
   Prayerful companions (spiritual family) must be bonded to each survivor.
   The survivors must endeavor to stay on their jobs, in school or providing service elsewhere in order to continue functioning.
4. Associated therapists must be prepared.
   Crisis plans must be prepared.
   A working understanding between therapist and community leaders is needed.
5. Church facilities and resources must be prepared.
   A library of books and tapes is needed.
   There must be an environment safe from unexpected intruders, from sharp or dangerous objects and from hazards for children.
   Music and materials for worship and expression must be provided for the immature and wounded.
6. A program must be developed.

C.A.R.E. describes a church-based program in its book *Care-Giving: The Cornerstone of Healing*. This book has many guidelines, questionnaires and instructions. C.A.R.E. (3069 S. M–37, Baldwin, MI 49304, (616) 745–0500) will visit churches and develop programs.

KBJ Solutions describes a small, support group–sized program in its book *A Community of Healing* (P.O. Box 20735, Knoxville, TN 37940, (423) 577-4279).

Model A. This model assumes that church members have a certain familiarity and comfort with traumatized people. Such churches often have high numbers of trauma survivors on the church or pastoral staff (spouses included). The volunteer leaders are usually quite gifted. This multitrack program sets aside two-hour blocks of time on two or more days of the week during which survivors and their prayerful companions may gather for:

Group praise and worship

Reading, listening to tapes and contributing to the library

Developing a prayer life

Growth-oriented sharing groups

Experiencing the presence of God

Soaking prayer for memories

Community lectures (perhaps twice a month) for partners, friends and supporters

Playtime for spontaneous expression without fear

Model T. This is a model based on heavy training in lay counseling skills for church members. This training is usually carried out by professional counselors or well-trained pastoral care staffs. Church members are trained for two years in weekly seminars covering prayer, healing, deliverance and a wide range of situations designed to enrich the whole church. These lay counselors extend the reach of pastoral care by providing the intimate nurture and oversight of each survivor while directing serious problems for timely help from better trained counselors.

Simple model. Prayer and praise are the components of this model. Church members and survivors meet twice during the week in four-hour blocks of time. The first block is for prayer, during which the survivors' lives are "soaked" in prayer. The second block is for praise. Caring people are available to meet and teach young personalities about prayer and praise. They will take upset people aside to teach and comfort them until they can rejoin the rest of the group. One church attempted to add discipleship to this model but it did not work. Play, however, can be added.

7. Establish a responsibility structure.

Pastor's responsibilities

Spiritual covering

Prayer support of therapists, ministry teams, survivors

Validating the condition and needs of the weak and wounded

Distributing helpers as needed

Discovering and developing spiritual gifts

317

Encouraging a spirit and vision for adoption in the spiritual family

Therapist's responsibilities

Teaching on bonding and the removal of fear bonds

Crisis interventions

Educating clients, support people, church and family members in trauma recovery

Guiding the trauma team

Helping set boundaries

Finding their own prayer support base and network

Community member's responsibilities

Assisting in tasks of daily living (e.g., childcare, transportation, safety)

Intercessory prayer for survivor, pastor, therapist, prayer team

Maintaining the spiritual health of the prayer team

Explaining and advocating the ministry to the church

Learning to minister

Learning to set boundaries for themselves and for the weak and wounded that give life

Networking with other ministries

Carrying the financial responsibility in partnership with the church

Responsibilities for weak, wounded spiritual children

Commitment to truth

Encouraging the strong, living parts of themselves

Giving what they have received

Working on their own maturity

Guidelines for Prayer Teams (from the *LIFE* Model)

E. James Wilder, Ph.D., and Charles H. Kraft, B.D., Ph.D.

Praying in teams is advisable for several reasons. Since the Holy Spirit works differently through different people, a team makes available a multiplicity of gifts. This provides greater insight, experience, power and ability to express love. Teams function well to serve at least four purposes: intercession; prayer support (soaking in prayer); physical and/or emotional healing; and deliverance. Any given ministry team may involve more than one of these functions.

Care of the Prayer Ministry

Whatever the purpose of the team, it is important to avoid confusion by having one person in charge. For intercession or prayer support, the team can consist of many people. Though the leader guides the session, the usual process allows individuals to lead as they feel prompted by the Holy Spirit.

Healing and deliverance teams need to be limited in size and be run with a firm hand to avoid confusing the recipient. Teams of three or four are usually best.

Though the leader may ask others for input or allow others to take the lead, the recipient should have to focus on only one person at a time.

It is important, however, to give opportunity for input from the members of the team. One approach that allows everyone to participate in a nonintrusive way is to have team members write down on slips of paper any insights that come to them during the session, and place them where the leader can refer to them easily as he or she works with the recipient.

Intercessors are those gifted in tackling a problem with tenacity, as Abraham did when he begged God to refrain from destroying Sodom (see Genesis 18:20–33). As intercessors pray they typically hear from God, through words or pictures, how He wants them to pray. They are also often given prophetic insight into how their prayers will be answered. Support pray-ers may have less specific gifting but be no less tenacious in dealing with an issue in prayer. Both kinds of prayer teams are important to healing and deliverance ministries. Intercessors should be alerted to pray ahead of time for ministry sessions. Support pray-ers, many of whom may be intercessors, should be praying before, during and after healing and deliverance ministry takes place.

Healing and deliverance teams should be led by persons with demonstrated gifts in these areas. Leaders should possess personal maturity in addition to their gifting, which allows them to lead responsibly. Others on the team may have demonstrated support gifting or may have the gifting necessary to lead healing teams, but lack experience. The most valuable gifts are those that enable the person to gain insight from the Holy Spirit concerning the recipient and how best to approach problems. Often intercessors and other pray-ers are good support personnel on healing and deliverance teams. They usually do not know whether they have specific ministry gifts until they participate several times on such teams.

Care of the Prayer Team

An important function of any ministry team, whether focused on healing or prayer, is providing an example to those in need. First, those responsible for ministry should be exemplary in their Christian walks. They should model compassion to those in need and teach others how to minister by their example. Often those who receive prayer ministry become the most effective in ministering to others because they are able to follow the example of those whom God used to free them.

In the process of ministry, God also attends to those who do the ministry. He brings much blessing and maturity through the spiritual, emotional and physical closeness that teams develop. He also blesses in mighty ways through the consciousness that what we do at the human level is impossible without the love and empowerment of the Holy Spirit. Ministry teams receive blessing beyond measure through constant involvement in doing things they know they cannot do, unless the Holy Spirit is there to provide the insight and power.

The fact that we cannot do such ministry without the Holy Spirit teaches us that we dare not become proud of our own abilities. We must go into every session humbly and prayerfully, with full knowledge that we work with a Senior Partner who is God Himself. We need to examine our attitudes and impressions constantly, then, lest we be guilty of pride and self-confidence rather than the humility and God-confidence that God can bless. In this way we do not mistake our agenda for God's, or use God's words to take control ourselves. We do not use God's work as a way to avoid our own problems, or prayer as a way to avoid responsibility for our actions or passivity. We do not attempt to prove our faith and hope in God at someone else's expense. Loving action has precedence over our faith and hope. And remember, God always wraps His power in love. So should we.

Care of the Recipient

Ministry is guided by three factors: Scripture, the Holy Spirit and loving relationships. It is essential to have someone present with the ministry team who can function as a spiritual parent to the recipient. This person can function both during and after ministry to support and advise the recipient as he or she would his own child. This helps prevent excesses and abuses of personal and spiritual power.

Intercessors can be especially helpful to those on healing teams by focusing their prayers on areas of a recipient's weakness or demonization. As we battle spiritual powers, those who can strengthen the recipient in spiritual ways are crucial to the healing that God wants to bring about. Often the Lord shows intercessors and support pray-ers facts about the person or battle that are to be prayed about but not shared with the recipient. God often gives counsel and Scripture portions that *are* to be shared to strengthen both pray-ers and those receiving ministry.

Prolonged "soaking prayer" by support prayer teams serves many important functions. Prior to healing and deliverance ministry, it softens up enemy defenses. During ministry it weakens the enemy and strengthens the recipient and team. Prayer also strengthens everyone between sessions. Often God gives encouraging words and Scriptures to these pray-ers to be passed along to other participants. In addition to its strengthening function, soaking prayer is particularly helpful for participants in the process of identity transformation. They experience themselves differently when soaked in prayer in the presence of God. In this way they produce constructive habits to replace those that kept them in bondage.

The wounded need both healing and support. The purpose of healing and deliverance teams is to open and explore wounds that are often very deep. Members of prayer teams as well as spiritual family members, then, are to provide support for the person undergoing spiritual surgery. It is a joint effort between the various team members, the community and the Holy Spirit to bring the recipient to freedom and a new course for life.

Guidelines for Spiritual Adoptions (from the *LIFE* Model)

E. James Wilder, Ph.D., and Rick Koepcke, M.A., M.F.C.C.

Spiritual adoption is not a technique; it is an eternal family bond that changes the family structure permanently for parent, adopted child, brother or sister, and for other family members. The nature of this bond will profoundly and permanently alter the personalities and character of both participants. This bond can be created only by God and must be undertaken only under the guidance of the Holy Spirit by those prepared to receive family members. Spiritual adoption is not a method to promote recovery (as recovery may or may not follow) but is intrinsic to normal spiritual growth. Spiritual adoption affects every level of the community and family and is not without pain.

Spiritual parenting with very wounded children is like rearing an abused child. Attention must be paid to the two types of trauma these children have suffered.

Guidelines for Spiritual Adoptions

Type-A trauma arises from the absence of necessary love and care. This produces feelings of abandonment, rejection, despair, loneliness, loss, depression and grief. These feelings remain frozen inside the child/adult and thaw in the presence of love. Comfort, care and love bring out the pain very quickly. New spiritual parents commonly assume that more love will make the pain go away. Instead it thaws more pain, making their child feel more abandoned, rejected and unloved. Immature people (often called codependent) may break bonds at this point, noting correctly that the more they care, the worse it gets. Supportive therapies, counseling and prayer ministries may yield the same result. It requires the greatest care, patience, restraint and self-control (in other words, maturity) to avoid "thawing" adopted children too quickly. Spiritual parents are careful because they will share this child's pains the rest of their lives.

Type-B trauma refers to the bad things that have happened. Spiritual adoption brings with it the responsibility to stop damage that is continuing at either a physical or a spiritual level. It also requires parents to seek the healing, redemption and restoration of damaged areas. While adoption helps prevent and restore type-B trauma, restoration is often incomplete and always depends on God. The primary responsibility in adoption is to grow bonds of love, which bring maturity and fruit.

Authenticity of Adoption

1. Parents must know why they want to adopt. Whose idea was it—yours, the adoptee's or the Holy Spirit's? It is always and only God who reveals our relationships in the spiritual family and develops awareness in our hearts of what He has already done.
2. Spiritual parenting is not role play. A parent is a parent in all situations and at all times. A parenting relationship that exists only in certain situations is a potentially dangerous fantasy role play. Unlike role play, adoptions are limited by maturity, capacity and need rather than by context-specific roles.
3. Even when adoption is ordained by God, we cannot make it work. Unless the Lord builds the house, they labor in vain who build it.
4. Spiritual adoption is not based on outcome. Love will not repair most damage and healing may not remove it.
5. God selects parents with sufficient maturity. Elders, especially at the "empty nest" point in life, make the best spiritual parents.

Spiritual Parenting Requirements

1. Parents must be aware of what a child needs from Mother, Father, siblings and community. Each parent must determine the nature of his or her own bond ("I am Mother" or "I am Father"). If at all possible, don't be a single parent.
2. Follow "Guidelines for Redemptive Bonding" in the following section.
3. Parents must be able to withstand and function in painful situations when the pain may never entirely be removed.
4. Parents are adopting a "high-need" child with exceptional problems and demands. The task will require more time, energy, resources and care than having a nontraumatized child of the same emotional age.
5. Parents must be aware of the developmental age or ages of the person they are adopting and match their efforts with the level of development.

Appendix of Guidelines

6. Allow for adoptions to match the adoptee's maturity and needs. Some people need only a father or mother in certain areas of their lives, while others have needed a complete family from infancy.
7. Spiritual parents help their children become strong enough to leave them and come and go without fear.

Growth for Spiritual Parents

1. Parents must recognize gaps in their own development and know where they are likely to get stuck reparenting. Parents must find healing for themselves and provide other supplemental parents for the adopted child.
2. Adoptive parents must learn to love and honor the individual's abusive natural parents without condoning any evil behavior.
3. Parents must recognize that spiritual parenting is a redemptive process for themselves. This is much of the joy of reparenting.
4. Adoptive parents of abused children must be willing to show their own faults and dangers early in the relationship; otherwise the adoptees will waste time looking for them and feel betrayed when they find their parents' dangerous points.

Sons and Daughters

1. Adopted children must choose progressively to honor and submit to their new parents out of love.
2. Adopted children must look to see what God is doing with the people He gives them. They should not be surprised when their adoptive parents do not fill the role in the ways they expect.
3. Spiritual bonds are different than biological family bonds. Adopted children must not expect the natural family (biological relatives) of their new parents to acknowledge a spiritual relationship with them.
4. Spiritual adoption helps give adopted children the strength to feel their pain and let their old hopes die. They will need help taking this slowly. Until they are healed, it will hurt more, not less, to be adopted.

Community Support

1. Parents must be able to identify and tell others what they *cherish* about this child.
2. Parents must introduce their adopted children slowly but extensively into their community and be prepared to explain and interpret for others the nature of their relationship. They should expect discomfort, doubt, disbelief and censure.
3. One central goal is complete adoption by the whole community—parents, siblings, relatives and church.
4. Parents must seek to redeem everything.

Spiritual Siblings

1. Brother-to-brother, sister-to-sister and brother-to-sister bonds need to be created by Christ and brought to life by the Holy Spirit. We cannot simply create them when we want to.

2. Brothers and sisters must introduce each other to their families and communities. They will need to explain their spiritual relationships to others.
3. Adopted siblings recognize their relationships as permanent and eternal. They are prepared to work on differences, hurts and disappointments without breaking bonds.
4. Adopted siblings discover and encourage one another to live out of the hearts that Jesus gave them.
5. Adopted siblings do well to study the "Guidelines for Redemptive Bonding" (following).

Guidelines for Redemptive Bonding

1. Begin by accepting the fear bonds as your first connection; it is usually all the survivor knows.
2. Avoid all intensity or trauma bonding by staying calm during intense emotion, then moving close after the intensity has started to subside slightly.
3. Add love bonds to fear bonds until the fear bonds can be dropped.
4. Form bonds according to the structure of the spiritual community. If you will be a parent, form parental bonds; if you will be a sibling, form sibling bonds; if you will be an adopted child, form child bonds.
5. Be clear about the kind of bond you are forming—parent-child or sibling-sibling.
6. Expect suffering and pain. The stronger the bond, the more pain it will probably have to sustain.
7. Remember, bonds form best during hard times.
8. Review your objectives and the nature of your bond and speak them often.
9. Admit failures but do not break bonds.
10. Always build toward *strong, permanent* bonds.
11. Establish your bond through public ceremony or confession with symbols and stories.
12. Expect rejection, misunderstanding, criticism, judgment, doubt, suspicion, hostility, abandonment and distancing from others, especially when things get worse and you could really use some help, understanding and support. Use this time to purify your bonds and motives and to interpret clearly the bond to the person you are bonding with, as well as with the skeptics. Be very patient with them all.
13. Teach others how to form love bonds. There are two ways:
    a. *Building joy.* Joy produces love bonds when people are genuinely glad to be together. The main sources of joy are nonverbal—a face that lights up to see us and a warm tone of voice. Touch is third, but it may have the opposite results with sexually abused people.
    b. *Returning to joy.* Meeting people in their unhappy feelings, sharing these feelings and letting the people know you are still glad to know them returns them to joy. The six biggest negative feelings are sadness, anger, terror, shame, disgust and hopeless despair.
14. Characteristics of a healthy bond are:
    a. It grows stronger by moving closer and moving apart.
    b. It grows stronger by sharing positive and negative emotions.
    c. It helps all parties feel stable and act like themselves.

d. It provides freedom and connection.

e. It stretches limits and capacities slightly to promote growth.

Guidelines for Identity Change

Characteristics of All Identity Change

1. Insight alone will not transform identities.
2. Identity change is a crisis experience. It is self-limiting in duration. It is not a growth experience.
3. No one can understand his or her new identity ahead of time.
4. Identity change requires the relinquishing of an old identity *before* finding a new one. Consequently it is terrifying for those who lack trust.
5. Identity change cannot be accomplished by any person alone. At best, people can disintegrate and wait to see what happens.
6. New identities are established by the community-of-the-self.

DESIRABLE CHARACTERISTICS IN A NEW IDENTITY

1. A new identity must be greater (more inclusive) than the previous one in order to be helpful.
2. The ideal identity is an accurate one that fits the person rather than idealizing him or her.
3. Most identities are too positive when it comes to abilities and too negative when it comes to value.

IMPORTANT DISTINCTIONS

1. Distinguish carefully between identity transformation (which requires and precipitates a crisis of death) and growth issues (which require identity repair and nurture).
2. It is helpful to distinguish two kinds of identity change. The first occurs naturally at the transformation points in normal human maturity. At these transitions our younger identities die and we move on to a new stage of life (for example, we become adults instead of children). The second kind of transformation is redemptive or corrective. These allow a defective identity to die in favor of a new and more accurate one.
3. Distinguish carefully between developmental arrests caused by trauma and those caused by missing the normal identity change points. A male may have failed to become a man by age 35, for example, because of extensive abuse when he was nine (trauma) or because, from age thirteen on, he has not found anyone to help him through the transformation from boy to man. Both require help, but the traumatized individual requires healing as well.

Characteristics of Normal Identity Change in Human Maturity

1. Transformation can occur naturally at birth, weaning, puberty, parenthood, when children leave home, and death.

324

2. Transformation can occur when traumas are resolved, allowing normal growth to resume and reach a natural change point.
3. After traumas that stopped development have been resolved, recovery (growth that was suspended) occurs at the rate of about one month for each year. If the trauma happened at age three, for example, and the person is now 23, the twenty years of growing that were missed will take about twenty months once the trauma is resolved.

Steps to Normal Identity Change

1. Maturity of the present identity must be complete.
2. The nature of the identity change must be explained to the applicant—for example, "You will go from girl to woman."
3. Those who understand the nature of the new identity carefully precipitate a symbolic crisis to facilitate a rapid disintegration and reintegration of identity.
4. The new identity must be checked quickly to remove painful "misfits" and be corrected to suit the person. David can say to Saul, for example, that Saul's armor does not fit his kind of warrior.
5. The new identity must be supported and shaped regularly for the first six to twelve months to allow it to become firm and to correct anomalies.
6. The person must grow into his or her new identity through instructed and supported trial and error.

Characteristics of Redemptive or Corrective Identity Change

1. Redemptive identity change is needed when one is separated in some way from part of his or her complete identity. This separation is always painful but often motivated by the individual's desire to avoid a pain-filled part of himself from which he does not know the path back to joy. (Remember, joy means, "This person is glad to be with me here.")
2. When parts of the identity are separated, they are kept apart by pain, which must come out before the parts can be reunited. This pain is created by a lie (or distortion of the true identity in the heart).
3. Most identity change comes after we stop avoiding (or are unable to avoid) pain.
4. After it gets worse, it gets worse. Dying is hard.
5. We cannot face any pain greater than our greatest joy.
6. People who avoid emotional pain will usually not experience transformation no matter what they intend, attempt or promise. It is impossible to return to joy if one has not gone first into the pain.
7. Falling in love is *always* an attempt to change one's own identity. It indicates an identity that is too small for the one falling in love.
8. Obsessions are an attempt to avoid identity disintegration due to the intrusion of some rejected bit of self.
9. Redemptive transformation can occur spiritually at regeneration, deliverance, inner healing and infilling by the Holy Spirit, and at times of crisis, failure or surrender (death).
10. Many identity changes succeed in changing only a portion of the person, leaving other portions unchanged and still separated. This produces "some-

times true" identities that are true when they are true and not when they are not. Those who love people with partially transformed identities are not sure what to believe or trust. This condition is common.

11. During a corrective identity change, a person will disintegrate to the functional age at which his or her personality distortion (lie) occurred. This disintegration is called regression. Regression is not present in the identity changes of normal human maturity.

12. During regression people temporarily lose the effective use of abilities they acquired at later ages. This loss is most crucial if they drop below age five, when logical filtering of verbal statements is acquired. This *logical filtering crossover point* is reached during regressions that go younger than age five. At that point people begin to suspend their own judgment and let others tell them who they are.

Once past this crossover point, extreme accuracy of perception and speech is required. Above it, a guess that is partly right will usually help someone. Below the crossover point, an observation that is only partly wrong will hurt the person. In talking to someone who has not begun to disintegrate about his or her anger, for example, it is helpful to suggest that his failure to call home might be caused by anger at his father, even though this is only twenty percent of the reason. Once below the regression crossover point where logical filtering stops, however, the person will take such a statement as a terrible distortion of his identity. Even a description that is 98 percent true will produce a sense of being hurt. Friendships, especially among survivors, often fall apart at just this point.

Since some people live chronically below the five-year-old logical filtering point, they take all statements they hear from others as definitions of themselves. These people suffer terribly during sermons, feeling alternately horrible about themselves or very misunderstood by the preacher. They are unable to apply any partially correct observations correctly; instead they feel hurt and misunderstood.

We can drink orange juice because our digestion filters it into nutrients and keeps out what we cannot handle. If we transfused orange juice directly into our bloodstreams, we would cause great harm. For people who disintegrate to pre-five levels, we must "transfuse" them with only the purest truth about their identities until they can filter again for themselves. The main components of this truth are that they are greatly loved, that we share their pain and that we are still delighted to be with them.

Guidelines for Assessing Resources

1. *Health.* Overall physical health sets limits on energy available for recovery. Frequent back surgery, being in a wheelchair or battling cancer or chronic fibromyalgia syndrome (FMS), for example, diverts time, energy, relationship demands and money from recovery.

2. *Education and intelligence.* Intelligent and creative people can use these traits to help recover, as they used them to avoid some of the impact of their abuse. The better their education, the more they will be able to use ideas to help guide their recovery. Those who lack these resources must

326

learn from experience and example—both of which require far more time and personal investment.

3. *Job skills and employment.* Adequate employment meets many social, self-esteem, security and motivational needs. Those who have no work, or those with work that depletes and exhausts them, or those who work under threats and contempt or harassment, will be far more unsatisfied and desperate and prone to crisis.

4. *Positive life experiences.* For an individual to experience a safe place, to know someone he or she can trust, to be respected, to have someone take him or her seriously, and many other positive life experiences, improve his or her rate of recovery.

5. *Capacity for joy.* The individual's capacity to experience joy, to be enjoyed and to enjoy others, reflects the size of his or her joyful identity. Someone will not be able to handle pain greater than his or her capacity for joy.

6. *Maturity.* Does the person function at an infant, child, adult, parent or elder level of maturity? Does it vary under stress? Here are three major indicators of maturity: First, a person feels more satisfied when he or she takes care of himself than when others take care of him; second, he uses information to correct his feelings rather than using his feelings to rearrange and interpret information; and, third, he believes and acts as though two or more people can be loved and cared for at the same time.

7. *Income, finances and insurance.* Counseling, medical care and safe housing are all improved by having sufficient financial resources.

8. *Shelter and safety.* Those who depend on abusive people for shelter or who are subject to harassment, abduction, crime and attack make very limited progress. Shelter should be safe and provide an environment of safe people.

9. *Recovery time.* Those who can take time off in a safe place where they do not have to take care of themselves for a few hours or days after discovery and treatment for traumatic memories can grieve and be healed of many more wounds in a given time period.

10. *Friends.* Having someone who enjoys you and takes you out to play after the grief is done, or who stands by in the hour of crisis, enables you to use your energy to face the pain instead of simply coping with the present or fears of the future.

11. *Spiritual/personal.* Those having a personal relationship with God and knowledge and confidence in His care face the unknown with more assurance. They also do better when they feel powerless and out of control and have comfort for their fears and pain. This is a huge factor in recovery.

12. *Spiritual/church community.* In addition to personal faith, the existence of a supportive spiritual family that brings God to the center of healing and community life is crucial. It should include spiritual parents, brothers and sisters, ministry teams, encouragers and those who equip all the others. This stable environment should stand firm in the face of evil and fear, creating a safe nest of love. It should be the source of the ministries of healing, deliverance and adoption.

13. *Personality strengths.* Those with strong personalities and character withstand pain and fear better. Some strengths are harder to see when they emerge as stubbornness, defiance or skepticism. But these strengths helped

the person survive hard experiences and will help them through the even harder experience of recovery.

14. *Family.* The more elements of the family that are intact and supportive of recovery, the better that family will progress. These include adoptive families (spouses and spiritual families), parents, siblings, other relatives and children. The fewer of these that must be lost to the effects of evil, the less grief there will be.

Guidelines for Assessing Resources

Resources	Poor	Fair	Excellent	Need to receive	Have to give
Health		_____	_____		[ ]	[ ]
Education		_____	_____		[ ]	[ ]
Intelligence		_____	_____		[ ]	[ ]
Job skills Employment		_____	_____		[ ]	[ ]
Positive life experiences		_____	_____		[ ]	[ ]
Adequate income		_____	_____		[ ]	[ ]
Adequate shelter		_____	_____		[ ]	[ ]
Safety		_____	_____		[ ]	[ ]
Recovery time		_____	_____		[ ]	[ ]
Friends		_____	_____		[ ]	[ ]
Personal spiritual life		_____	_____		[ ]	[ ]
Personality strengths		_____	_____		[ ]	[ ]
Spiritual community		_____	_____		[ ]	[ ]
Family		_____	_____		[ ]	[ ]
Capacity for joy		_____	_____		[ ]	[ ]

Resources I most need to receive

Resources I most need to give

(Permission granted to reproduce this form for personal use.)

329

NOTES

The Professional Preface

1. Dr. Dallas Willard's term. He is a theologian, scholar, author and professor of philosophy at the University of Southern California.

2. Dr. Charles H. Kraft, professor of anthropology and intercultural communication at Fuller Theological Seminary's School of World Mission. Personal communication.

3. Robert J. Lifton, *The Nazi Doctors: Medical Killing and the Psychology of Genocide* (New York: Basic, 1986).

The Essential Introduction

1. Stanley Hauerwas and William H. Willimon, *Resident Aliens: Life in the Christian Colony* (Nashville: Abingdon, 1989), p. 12.

2. Michael Kelley, *The Burden of God: Studies in Wisdom and Civilization from the Book of Ecclesiastes* (Minneapolis: Contra Mundum, 1993).

3. Newton R. Russell, "Ritualized Crimes against Children," a speech to the National Crimes against Children Conference, Washington, D.C., September 19, 1993.

4. James Noblitt and Pamela Perskin, *Cult and Ritual Abuse* (Westport, Conn.: Praeger, 1995), pp. 166–168.

5. See text relating to endnote 19 in chapter 1.

Chapter 1: The Struggle

1. *America's Best Kept Secret: A Look at Modern-Day Satanism* (Passport Enterprises, 1988). *Passport* magazine's educational videotape on Satanism.

2. The fact that high school students call themselves Satanists does not mean they are connected with any group or tradition. Anyone who wants to can call himself a Satanist and what he is doing Satanism. Nonetheless these young experimenters in occult practices identified themselves to their classmates as Satanists.

3. Ronald Enroth and J. Gordon Melton, *Why Cults Succeed Where the Church Fails* (Elgin, Ill.: Brethren, 1985), p. 75.

4. Roland C. Summit, "The Dark Tunnels of McMartin," *The Journal of Psychohistory*, Vol. 21, No. 4, spring 1994, pp. 397–416.

5. Taken from the text of Senator Russell's speech "Ritualized Crimes against Children." In the section of his speech devoted to comments by law enforcement personnel, California State Senator Russell quotes Ed Szendry, supervising investigator for the Butte County District Attorney as saying, "Law enforcement cannot always promise the successful prosecution of such cases and, therefore, should not necessarily be considered the benchmark by which these cases are evaluated. . . . I don't foresee us getting a handle on ritualistic abuse in the immediate future."

6. James G. Friesen, *The Truth about False Memory Syndrome* (Lafayette, La.: Huntington House, 1996), pp. 93–94.

7. "Justice Ill Served: Who Speaks for Baby X?" *South Idaho Press*, September 15, 1991, p. 4.

Notes

8. For a detailed account of a trial involving ritual abuse and the interactions of therapists with children, read Jan Hollingsworth, *Unspeakable Acts* (New York: Congdon & Weed, 1986).

9. Credibility problems are discussed in "Theoretical and Personal Perspectives on the Delayed Memory Debate," presented by Jennifer J. Freyd, Ph.D., on August 7, 1993, at "Controversies around Recovered Memories of Incest and Ritualistic Abuse," a continuing education conference in Ann Arbor, Michigan. Dr. Freyd is professor of psychology at the University of Oregon and daughter of the founders of the False Memory Syndrome Foundation (FMSF). Other sources are Hollingsworth, *Unspeakable*, and David L. Calof, "A Conversation with Pamela Freyd, Ph.D., Co-Founder and Executive Director, False Memory Syndrome Foundation, Inc., Part I," *Treating Abuse Today*, Vol. 3, No. 3, pp. 25–31.

10. VOCAL is an organization composed largely, according to Hollingsworth, of accused and convicted child molesters (*Unspeakable*, p. 345).

11. False Memory Syndrome Foundation, Inc., "Dear Friends" letter, February 20, 1992, p. 1, as quoted by David Calof in "A Conversation," p. 26.

12. Calof, "A Conversation," p. 26.

13. Hollingsworth, *Unspeakable*, p. 395.

14. Friesen, *False Memory Syndrome*, pp. 15–17.

15. *The Journal of Paedophilia* (winter 1993, Vol. 3, No. 1, pp. 3–4), quoted by Calof, "A Conversation," p. 28. Also quoted in the video *False Prophets of the False Memory Syndrome* by Cavalcade Productions (7360 Potter Valley Rd., Ukiah, CA 95482; (800) 345–5530 or (707) 743–1168 in California). Further analysis of this interview can be found in Noblitt and Perskin, *Ritual Abuse*, p. 181.

16. James Webb, *The Occult Underground* (LaSalle, Ill.: Open Court, 1974), p. 141.

17. David J. Lotto, "On Witches and Witch Hunts: Ritual and Satanic Cult Abuse," *The Journal of Psychohistory*, Vol. 21, No. 4, spring 1994, p. 392.

18. *Children at Risk*, video (Ukiah, Calif.: Cavalcade Productions, 1992).

19. Harvey M. Weinstein, *Psychiatry and the CIA: Victims of Mind Control* (Washington, D.C.: American Psychiatric Press, 1990), p. 268.

20. Michael Nicholson, "Escape from Sarajevo," condensed from *Natasha's Story*, *Reader's Digest*, March 1994, p. 123. Nicholson was a 25-year veteran reporter sent to cover a war that has killed more than 17,000 children.

21. For example, Bessel A. van der Kolk, M.D., *Psychological Trauma* (Washington, D.C.: American Psychiatric Press, 1987).

22. Daniel J. Siegel, M.D., "Cognition, Memory and Dissociation," *Child and Adolescent Psychiatric Clinics of North America*, Vol. 5, No. 2, April 1996, pp. 509–536.

23. Ibid., p. 513.

24. Daniel J. Siegel, in a lecture in the continuing education seminar "Understanding and Treating Trauma: Developmental and Neurobiological Approaches" at the University of California, Los Angeles, February 1, 1998.

25. Deborah A. Lott, "Brain Development, Attachment and Impact on Psychic Vulnerability," *Psychiatric Times*, May 1998, <http://www.mhsource.com/edu/psytimes/p980547.html>.

Chapter 2: The Dragon's Lures

1. E. James Wilder, *Life Passages for Men* (Ann Arbor, Mich.: Servant, 1993). Republished as *The Stages of a Man's Life: A Guide for Men and Women* by Quiet Waters Publications, P. O. Box 4955, Springfield, MO 65808, FAX (417) 887–1484, <QWP@usa.net>.

2. Thomas Wedge, *The Satan Hunter* (Canton, Oh.: Daring, 1988), p. 42.

3. Webb, *Occult Underground*, pp. 39–44.

4. Dan Korem, *Powers: Testing the Psychic and Supernatural* (Downers Grove, Ill.: InterVarsity, 1988), p. 188.

5. Bob Altemeyer, Ph.D., "The Authoritarian Personality," *The Harvard Mental Health Letter*, Vol. 7, No. 3, September 1990, pp. 4–6.

6. Ibid., p. 6.

7. See Webb, *Occult Underground*, and *The Occult Establishment* (LaSalle, Ill.: Open Court, 1976), for an extensive development of this creative end of the occult.

8. Webb, *Occult Establishment*, p. 2.

9. Johanna Michaelsen, *Your Kids and the Occult* (Eugene, Ore.: Harvest House, 1989), p. 28.

10. Volney P. Gay, *Understanding the Occult: Fragmentation and Repair of the Self* (Minneapolis: Fortress, 1989), p. 85.

11. Irene Park, *The Witch That Switched* (Spring Hill, Fla.: 1980).

12. Larry Kahaner, *Cults That Kill* (New York: Warner, 1988), p. 84.

13. Dr. Charles H. Kraft. Personal communication.

Chapter 3: Preparing Children for the Dragon

1. Allan N. Schore, *Affect Regulation and the Origin of the Self: The Neurobiology of Emotional Development* (Mahwah, N.J.: Lawrence Earlbaum, 1996), pp. 10–13.

2. Schore, *Affect Regulation*, pp. 71–82.

3. See Mary D. S. Ainsworth, Mary C. Blehar, Everett Walters and Sally Wall, *Patterns of Attachment* (Hillsdale, N.J.: Lawrence Earlbaum, 1978).

4. Schore, *Affect Regulation*, pp. 92–98.

5. Van der Kolk, *Psychological Trauma*, p. 115.

6. See Wilder, *Life Passages*.

7. See Ronald Enroth, *Churches That Abuse* (Grand Rapids: Zondervan, 1992), and *Recovering from Churches that Abuse* (Grand Rapids: Zondervan, 1994).

8. The necessary identity transformations in our normal life span are described in considerable detail in Wilder, *Life Passages*. Both men and women experience the same stages and transformations so the information is generally applicable.

9. Pat Pulling, *The Devil's Web* (Lafayette, La.: Huntington House, 1989), p. 35.

10. Enroth and Melton, *Why Cults Succeed*, pp. 59–61.

11. Johanna Michaelsen, *Like Lambs to the Slaughter* (Eugene, Ore.: Harvest House, 1989), p. 263.

Chapter 4: The Red Dragon's Lair

1. Tim Cahill, "We Are Not Men; We Are Roto," *Los Angeles Times Magazine*, January 6, 1991, p. 19.

2. Dr. Carlos A. León, "*La Violencia* in Colombia," *American Journal of Psychiatry*, 125:11, May 1969.

3. León, "*La Violencia*." All the specific information in this chapter about Colombian violence is cited from Dr. León unless otherwise noted.

4. "The Cold War Experiments (Americans as Guinea Pigs)," *U.S. News & World Report*, January 24, 1994, pp. 33–38.

5. Michael D. Langone, Ph.D., and Linda Blood, *Satanism and Occult-Related Violence: What You Should Know* (Weston, Mass.: American Family Foundation, 1990), pp. 11–12.

6. Russell Miller, *Bare-Faced Messiah: The True Story of L. Ron Hubbard* (New York: Henry Holt, 1987), pp. 112–121.

7. Ibid., p. 113.

8. Lawrence Wright, *Saints and Sinners* (New York: Knopf, 1993), p. 144.

9. For a more in-depth look at the results and patterns produced by Satanism, read *Uncovering the Mystery of MPD* by James Friesen, Ph.D. The fourth chapter describes the effects of several types of involvement with Satanism. (Currently published by Wipf & Stock Publishers, Eugene, Ore., phone (514) 485–5745, FAX (514) 465–9694, <WSPub@academic-books.com>.)

10. Like all the stories in this book, Dave's is a composite of the experiences of several people, as told to me. Certain of the elements in Dave's story, unlike other stories, have been altered slightly to prevent anyone from using this technique to change someone's identity successfully. While the level of trauma has been represented accurately, the actual procedure has been obscured. This will be obvious to expert readers but should not hinder the average reader from seizing the point: Personalities can be disintegrated.

11. Maury Terry suggests in *The Ultimate Evil* that part of the motives for the Son of Sam killings in New York were jealousy and revenge over sexual liaisons between cult members. Money, drug deals, movie rights and other business deals have also led to violence and

death. Business deals are sealed with fear, not legal forms. One should be careful with people who get revenge.

Chapter 5: Dragon Love

1. See Ainsworth, et. al., *Patterns of Attachment.*
2. You may recognize this line of argument as essentially humanistic and not based on a biblical worldview. Please indulge me as I meet our culture on its own terms. Even within a materialistic worldview, optimism about intelligence cannot be maintained.
3. *A Nation's Shame: Fatal Child Abuse and Neglect in the United States*, Fifth Report, U.S. Advisory Board on Child Abuse and Neglect, Washington, D.C., April 1995.
4. Miller, *Bare-Faced Messiah*, p. 113.

Chapter 6: Christmas Savings Bonds

1. Enroth and Melton, *Why Cults Succeed*, p. 51.
2. Nicky Cruz, *Devil on the Run* (Melbourne, Fla.: Dove, 1989), p. 103.
3. Bob Larson, *Satanism: The Seduction of America's Youth* (Nashville: Thomas Nelson, 1989), p. 46.
4. James B. Jordan, *Through New Eyes* (Brentwood, Tenn.: Wolgemuth & Hyatt, 1988). Also of help is his tape series *The Art of Interpretation* (BASJORDAN–1C), available from Great Christian Books, Wilmington, Del.
5. Michaelsen, *Your Kids*, pp. 27–28.
6. Paul C. Vitz, "The Use of Stories in Moral Development," *American Psychologist*, Vol. 45, No. 6, June 1990, pp. 709–720.
7. If you would like an extended example of ways to teach values and create bonds through stories, see my book *Just Between Father and Son* (Downers Grove, Ill.: InterVarsity, 1990). The book is out of print but available from The Archives Bookshop, (626) 797-4756 or from <archivesb@aol.com>. Especially good for those who need help with symbols are *Tales of the Kingdom* and *Tales of the Resistance* by David and Karen Mains (Elgin, Ill.: Chariot, 1983 and 1986). *A Bridge of Love* by Barbara Moon is particularly suited for dissociators and available from 615 Rivercrest Dr., Woodstock, GA 30188, (770) 591-3731.

Chapter 7: Gifts of Prevention

1. Volney P. Gay, *Understanding the Occult: Fragmentation and Repair of the Self* (Minneapolis: Fortress, 1989).

Chapter 8: Gifts of Restoration

1. For more information on multiple personalities and other forms of personality disintegration common among satanic ritual abuse survivors, see *Uncovering the Mystery of MPD* by Dr. James Friesen.
2. For information regarding this prayer ministry of John and Paula Sandford, contact Elijah House, 1000 S. Richards Rd., Post Falls, ID 83854, (208) 773-1645.
3. Some good books on spiritual warfare include: *A Believer's Guide to Spiritual Warfare* by Thomas B. White (Ann Arbor, Mich.: Vine, 1990); *Defeating Dark Angels* by Charles H. Kraft (Ann Arbor, Mich.: Vine, 1992); *I Give You Authority* by Charles H. Kraft (Grand Rapids, Mich.: Chosen, 1997); and *The Handbook for Spiritual Warfare* by Dr. Ed Murphy (Nashville: Thomas Nelson, 1992). Any of the works of Neil T. Anderson or Mark Bubeck are likely to be helpful as well.
4. E. Thomas Brewster and Elizabeth S. Brewster, *Bonding and the Missionary Task: Establishing a Sense of Belonging* (Pasadena, Calif.: Lingua House, 1982). (626) 584-5200.
5. See "The Professional Preface" to this book.
6. *Care-Giving: The Cornerstone of Healing* by Cheryl S. Knight and Jo Getzinger is available from C.A.R.E., Inc., 3069 S. M-37, Baldwin, MI 49304. Phone (616) 745-0500, FAX (616) 745-9662.
7. Dr. Ed Smith developed the TheoPhostic approach that, while failing to be compelling theoretically at the time of this writing, bases its results on a deep faith that Jesus is truth and that He reveals the truth, which brings lasting healing. Unlike most methods, Dr. Smith's does not depend on the counselor to know, defend, teach or persuade the client of truth.

Notes

Dr. Smith can be contacted at his Alathia Retreat Center, P.O. Box 489, Campbellsville, KY 42719. Phone (888) 467-3757, FAX (502) 789-2867.

8. Anton LaVey, *The Compleat Witch or What to Do When Virtue Fails*, pp. 197–199, quoted in *Satanic Ritual Abuse and Mormonism* by Jerald and Sandra Tanner (Salt Lake City: Utah Lighthouse Ministry, 1992), p. 36.

9. Schore, *Affect Regulation*, pp. 355–369.

Chapter 9: Gifts of Maturity

1. From the *LIFE* Model of Redemption and Maturity. See "The Professional Preface."

2. See Jeff VanVonderen, *Tired of Trying to Measure Up* (Minneapolis: Bethany, 1989).

3. Kelley, *Burden*, p. 75.

4. Before this death, pain means we lack value. After this transformation, pain becomes a sign that our value cannot be taken away. This makes no sense before death, however, and even sounds sadistic or crazy-making.

5. Some scholars make a case that a long time passed while Abraham lived in the land of Abimelech, after which the events with Isaac took place. Others read it that Abraham was with Abimelech a long time and that the events in the land of Moriah transpired after he had been there awhile. Some Hebraists make much of the evidence suggested by the Hebrew word for *lad*, *na`ar*. Ishmael was called a lad at fourteen-plus. Joseph was a lad at seventeen, out tending sheep. Even Benjamin in Genesis 43 was a lad at a possible thirty years of age. All we know for sure is that this event took place before Sarah died when Isaac was 36.

Chapter 10: The Gifts of Christ

1. W. T. Purkiser, et al., *Exploring Our Christian Faith*, revised edition (Kansas City, Mo.: Nazarene Publishing, 1978), p. 223.

2. Ronda S. Perry, *A Community of Healing: Supporting an Adult Survivor of Satanic Ritual Abuse* (Knoxville, Tenn.: KBJ Solutions, 1998). Available through KBJ Solutions, P.O. Box 20735, Knoxville, TN 37940, (423) 577–4279.

3. In his plea for spiritual fatherhood, Pastor Jack Hayford describes Paul's view of spiritual family. Paul calls Abraham "the father of us all" in Romans 4:16 (NKJV). Hayford also answers the objection raised by Protestants about Jesus' words in Matthew 23:9: "Do not call any man on earth 'father.'" This, Hayford explains, was an attack on the Pharisees' claim to the title *fathers in Israel*, thereby making themselves the source of life. Spiritual fatherhood is only for dependent men who give the life they have received from God. See Jack Hayford, *Pastors of Promise* (Ventura, Calif.: Regal, 1997), p. 37.

4. See Trula Michaels LaCalle, Ph.D., *Voices* (New York: Dodd, Mead, 1987).

5. See Joan Frances Casey, *The Flock* (New York: Knopf, 1991).

6. Serafina Anfuso, Ph.D., "Spiritual Bonding," *The Journal of Christian Healing*, Vol. 15, Nos. 2 & 3, summer/fall 1993, pp. 28–43.

7. Wilder, *Life Passages*, p. 198.

8. Larry Crabb, *Finding God* (Grand Rapids: Zondervan, 1993).

9. For a useful and succinct treatment of this topic, see *Emotional Dependency* by Lori Rentzel (Downers Grove, Ill.: InterVarsity, 1990).

Chapter 11: Redemption Comes to My House

1. Kitty's life stabilized when she began taking a serotonin re-uptake inhibitor that did not produce sympathomimetic metabolites. This medication had just been introduced.

2. Barbara Moon, *A Bridge of Love*, is a story that grew out of living with dissociators in the initial stages of finding their traumas. Available from 615 Rivercrest Dr., Woodstock, GA 30188, (770) 591–3731.

BIBLIOGRAPHY

Alexander, Brooks. *The Occult.* Downers Grove, Ill.: InterVarsity, 1983.

Allison, Ralph. *Minds in Many Pieces.* New York: Rawson, Wade, 1980.

Altemeyer, Bob, Ph.D. *The Authoritarian Personality.* The Harvard Mental Health Letter, Vol. 7, No. 3, September 1990, pp. 4–6.

"America's Best Kept Secret: Special Report." *Passport Magazine,* fall 1986.

America's Best Kept Secret: A Look at Modern-Day Satanism (video). Passport Enterprises, 1988.

Anderson, Neil T. *The Bondage Breaker.* Eugene, Ore.: Harvest House, 1990.

_____. *Victory Over the Darkness.* Ventura, Calif.: Regal, 1990.

Anderson, Neil T. and Steve Russo. *The Seduction of Our Children.* Eugene, Ore.: Harvest House, 1991.

Ankerberg, John and John Weldon. *The Secret Teachings of the Masonic Lodge.* Chicago: Moody, 1989.

Brewster, Thomas E. and Elizabeth S. Brewster. *Bonding and the Missionary Task: Establishing a Sense of Belonging.* Pasadena: Lingua, 1982.

Braswell, George W. Jr. *Understanding Sectarian Groups in America.* Nashville: Broadman, 1986.

Brown, David, Allan Scheflin and Gary D. Hammond. *Memory Trauma, Treatment and the Law.* New York: W. W. Norton, 1997.

Brown, Dee. "Adult Survivors of Satanic Ritualistic Abuse." Audiotape recorded at Consortium of California Child Abuse Councils conference, February 1987.

Carling, Paul J. *Return to Community: Building Support Systems for People with Psychiatric Disabilities.* New York: Guilford, 1995.

Carr, Joseph. *The Lucifer Connection.* Lafayette, La.: Huntington, 1987.

"Satanism Haunts Tales of Child Sex Abuse." *Chicago Tribune,* July 29, 1985.

Children at Risk (video). Ukiah, Calif.: Cavalcade Productions, 1992.

Cruz, Nicky. *Devil on the Run.* Melbourne, Fla.: Dove, 1989.

DeMar, Gary. *Surviving College Successfully.* Brentwood, Tenn.: Wolgemuth & Hyatt, 1988.

Duzán, María Jimena. *Death Beat.* New York: HarperCollins, 1994.

Enroth, Ronald. *The Lure of the Cults and New Religions.* Downers Grove, Ill.: InterVarsity, 1987.

_____. *Churches That Abuse.* Grand Rapids: Zondervan, 1992.

_____. *Recovering from Churches That Abuse.* Grand Rapids: Zondervan, 1994.

_____. *What Is a Cult?* Downers Grove, Ill.: InterVarsity, 1982.

_____ and J. Gordon Melton. *Why Cults Succeed Where the Church Fails.* Elgin, Ill.: Brethren, 1985.

Bibliography

Fraser, George A., M.D., F.R.C.P.C., ed. *The Dilemma of Ritual Abuse: Cautions and Guides for Therapists*. Washington, D.C.: American Psychiatric Press, 1997.

Frederickson, Bruce G. *How to Respond to Satanism*. St. Louis: Concordia, 1988.

Friesen, James G. *The Truth about False Memory Syndrome*. Lafayette, La.: Huntington, 1996.

_____. *More Than Survivors: Conversations with Multiple-Personality Clients*. Nashville: Thomas Nelson, 1992.

_____. *Uncovering the Mystery of MPD*. Nashville: Thomas Nelson, 1991.

Fox, Loreda L. *The Spiritual and Clinical Dimensions of Multiple Personality Disorder*. Salida, Col.: Sangre de Cristo, 1992.

Gay, Volney P. *Understanding the Occult*. Minneapolis: Fortress, 1989.

Getz, Gene A. *Sharpening the Focus of the Church*. Wheaton, Ill.: Victor, 1984.

Groothuis, Douglas R. *Confronting the New Age*. Downers Grove, Ill.: InterVarsity, 1988.

_____. *The New Age Movement*. Downers Grove, Ill.: InterVarsity, 1986.

_____. *Unmasking the New Age*. Downers Grove, Ill.: InterVarsity, 1986.

Hayford, Jack W. *Pastors of Promise*. Ventura, Calif.: Regal, 1997.

Harris, Marvin. *Cows, Pigs, Wars and Witches*. New York: Vintage, 1974.

Herman, Judith H. *Trauma and Recovery*. New York: Basic, 1992.

Hauerwas, Stanley and William H. Willimon. *Resident Aliens*. Nashville: Abingdon, 1989.

Hieronimus, Robert, Ph.D. *America's Secret Destiny*. Rochester, Vt.: Destiny, 1989.

Hill, Sally and Jean Goodwin. "Satanism: Similarities between Patient Accounts and Pre-Inquisition Historical Sources." *Dissociation*, March 1989.

Hollingsworth, Jan. *Unspeakable Acts*. New York: Congdon & Weed, 1986.

Hubner, John and Lindsey Gruson. *Monkey on a Stick*. Orlando: Harcourt Brace Jovanovich, 1988.

Hunt, Dave. *The Cult Explosion*. Eugene, Ore.: Harvest House, 1978.

Jaranson, James M., M.D., and Michael K. Popkin, M.D. *Caring for Victims of Torture*. Washington, D.C.: American Psychiatric Press, 1998.

Johnston, Jerry. *The Edge of Evil*. Dallas: Word, 1989.

Jordan, James B. *Through New Eyes*. Brentwood, Tenn.: Wolgemuth & Hyatt, 1988.

Kahaner, Larry. *Cults That Kill*. New York: Warner, 1988.

Kraft, Charles H. *Deep Wounds, Deep Healing*. Ann Arbor, Mich.: Servant, 1993.

Kelley, Michael. *The Burden of God*. Minneapolis: Contra Mundum, 1993.

Kelley, Susan J. "Ritualistic Abuse of Children." *Cultic Studies Journal*, Vol. 5, p. 228.

Knight, Cheryl S. and Jo M. Getzinger. *Care-Giving, the Cornerstone of Healing*. Port Huron, Mich.: Hope, 1994.

Koch, Kurt. *Christian Counselling and Occultism*. Grand Rapids: Kregel, 1972.

Korem, Dan. *Powers Testing the Psychic and Supernatural*. Downers Grove, Ill.: InterVarsity, 1988.

Langone, Michael D. and Linda O. Blood. *Satanism and Occult-Related Violence: What You Should Know*. Weston, Mass.: American Family Foundation, 1990.

Larson, Bob. *Satanism: The Seduction of America's Youth*. Nashville: Thomas Nelson, 1989.

LaVey, Anton Szandor. *The Satanic Bible*. New York: Avon, 1969.

Leithart, Peter J. *The Kingdom and the Power: Rediscovering the Centrality of the Church*. Phillipsburg, N.J.: P&R, 1993.

Lifton, Robert J. *The Nazi Doctors*. New York: Basic, 1986.

"A Choice to Share Death: Final Act of Couple's Mystical Beliefs Confirmed 6 Years Later." *The Los Angeles Times*, April 1, 1989.

Bibliography

"Satanists' Trail: Dead Pets to a Human Sacrifice." *The Los Angeles Times*, October 19–20, 1988.

Lotto, David. "On Witches and Witch Hunts: Ritual and Satanic Cult Abuse." *The Journal of Psychohistory*, Vol. 21, No. 4, spring 1994, pp. 373–396.

Marrs, Texe. *Dark Secrets of the New Age*. Westchester, Ill.: Crossway, 1987.

Martin, Walter. *The Kingdom of the Cults*. Minneapolis: Bethany, 1985.

Medve, Pamela. "Former Satanist Decries Occult." *Star News*, May 29, 1990, pp. A-3–A-4.

Michaelsen, Johanna. *Like Lambs to the Slaughter*. Eugene, Ore.: Harvest House, 1989.

————. *Your Kids and the Occult*. Eugene, Ore.: Harvest House, 1989.

Mithers, Carol L. *Therapy Gone Mad*. Reading, Mass.: Addison-Wesley, 1994.

Morgan, Robin. *The Demon Lover*. New York: W. W. Norton, 1989.

Murphy, Edward F. *The Handbook for Spiritual Warfare*. Nashville: Thomas Nelson, 1992.

Nobit, James R. and Pamela S. Perskin. *Cult and Ritual Abuse: Its History, Anthropology, and Recent Discovery in Contemporary America*. Westport, Conn.: Praeger, 1995.

North, Gary. *Unholy Spirits*. Ft. Worth, Tex.: Dominion, 1986.

Oke, Isaiah. *Blood Secrets*. Buffalo: Prometheus, 1989.

Park, Irene Arrington. *The Witch That Switched*. Spring Hill, Fla.: 1980.

Parker, Russ. *The Occult: Deliverance from Evil*. Downers Grove, Ill.: InterVarsity, 1989.

Phillips, Phil and Joan Hake Robie. *Halloween and Satanism*. Lancaster, Pa.: Starburst, 1987.

Pratney, Winkie. *Devil Take the Youngest*. Shreveport, La.: Huntington, 1985.

Pulling, Pat. *The Devil's Web*. Lafayette, La.: Huntington, 1989.

Raschke, Carl A. *Painted Black*. San Francisco: Harper & Row, 1990.

Research Update: Occult Crime: Law Enforcemant Primer. Sacramento, Calif.: Office of Criminal Justice Planning, Vol. 1, No. 6, winter 1989–1990.

Reisser, Paul C., M.D., Teri K. Reisser and John Weldon. *New Age Medicine*. Downers Grove, Ill.: InterVarsity, 1987.

Rentzel, Lori. *Emotional Dependency*. Downers Grove, Ill.: InterVarsity, 1990.

Ritualistic Abuse: A Professional Overview (video). Ukiah, Calif.: Cavalcade Productions, 1987.

Rodney-Wilson, Kathleen. "Healing Survivors of Satanic Sexual Abuse." *The Journal of Christian Healing*, Vol. 12, No. 1, spring 1990, pp. 9–12.

Ross, Colin A. *Satanic Ritual Abuse: Principles of Treatment*. Toronto: University of Toronto Press, 1995.

Ryder, Daniel. *Breaking the Circle of Satanic Ritual Abuse*. Minneapolis: CompCare, 1992.

Sanders, Ed. *The Family*. New York: Signet, 1990.

Sandford, John and Mark. *Deliverance and Inner Healing*. Grand Rapids: Chosen, 1992.

Sands, Susan H., Ph.D. "What Is Dissociated?" *Dissociation*, Vol. VII, No. 3, September 1994, pp. 145–152.

Sakheim, David K. and Susan E. Devine. *Out of Darkness: Exploring Satanism and Ritual Abuse*. New York: Lexington, 1992.

Schore, Allan N. *Affect Regulation and the Origin of the Self: Neurobiology of Emotional Development*. Hillsdale, N.J.: Lawrence Erlbaum Associates, 1994.

Schwarz, Ted and Duane Empey. *Is Your Family Safe? Satanism*. Grand Rapids: Zonder-van, 1988.

Siegel, Daniel J., M.D. *The Developing Mind: Toward a Neurobiology of Interpersonal Experience*. New York: Guilford, 1999.

Sire, James W. *Shirley Maclaine and the New Age Movement*. Downers Grove, Ill: Inter-Varsity, 1988.

Bibliography

Shaw, Jim and Tom McKenney. *The Deadly Deception*. Lafayette, La.: Huntington, 1988.

Shuster, Marguerite. *Power, Pathology, Paradox*. Grand Rapids: Zondervan/Academie, 1987.

Smith, Michelle and Lawrence Pazder, M.D. *Michelle Remembers*. New York: Pocket, 1980.

Spencer, Judith. *Suffer the Child*. New York: Pocket, 1989.

Summit, Roland C. "The Dark Tunnels of McMartin." *The Journal of Psychohistory*, Vol. 21, No. 4, spring 1994, pp. 397–416.

Tanner, Jerald and Sandra. *Satanic Ritual Abuse and Mormonism*. Salt Lake City: Utah Lighthouse Ministry, 1992.

Tendler, Rebecca, Ph.D. "The Treatment of Narcissistic Injury in Dissociative Identity Disorder Patients: The Contributions of Self Psychology." *Dissociation*, Vol. VIII, No. 1, March 1995, pp. 45–52.

Terry, Maury. *The Ultimate Evil*. Garden City, N.Y.: Dolphin, 1987.

Terr, Lenore. *Too Scared to Cry: Psychic Trauma in Childhood*. New York: Harper & Row, 1990.

_____. *Unchained Memories*. New York: Basic, 1994.

VanVonderen, Jeff. *Tired of Trying to Measure Up*. Minneapolis: Bethany, 1989.

van der Kolk, Bessel A. *Psychological Trauma*. Washington, D.C.: American Psychiatric Press, 1987.

_____, Alexander C. McFarlane and Lars Weisaeth, eds. *Traumatic Stress*. New York: Guilford, 1996.

Wagner, C. Peter and F. Douglas Pennoyer, eds. *Wrestling with Dark Angels*. Ventura, Calif.: Regal, 1990.

Webb, James. *The Occult Establishment*. LaSalle, Ill.: Open Court, 1976.

_____. *The Occult Underground*. LaSalle, Ill.: Open Court, 1974.

Wedge, Thomas W. *The Satan Hunter*. Canton, Oh.: Daring, 1988.

Weinstein, Harvey M. *Psychiatry and the CIA: Victims of Mind Control*. Washington, D.C.: American Psychiatric Press, 1990.

Weldon, John and James Bjornstad. *Playing with Fire*. Chicago: Moody, 1984.

White, Thomas B. *A Believer's Guide to Spiritual Warfare*. Ann Arbor, Mich.: Vine, 1990.

Whitfield, Charles L. "How Common Is Traumatic Forgetting?" *The Journal of Psychohistory*, Vol. 23, No. 2, fall 1995, pp. 119–130.

_____. *Memory and Abuse: Remembering and Healing the Effects of Trauma*. Deerfield Beach, Fla.: Health Communications, 1995.

Wilder, E. James. *Life Passages for Men*. Ann Arbor, Mich.: Vine, 1993.

_____. *Rite of Passage*. Ann Arbor, Mich.: Vine, 1994.

_____. *The Stages of a Man's Life: A Guide for Men and Women*, Springfield, Mo.: Quiet Waters Publications, 1999.

Wright, Lawrence. *Saints and Sinners*. New York: Knopf, 1993.

INDEX

Index

Index

occult, 65–68; personal, 67–68; practical, 67; uncommon, 65–68
Korem, Dan, 59
Kraft, Dr. Charles H., 17, 42, 72, 310
Ku Klux Klan, 23

Larson, Bob, 162
LaVey, Anton, 57, 108, 110, 158, 161, 179–80, 209
law enforcement, 34–35, 203
Lenin, Vladimir, 117
León, Dr. Carlos, 101
Lewis, C. S., 20
lies, 209
LIFE Model, 13–15, 82, 204, 229–30
"Lincoln Duncan" (Simon), 251
Lindsey, Hal, 202
literature, 189
love, 124–25
love bonds, 122–26, 223–24; as basis of Christian faith, 63; and Christ's death, 148; community based on, 234, 275; and community-of-the-self, 224; with fathers, 162; and fear, 195–98; and the fruit of the Spirit, 210–11; with the newly adopted, 265; between parents and children, 174–75; with spiritual family, 263; and the spiritual world, 188; standards for, 193; structures responsible for, 78
love spells and potions, 32, 59, 68, 98
Luciferians, 21, 22–23

magic, 59
magick, 20, 59, 109, 113, 115, 178, 248; black, 109; sexual, 113, 132, 158, 174
magus, 178
Mansfield, Jayne, 108
Manson, Charles, 20, 35
marriage, 234–35
Marx, Karl, 117
Mary, 254, 261–62
Matamoros, Mexico, 105–6
maturity, 222–52, 281–87; blockage of, 229, 236–39; and dependency, 281–85; evil and, 238–39; and growing a mature self, 228–30; normal human, 13–18; redemption and, 287; and the self, 236–39; spiritual, 226, 247–48, 285–86; and spiritual adoption, 281–85; stages of, 14–15, 237–38
McMartin Preschool, 35
media, 39, 119
mediums, 68, 120
Melton, Dr. J. Gordon, 33

memory, 43–48; left-hemispheric, 44–45, 111; right-hemispheric, 43–45; of trauma, 46–48
memory retrieval, 46–48
Milosevic, Slobodan, 41
mind control, 20, 33, 40–41, 61–64, 105, 111
Moon, Barbara, 310
Moses, 299
mothers, 81, 170
Mr. Choice, 194–95
multiple personalities, 111, 200
murder, 34, 38, 99–101, 105, 120, 191, 194–95, 202
music, 189, 246

NAMBLA, 22
Naomi, 193
nature lovers, 188–89
Nazis, 18, 43
Nazism, 21, 70
needs, 52–56
neglect, 80, 90–91, 97–98, 130. *See also* trauma, type-A
neo-Druids, 23
neo-Nazis, 22, 23
New Age, 21, 67, 69, 164, 172, 186
New World Order, 23
Night Stalker, 35
Noblitt, Dr. James, 23
numbers, 147

obedience, 86–87
occult. *See* cults
occultists, 156
Order of the Solar Temple, 23
organized crime, 21, 22, 23
Osborn, Ozzie, 30
OTO (Ordo Templi Orientis), 21, 107
Ouija board, 30, 58

paganism, 21, 23–24, 155, 164, 212, 213
Paidika: The Journal of Paedophilia, 37
pain, 76–77, 84–89, 175–77, 285–86
Palo Mayombe, 21, 106
parapsychology, 59
parents: and children's identity, 80–84; and power, 168–73; protecting children, 166–93; requirements for, 82. *See also* spiritual parenting
Parsons, John Whiteside (Jack), 107, 109, 137
passivity, 127
pastoral care, 17–18
paternal involvement, 101
Paul the apostle, 155, 213, 236–37, 246–47, 278
Peace Child (Richardson), 163

Index

Index

Sly and the Family Stone, 20
Smith, Dr. Ed, 206
sodomy, 84–85
Son of Sam, 35
sorcery, 59, 178. *See also* magick
spells, 59, 67, 82
spirit guides, 68–69, 111, 128
spirits, 68–69, 223
spiritual adoption, 13–18, 269–86; and
    apostle John and Mary, 261–62; for cult
    survivors, 277; dependency and,
    281–85; and dependency, pain, and
    spiritual maturity, 285–86; and family,
    267; maturity and, 281–85; and parent-
    ing, 277–81; and redemption, 137–41,
    259
spiritual gifts, 15, 16. *See also* gifts of the
    Spirit
spirituality, 184–90; guides to, 185–86,
    188–90; and touring styles, 188–90;
    tours of, 186–90
spiritual parenting, 277–81, 283–84, 309
spiritual warfare, 201, 275, 299, 303
stories: bad, 148, 151–52, 154; Christian,
    202; reclaiming, 201–2; and repair of
    the community-of-the-self, 243–35; and
    symbols, 142–43, 144–45, 165; toxic,
    216–17
strangers, weak and wounded, 255, 257–58,
    269–75
supernatural. *See* spirituality
symbols, 17, 117, 142–57, 162–65; abstract,
    147–48; battle for, 155–62; Bible, 146,
    147–48, 150–51; blood, 147–48; and
    bonds, 144–45, 155–62, 165; Christian,
    154; Christmas, 142–44, 145–46, 147,
    148–49; culture-wide, 144; defense of,
    162–65; eating, 150–51; and eternal
    bonds, 148–52; family-wide, 143–44; fish, 147;
    food, 149–50; global, 144; and God,
    162–65; and identities, 144–45; and
    numbers, 147; and objects, 145–47;
    occult, 154; private, 143; reclaiming,
    201–2; and relationships, 152–54; and
    repair of the community-of-the-self,

243–45; and stories, 142–43, 144–45,
    165; truth and, 17

Taxil, Leo, 39
teachers, 190
teenagers. *See* young adults
telekinesis, 22, 58–59
Theosophical Society, 21
therapy, 37, 40, 111
Torquemada, Tomás de, 38
torture, 34, 38, 42, 101–3, 105, 113–14
trance state, 86, 111, 114
transformation, 228–30, 232–33, 262–69
trauma; cause of immaturity, 14; teams,
    199–220, 273–74; type-A, 14, 17, 90–91,
    111, 229, 268, 287; type-B, 14, 84–89,
    111, 229
truth, 48–49, 71–72, 141, 208–9
Tucker, Karla Faye, 103

uncommon, becoming, 106–10
Underwager, Dr. Ralph, 36–37
Unspeakable Acts, 117

VOCAL, 36
vodoun, 23
voodoo, 20, 21

weak bonds, 126–27, 131–32, 195–97; in
    churches, 135; family, 126–27; father,
    157–60; problems with, 125
weaknesses, 208
Webb, James, 59
white supremacists, 22
whore of Babylon, 107
Wicca, 21, 24, 170, 186–87, 284
Willimon, 19
Winfrey, Oprah, 39
witchcraft, 21, 23, 24, 66, 67, 105, 156, 164,
    170, 178, 284; "Christian," 93–95
witch doctor, 178

young adults, 50–72; and affection, 173–74;
    needs of, 52–56, 70–72; and Satanism,
    97–98

344

E. James Wilder, a licensed clinical psychologist, has an M.A. in theology from Fuller Seminary, a Ph.D. in clinical psychology from Fuller Graduate School of Psychology and is ordained in the Church of the Nazarene. He is director of Shepherd's House, an outpatient treatment center in Van Nuys, Calif. His specialties include community-based treatment, identity change, trauma recovery, maturity for men, husbands of incest survivors, fatherhood, spiritual family formation and adult third-culture kids.

Wilder has written *Life Passages for Men* (Servant, 1993) and *Just Between Father and Son* (InterVarsity, 1991) and speaks across the country on spiritual warfare, spiritual community, prayer and maturity. He and his wife, Kitty, have two grown sons, a grandchild and a growing spiritual family and live in Pasadena.